RELIGION AND MORALITY IN AMERICAN SCHOOLING

Edited by

Thomas C. Hunt and Marilyn M. Maxson

UNIVERSITY
PRESS OF
AMERICA

Copyright © 1981 by
Thomas C. Hunt and Marilyn M. Maxson
University Press of America, Inc.^{TM}

P.O. Box 19101, Washington, DC 20036

Printed in the United States of America

ISBN: 0-8191-1585-1 Perfect
0-8191-1584-3 Case
Library of Congress Number: 81-40154

CONTENTS

iii

PREFACE

The evidence of history clearly attests to the central place which morality and moral/ethical concerns have occupied in the conduct of American schooling, public and private. Originally based on the premises of revealed religion, the foundation for moral education in the public schools started to evolve to natural bases (the South generally excepted) in the last quarter of the nineteenth century. Democratic citizenship, rather than mainstream Protestantism, came to embody the moorings of moral/ethical education.

Ample data exist (one illustration being recent Gallup Polls on the American public's attitudes toward education) to demonstrate that concern over moral education remains a major issue in the conduct of schooling. This book was conceptualized and written to address some of the salient issues relative to the place of religion and morality in American schooling today.

The first section is an Introduction. It contains two articles, the first of which provides the reader with an historical overview of the evolution of moral education in public schools in the nineteenth and twentieth centuries. The second probes the constitutional issues which pertain to religion and schooling.

The second part contains articles on the schools of three (of the many) religious persuasions which maintain schools. The denominations whose schools are explicated are 1) Catholic, 2) the rapidly growing Christian Day (evangelical and fundamentalist), and 3) Jewish Day schools.

It is the third section, however, which comprises the major thrust of the book. Several articles, written from diverse perspectives, address the perplexing question of how the public schools can, do, and should conduct moral education in a culturally heterogeneous society. Several other articles in this section focus on particular dilemmas which face the public schools in religion and morality today.

The editors are aware that, due to limitations imposed by cost and space factors, several important aspects related to the topic unfortunately had to be omitted. Among these are the question of parental rights in education, particularly in the transmission of values; student rights; the right of the state to regulate non-public, church-affiliated schools; and the potentially explosive issues of educational vouchers and tuition tax credits. A number of published works exist on these topics, some of which are listed in the "Selected Bibliography" section at the end of this Preface.

It is the editors' sincere hope that this volume, by shedding light on some pertinent critical aspects of the issues, will evoke considerable thought and discussion. It is our further hope that this thought and discussion will generate an increased understanding of the complexity of the issues involved on the part of its readers. Finally, it is our wish that the insights garnered and the knowledge and understanding obtained from this volume ultimately will benefit all who are involved in one capacity or another in the process of American schooling.

The editors wish to express their appreciation to those individuals without whose aid this volume would not have been possible. First of all we would like to acknowledge our gratitude to the authors for the high scholarly quality of their articles. The support and encouragement of Dr. Thomas G. Teates, Director of the Division of Curriculum and Instruction, was indispensable to the successful completion of this venture. Also, we wish to acknowledge the patience and thoroughness of our secretary, Ms. Susan Blanton, whose accuracy and perseverance in typing and proofing the manuscript were of immeasurable value in our efforts. Finally, we are indebted to Ms. Helen Hudson, Editorial Assistant of the University Press of America, for answering the many questions we addressed to her while this book was in preparation. To each of these persons we say a most sincere "Thank you!".

Thomas C. Hunt and Marilyn M. Maxson

February 1981
Blacksburg, Virginia

SELECTED BIBLIOGRAPHY

American Association of School Administrators, Commission on Religion and Education. Religion in the Public Schools (Washington: American Association of School Administrators, 1964).

Arons, Stephen. "The Separation of School and State: Pierce Reconsidered." Harvard Educational Review. 46 (February 1976), pp. 76-104.

Association for Supervision and Curriculum Development. The School's Role as Moral Authority (Washington, D.C.: Association for Supervision and Curriculum Development, 1977).

Bird, Wendell R. "Freedom from Establishment and Unneutrality in Public School Instruction and Religious School Regulation." Harvard Journal of Law and Public Policy. 2 (June 1979), pp. 125-205.

Boles, Donald E. The Bible, Religion and the Public Schools. 3rd Edition (New York: Collier Books, 1966).

Buetow, Harold A. Of Singular Benefit: The Story of U.S. Catholic Education (New York: The Macmillan Company, 1970).

Butts, R. Freeman. The American Tradition in Religion and Education (Boston: The Beacon Press, 1950).

Butts, R. Freeman. The Revival of Civic Learning: A Rationale for Citizenship Education in American Schools (Bloomington, IN.: Phi Delta Kappa, 1980).

Coons, John E. and Stephen D. Sugarman. Education by Choice: The Case for Family Control (Berkeley: University of California Press, 1978).

Educational Policies Commission. Moral and Spiritual Values in the Public Schools (Washington: National Education Association, 1951).

Gartner, Lloyd P. (ed.). Jewish Education in the United States: A Documentary History (New York: Teachers College Press, 1969).

Hunt, Thomas C. "Public Schools and Moral Education: An American Dilemma." Religious Education. 74 (July-August 1979), pp. 350-372.

Itzkoff, Seymour W. A New Public Education (New York: David McKay, 1976).

Kennedy, William B. The Shaping of Protestant Education (New York: Association Press, 1966).

Kliebard, Herbert M. (ed.). Religion and Education in America: A Documentary History (Scranton, PA.: International Textbook Company, 1969).

Malbin, Michael J. Religion and Politics: The Intentions of the Authors of the First Amendment (Washington: American Enterprise Institute for Public Policy Research, 1978).

Michaelsen, Robert. Piety in the Public School (New York: The Macmillan Company, 1970).

Piediscalzi, Nicholas and William E. Collie. (eds.). Teaching about Religion in Public Schools (Niles, IL.: Argus Communications, 1977).

Pierce v. Society of Sisters 268 U.S. 510 (1925).

Purpel, David and Kevin Ryan. (eds.). Moral Education ... It Comes with the Territory (Berkeley, CA.: McCutchan Publishing Corporation, 1976).

Richey, Russell E. and Donald G. Jones. (eds.). American Civil Religion (New York: Harper and Row, 1974).

School District of Abington Township v. Schempp 374 U.S. 203 (1963).

Sizer, Theodore R. (ed.). Religion and Public Education (Boston: Houghton Mifflin Company, 1967).

Tyack, David B. "The Kingdom of God and the Common School." Harvard Educational Review. 36 (Fall 1966), pp. 447-469.

Wisconsin v. Yoder 406 U.S. 205 (1972).

SECTION ONE

INTRODUCTION

Religion, Morality and Schooling:
Forging the Nineteenth Century
Protestant Consensus

Harvey G. Neufeldt

The recent furor over the ruling of Tennessee's
Attorney General relative to prayer in connection
with a school function illustrates once again that
Americans have found the Supreme Court decisions on
prayer and Bible reading in the public schools unacceptable. The controversy erupted over a football team's practice of having a brief prayer prior
to the game. When the Attorney General, in response to a request for a ruling on the matter,
suggested that the practice was unconstitutional,
several football coaches denounced the decision and
"heroically" suggested that prayer would continue.
One coach even detected the possibility of a Communist conspiracy. It would appear that football
and prayer were both American. These responses as
well as recent attacks by conservative groups on
secular humanism in the schools and current drives
by pressure groups for a constitutional amendment
that would permit Bible reading as a devotional
exercise in the public schools reinforces David
Tyack's observation of a decade ago. Writing in a
day when emotional outbursts over the Supreme
Court decisions of 1962 and 1963 relative to Bible
reading and prayer in the public schools were still
very much in evidence, Tyack stated:
> The present clash of religious folkways
> and legal interpretation is not the
> first time that the church-state issue
> has injected itself into politics nor,
> it is safe to say, will it be the last.[1]

To understand these clashes, it is necessary,
as Tyack has pointed out, to go beyond a philosophical analysis on the merits of state aid to
parochial schools and to merely restudy the legal
merits of specific court cases themselves. Although these are important, it is also necessary
that one gain an understanding of the role religion
played in the common or public schools as schoolmen,

3

politicians, and clergymen sought to use religion and schooling in their attempts to create a cohesive community.[2]

The purpose of this article is to trace the rise and development of a Protestant consensus relative to the place of morality and religion in the public schools from the era of Horace Mann to the decade of the 1920s. The latter date was selected as a suitable termination point for this study because it represents a high-water mark, so to speak, in the drive by Americanizers to use the schools to bring out a coerced uniformity throughout the community. Although attention will be given to individuals and groups who found the Protestant consensus relative to religion, morality and public schooling unacceptable, the major focus will be on the drive to establish an "American-Protestant" consensus upon the schools. Although a complete account of education must take into account both ends of the school-log so to speak, namely the teacher at one end and the student at the other, this paper will focus only on one end of the log. It will focus on what the adult generation, especially ministers, politicians, and teachers, sought to do to the student. The extent to which the student on the other end of the log agreed with this consensus is not analyzed. Although the common school was a nineteenth century creation, brief comments will also be made relative to religion and education in the Colonial era, the Revolutionary Period and the New Republic. A study of nineteenth century practices will demonstrate that many Americans assumed that in order for a nation to survive, it had to reach a consensus on values and on a world view. They also concluded that such a consensus could not be reached and maintained without the sanction of true religion, which for many Americans came to be defined as nonsectarian Protestantism. Since schooling was to promote virtue and conformity, and since virtue and conformity were impossible without religion, schooling without religion was, by definition and logic, doomed to failure.

4

The Pre-1830 Legacy

Common school reformers did not begin their task of creating statewide free school systems in an historical vacuum. They inherited two centuries of educational practice. Several aspects need to be kept in mind when discussing education, religion and morality in the colonial era. First, education was not necessarily synonymous with schooling, although it is true that schooling had been firmly implanted in several colonies by 1650. Secondly, the church remained a powerful and often dominant force in colonial education. Furthermore, schooling, when compared to present day practices, had limited functions. The school was expected to reinforce the efforts of the family and the church in the socialization of the young, but not to replace them.[3]

Several patterns relative to church-state relations were evident in the colonies. In much of New England — Rhode Island being a major exception — there was a close tie between church and state with the Congregational Church enjoying the privileges of an established church. Religious dissent was discouraged, Roman Catholicism was not tolerated and public worship was a privilege extended only to the established church. In Virginia, the Anglican Church enjoyed the status of an established church, but the clergy seemingly did not wield as much influence as did their counterparts in New England. In both regions, neither the church nor the state accepted the notion that a government could safely separate citizenship from religious orthodoxy. In the middle colonies and in the Southern proprietary colonies religious and national diversity were prevalent, with Quakers being dominant in Pennsylvania; Roman Catholics at first and then Anglicans in Maryland; Presbyterians, Quakers and Anglicans in New Jersey; and Dutch Reformed and Anglicans in New York. Religious diversity brought with it more tolerance for religious differences in these colonies than was the case in New England. In New England, as Daniel Boorstin points out, religious dissent coupled with

the availability of new land, did not lead to
religious tolerance but rather to the creation of
new colonies.[4]

Whatever the legal status of religion within
the colonies, the role of religion loomed large in
all colonies. As Roy Nichols has pointed out, all
colonial settlements assumed that the "hand of the
Divine" was instrumental in their efforts. Good
citizenship was seldom divorced from religious belief and practice since virtue or morality was assumed to be rooted in church doctrine and religious
practice.[5]

Although schools had limited functions to
fulfill, these were not considered to be unimportant for the well being of the community. School
laws, such as the ones passed in Massachusetts and
Connecticut in 1642 and 1650 respectively, were
enacted primarily with the community's interests in
mind. Schooling was promoted to help instill
"values of harmony and homogeneity" as well as to
ensure that each child would grow up to be a self
supporting citizen and thereby avoid becoming a
burden on the community. Since homogeneity was the
norm in the religious realm, the religious doctrines of the dominant or supporting church would
be taught in the schools.[6]

The Great Awakening, the Enlightenment, and
the influx of immigrants in the eighteenth century
undermined the attempts to maintain likemindedness
and harmony within the colonies. Although these
developments did not lead to an official separation
of church and state, they did serve to break up
religious uniformity in New England and Virginia
and push the colonies gradually towards the acceptance of the concept of voluntarism in religion.
The Great Awakening was especially important because it helped promote, as R. Freeman Butts has
pointed out, "a kind of liberty of religious conscience within Protestantism," but it also retained
the notion that Protestantism was superior to Roman
Catholicism as well as to all non-Christian religions. It was these beliefs in voluntarism and of

the superiority of Protestantism which would become part of the creed of Americanism and public schooling in the nineteenth century.[7]

As far as the pedagogical practices were concerned, they were heavily informed by a negative view of human nature. Original sin and human depravity were assumed. This gave rise to, what Barbara Finkelstein has called, "the tradition of intrusive child rearing," characterized by an "'over-controlling,' carefully planned regiment of protection and supervision." Manuals of conduct, sermons, and colonial laws all stressed the need for eternal vigilance over the lives of children in order to induce them "to be obedient, pious, diligent, civil, mannerly, and clean." Firm discipline including corporal punishment and stories depicting God's wrath and emphasizing the reality of death were utilized in the schools and the homes.[8]

The Revolutionary and the Early National periods also left their imprint on religion and the schools. The low level of immigration, characteristic of the late eighteenth and early nineteenth centuries, made it relatively easy to maintain, especially in the rural villages, homogeneous communities. Thus, not surprisingly, the district school with its localistic orientation, limited curriculum and limited functions, remained a dominant feature. Schools were not expected to teach much beyond the 3 R's and religion. The latter was entrusted not only to the teacher, or to books like the New England Primer, but also to local ministers. As late as the early nineteenth century, Massachusetts ministers would still periodically visit the local schools in order to catechize the students.[9]

Despite the catechizing efforts of local ministers, the Revolutionary period was also marked by a growth in free thought in religion. Instead of an emphasis on human depravity, it stressed a neutral view of man. It asserted the primacy of natural law and reason in human affairs, and

7

deemphasized the concept of a wrathful God. Proponents of religious free thought cooperated with non-established churches such as the Baptists in the struggle to separate church and state and to support the passage of the First Amendment.[10]

Historians have not reached an agreement as to the meaning of the First Amendment or on the intent of its promoters. Certainly it should not be assumed that Jefferson's and Franklin's generation were hostile to religion. There was a general assumption that religion was essential for the preservation of social order. In his Farewell Address, George Washington reminded his countrymen that religion, morality and education were essential for the preservation of a republican government. Many state governments had no difficulty in reminding their citizens that they were Christian states. Disestablishment of churches at the state level was not complete until Connecticut and Massachusetts abolished their provisions for tax support for religious purposes in 1818 and 1833, respectively.

Disestablishment at the state level and statements in state constitutions proclaiming religious liberty were not meant to be equated with neutrality in religious matters. What was usually meant was that there should be no sectarian Protestant tests for the privilege of participating in the political process. In 1787, religious tests for holding public office varied. Maryland and Massachusetts required a belief "in the Christian religion;" Georgia, New Hampshire, New Jersey, and North Carolina required a belief in the Trinity, while Pennsylvania required a belief in God as "the rewarder of the good and the punisher of the wicked." North Carolina finally dropped its Protestant test in 1835 but continued to require a belief in the existence of God.[11]

Despite the remaining religious and even Protestant tests for holding public offices, several trends were evident after the Revolution. One was the notion that citizenship need not be

tied to sectarian religious doctrine. To require
assent to specific sectarian doctrines would serve
to divide rather than to unite the community.
Furthermore, although Thomas Jefferson deliberately
omitted the study of the Bible and religion from
his plan for education for Virginia in 1779, this
was not typical of the Protestant majority of his
day. More in keeping with conventional wisdom was
Benjamin Rush's plan for education for Pennsylvania
in 1786 in which he concluded:

> religion is the foundation of virtue;
> virtue is the foundation of liberty;
> liberty is the object of all republican
> governments; therefore, a republican
> education should promote religion as
> well as virtue and liberty 12

Separating church and state was not meant to lessen
the impact of the church in society. By making
them voluntary, it was assumed that churches would
increase rather than decrease their efforts to
"propagate ... the common ethical principles essential to the survival of free institutions."13

The Public School Legacy

When Horace Mann accepted the position as
secretary to the Board of Education in Massachusetts in 1837, it was becoming evident that much
had changed in the Republic since the Revolutionary
period. In the late eighteenth century free
thought had been popular in the Republic, by 1810
it was being increasingly discredited. This was
graphically illustrated in the life of Thomas
Paine. During the American Revolution he was a
hero, yet when he died in 1809 he was viewed by
many as little more than a "lying, drunken
infidel."14 The Republic had felt the impact of
the Second Great Awakening, of the revivals and of
the activities of the benevolent religious societies that the Great Awakening had spawned. These
societies, such as the tract, Bible, Sunday School,
education and temperance societies, along with the
revival preachers had gone to battle to stem the
rising tide of "irreligion" and "infidelity." To a

remarkable extent they had won the battle and, in the process, stamped an unmistakable Protestant label upon the Republic.

One noticeable aspect of the revival movements and the benevolent societies was their emphasis upon the importance of interdenominational unity and the concerted action of all evangelical Protestants. In fact, Christian unity was depicted not only as a religious but also as a patriotic act. As one of the American Tract Society's publications in 1834 stated: "Union is strength." Consequently each Christian should "join heart and hand with all the friends of virtue and religion in efforts to bless this country and save mankind."[15]

The drive for Protestant unity was evident in several areas. One was the emphasis on revivals. Focusing on the method-revivals — rather than on the content-theology — enabled Protestants from various denominations to cooperate in building God's Kingdom, be it on the frontier in the West or in the urban area. Interdenominational unity was evident in the numerous benevolent organizations which joined to hold their annual meetings in New York City on the same week in May, a week known as Anniversary Week. In 1834, the following societies were represented on Anniversary Week: The American Tract Society, The American Bible Society, The American Seaman's Friend's Society, The American Antislavery Society, The Revival Tract Society, The American Peace Society, The New York Sunday School Union, The New York Colonization Society, The American Home Missions Society, The American Baptist Home Missions Society, The Seventh Commandment Society, The Presbyterian Education Society - United, The Foreign Missions Board, The New York Temperance Society, and The New York Infant and Sunday School Society. Interdenominational Protestant unity was also evident in the founding and control of private colleges, especially in the mid-West. Not surprisingly, this cooperation spilled over into the promotion of common schools in the West as well.[16]

Several historians have emphasized the conservative social, political and economic attitudes of the leaders of the revival movement and of the managers of the benevolent societies. And certainly there was a conservative bent, a note of fear, evident in these leaders which will be discussed later.[17] But the revival movements also unleashed a millenial fervor which was basically optimistic in its outlook concerning America's future. If only Christians — meaning evangelical Protestants — would unite to do good and fight sin, America could speed up God's millenial timetable in ushering in an age when goodness would be triumphant. This co-mingling of revivalism, millenialism, and Americanism gave a religious sanction to manifest destiny. But America could only fulfill its destiny if it remained an orderly, homogeneous, Protestant Republic. Not surprisingly, much of this emphasis spilled over into the public school movement. The end result was to place an unmistakable Protestant stamp upon the schools.

The traditional accounts of the controversies over the struggle to establish statewide public school systems easily lent themselves to two erroneous conclusions. One was the assumption that the controversy was, to a large degree, a struggle between schoolmen and churchmen. But, as David Tyack has pointed out, this is a questionable interpretation based largely upon Horace Mann's skirmishes with men like Reverend Mathew Hale Smith and Frederick Packard, recording secretary of the American Sunday School Union; or on the skirmishes between the New York City Public School Society and Bishop John Hughes. Another misconception that may arise is that the public school reformers sought to build a secular school system, one which would jettison much of the religious baggage of its colonial ancestors. It would be erroneous to assume that the controversy over the common school was a struggle between those who wanted schools which were pro-religion and those who wanted schools which were religiously neutral.[18]

Both the churchmen and schoolmen were

11

concerned over changes in nineteenth century America which were undermining the preservation of orderly, homogeneous communities. Both groups were willing to use the schools to help control the direction of change. One major area of concern was demographic changes brought about by the growth of urban centers, the rapid expansion of the West, and the influx of immigrants after 1825.

The growth of cities, including industrial centers, was viewed both positively and negatively. Cities offered opportunities for wealth and culture. Increasingly, the nation's most prestigious churches were found in large urban centers. But with urbanization and industrialization also came the visible concentration of the working poor in slums and ghettoes. Cities brought together a large number of people without property, without a stake in society. Yet at the same time conspicuous wealth increased, thus magnifying the social distances between the classes. Furthermore cities seemed to lack traditional patterns of social control which had been prevalent in rural villages.[19]

Along with the rapid growth of urban centers came the dramatic rise of the West. Prior to the Civil War, the West usually meant the territory between the states along the Atlantic Coast and the Mississippi River as well as several settlements along the Pacific coast. After the Civil War the West also came to mean the Great Plains and the mountain territories. The West, like the city, was viewed with both optimism and apprehension. As Henry Nash Smith has pointed out, it was not the "picturesque Wild West beyond the agricultural frontier" which many Americans idolized but rather the "domesticated West that lay behind it."[20] What was necessary was to somehow transform the frontier wilderness into a domesticated garden. The wild West was viewed as a religious and immoral wilderness. As one worker for the American Tract Society commented in 1845, here one could find Methodist, United Brethren, Baptist, Presbyterian, Episcopalian, Lutheran, and Roman Catholic churches as well as a deist lecturer all in one county.

12

Furthermore, it was also perceived as a social wilderness, where, according to an Episcopalian clergyman, a "changing social order, lack of respect for tradition," and continued population movement made it seem as if everything was "undisciplined and at random." Adding to this lack of discipline and order was a diversity of national or ethnic groups.[21]

But midst this gloom there was also a ray of hope. The wilderness could become an orderly, homogeneous community. As Rush Welter and David Tyack have pointed out, many believed the church and the school to be the keys to effecting this transformation. The West had great potential for meanness and destructiveness but also for greatness and creativity. Protestant Christianity walking hand in hand with schools and seminaries, public and private, was the answer. Not surprisingly, evangelical churchmen often accepted leadership roles in public and private education — the distinction between the two was not always clear — in their drive to remake the West into an orderly, Protestant community.[22] In the process they helped reinforce the notion that "Americanism and Protestantism were synonymous and that education and Protestantism were allies."[23]

The largest threat to the creation and preservation of a Protestant Republic came from the immigrant. Approximately 35 million immigrants entered the United States in the nineteenth century, many of whom adhered to the Roman Catholic religion. The values and lifestyle of the immigrant were often suspect. But above all, Roman Catholicism was commonly perceived to be a threat to liberty. As the managers of the American Tract Society warned its supporters in 1845, already one-sixth of America's population was made up of immigrants. "If a soulless, formal faith, and a loose morality, added to imperfect views of the nature of government, a diversity of languages" should prevail among these people, there would be grounds for concern especially since probably one-half of these immigrants were under the influence of priests who owed their "allegiance to a foreign spiritual and civil despotism." This anti-Catholic attitude was evident not only in publications of religious societies but in schoolbooks as well.[24]

In order to counteract the divisive impact of the city, the West, and the immigrant upon the American communities, Americans increasingly turned to the public school. In the process, its functions were expanded, especially when it came to the transmission of values. Piety or virtue was more important than scholarship in the battle to ward off the ill effects of a disorderly society, one in which disharmony and diversity rather than unity and consensus seemed to prevail. And as schools came to be viewed more as institutions of virtue than of scholarship, the role of religion again loomed large. This was evident in Hoarce Mann's ideology as well.

Horace Mann agreed that schools were important because of their potential impact in raising the moral level of the citizenry. In his Twelfth Annual Report (1848) he argued:

> In a republican government, legislators are a mirror reflecting the moral countenance of their constituents. And hence it is, that the establishment of a republican government, without well-appointed and efficient means for the universal education of the people, is the most rash and fool-hardy experiment ever tried by man.[25]

For Mann, then, moral education was the key; it was a major reason for the existence of the common school and for significantly expanding its function. As Herbert Kliebard has pointed out, Mann viewed education "as a way of making people better." The formula for progress was clear. For Mann it was simply stated in the Biblical injunction: "Train up a child in the way he should go, and when he is old he will not depart from it." Not only was the formula simple, it was also foolproof." If the conditions are complied with, Mann wrote, "it makes no provision for a failure."[26]

The question which Horace Mann faced was
whether or not the schools could inculcate morals
without relying on the sanctions of sectarian doctrines. Mann's solution was not to remove the
sanctions of religion _per se_, only those of
"sectarian" religion. In his Twelfth Report, Mann
took pains to point out that neither the Bible nor
Christianity had been removed from the state's public schools. What was ruled out in the public
schools was the teaching of sectarian doctrine
imparted for the purpose of inducing a child to
"join this or that denomination." Sectarian doctrine included an emphasis on human depravity,
therefore the books published by Frederick
Packard's Sunday School Union were banned. Teachers were expected to cull common teachings from all
Christians — actually Protestant groups. These
truths would also be transmitted to the students
through the use of stories, such as the ones found
in the McGuffey readers, and through Bible
reading.[27]

Horace Mann's rejection of the doctrine of
innate human depravity did not lessen the need for
religion and morality in the schools. Rather it
merely shifted the focus from heredity to environment which magnified the importance of nurture.
This emphasis would reappear in Horace Bushnell's
Christian Nurture (1847) which stressed three major
points. Conversion could be gradual, a process of
nurture and maturation; the child was born, in
Lockean terms, neither good nor bad; and God was
depicted as a God of love rather than a God of
wrath. For followers of Mann and Bushnell this
meant that the proper nurturing of the young was of
utmost importance, but also that nurture could
focus more on love than on fear. How much of the
theology of love found its way into school practice
is questionable.[28]

The controversies which surrounded Horace Mann,
then, were not disputes over whether schools should
teach morality and include religion. Right

believing in religious matters was deemed essential
to right behaving. Consequently an atheist, a
deist, or even a Jew or a Catholic could not be expected to act correctly. The question was whether
morality had to "rest upon a particular kind of
Christianity." Although some conservative Protestants said yes, in the end most Protestants closed
ranks in defense of a non-sectarian Protestantism,
especially when confronted with the influx of
Catholic immigrants.[29]

The shift from sectarian to non-sectarian
Protestant education is well illustrated in New
York City in the first half of the nineteenth
century. Since education had been traditionally
associated with religion and since New York City
was religiously diverse, little effort had been
made prior to 1805 to provide some form of communal
education. Matching funds provided by the State
legislature after 1795 for towns setting up their
own schools went to the City's ten church schools
and the African Free School. In 1805 a society was
organized, soon renamed the Free School Society, to
provide education for those children not being
served by an existing religious school. In 1807
the Society requested and received 5,000 dollars
from the State legislature and within two years it
was receiving a large portion of the City's allotment. In essence, the Free School Society was
becoming a non-sectarian Protestant organization.
Although Bible reading and religious exercises
(somewhat in a catechetical style) were carried on
daily, the Society's trustees sought to observe a
"scrupulous nonsectarianism." When several
churches, most notably the Bethel Baptist Church,
sought to expand their efforts into also operating
nondenominational schools, the Free School Society
opposed their plans if it meant that they would
share in the City's allotment. In 1825 the City
Common Council agreed with the Free School Society
and denied common school funds to any religious
society. The following year the Free School
Society was renamed the Public School Society and
was given permission to enroll any students, regardless of religious affiliation or class background.

New York City had, in effect, a non-sectarian Protestant school society.[30]

In the end, however, the Public School Society was unable to deliver what it promised — education for all children, especially the poor — under a nonsectarian umbrella. Beginning in the 1820s and increasing dramatically in the decades of the 1830s, 1840s and 1850s was a population shift brought about due to the massive influx of Irish Catholic immigrants. At first the Catholic leadership under Bishop John DuBois sought to work with the Public School Society. Bishop DuBois requested that sectarian Protestant principles and anti-Catholic references be deleted from the textbooks and that a Catholic teacher be hired by the Society. However, Bishop Du Bois' successor, Bishop John Hughes, rejected both the possibility and desirability of reaching a satisfactory compromise with the Society. Instead, he sought public funds to set up Catholic schools. In the end, Bishop Hughes lost his battle. The Public School Society was dissolved and made part of the New York's common school system. But no public monies were granted for the establishment of Catholic schools. As Timothy Smith has pointed out, in the controversy with the Catholics as with the Bethel Baptist Church earlier, "it was not secularism but non-denominational Protestantism which won the day." Although no public monies were to be used for sectarian religious instruction, the reading of the King James version of the Bible was required by the City Council. For those who found this concept of non-sectarian education unacceptable there was only one recourse; namely, to follow Bishop Hughes' lead in building a parochial school system.[31]

Non-denominational Protestantism won the battle not only in New York City but in the nation's schoolbooks as well. Catholicism rarely received a sympathetic hearing. Children were taught that virtue could only be identified with Christianity, and Christianity only with Protestantism. Although the harsh anti-Catholic notes were toned down somewhat after 1870, textbooks

17

continued to depict America as a Protestant country. Despite the negative portrayal of Catholicism, religion and moralisms loomed large in schoolbooks. Industry, frugality, chastity, and financial success were virtues that continually reappeared in the books. And alongside these virtues went religion. As Elson has pointed out, a "sense of God" just as "surely as a sense of nationalism" permeated all books. As late as 1880 the Webster Speller still contained at least one practice sentence on religion for every group of practice sentences. Science and math books taught that nature was created for man and man for God. The nineteenth century child read that this was God's world and that America would have a special place in it.[32]

The concepts of a Protestant Republic and a non-denominational Protestant school which had taken root in the pre-Civil War era continued to flourish in the late nineteenth and early twentieth centuries. As Americans witnessed labor unrest, slums, poverty and reoccurring waves of Roman Catholic immigrants they called for an "explicit teaching of behavior and patriotism." The public school was given this task. In the process the King James version of the Bible once again became the rallying point for nativists.[33]

Churchmen, educators and politicians all agreed that the Bible was the bedrock upon which American education was built. The National Teacher's Association in 1869 resolved that the Bible should be "devotionally read, and its precepts inculcated in all the common schools of the land." In 1885 the Massachusetts Legislature passed a constitutional amendment forbidding the use of public funds for sectarian schools but, at the same time, requiring that the Bible be read in the common schools. In 1894, Ohio's State Superintendent informed the N.E.A. convention "that excluding religion would impair the efficiency of the common schools." Two years later, Vermont's State Superintendent called for the "imperial and regenerating power" of the Bible to "pervade the

Nation's schools."[34] At the federal governmental
level, Senator Henry Blair of New Hampshire proposed a constitutional amendment in 1888 which
would require every state to establish and maintain
a public school system for all children, ages 6-16,
in which knowledge, "virtue, morality, and the
principles of the Christian religion" would be
taught. However no public monies were to go to any
school in which doctrines "peculiar to any sect"
would be taught. As Tyack has pointed out, the
Blair Bill was an attack on the Roman Catholic
population since Blair insisted that children
needed to be instructed in "that religion which is
the religion of the United States."[35]

The drive to link public schooling with "that
religion which is the religion of the United
States" was not without its dissenters. One source
of dissent, as mentioned previously, was the Roman
Catholic community. A most noticeable symbol of
this dissent was the parochial school.

In dealing with the Catholic dissent several
points need to be kept in mind. The history of the
public school's relations with the immigrant community was not only one of conflict. Timothy Smith
has pointed out that many immigrants viewed
schooling as the road to "personal gain." They did
not, as a whole, oppose compulsory education laws.
Furthermore, not all Catholic parents withdrew
their children from the public schools. Although
hindsight might suggest that the establishment of
parochial systems was inevitable, it did not appear
so to many Catholic leaders in the nineteenth century. But once the crusade for assimilation of
immigrants increased in tempo in the late nineteenth and early twentieth centuries, and as public
educators increasingly demonstrated an unwilling-
ness to accommodate the immigrant's interests, many
Catholic parents and leaders came to the conclusion
that the parochial school was the only viable option. One such group was the German Catholic
community which turned to parochial schools to preserve both its religion and language.[36]

19

Some, however, opted to stay within the public sector and to use their political influence to get some control over textbooks, course offerings, and staffing. For the Irish in New York City this meant working with Tammany Hall and its patronage system to encourage the hiring of young immigrant females as teachers and immigrant adults as school janitors, or to lobby for the removal of objectional materials from school books. The immigrant groups were successful in this as long as the decentralized ward system was prevalent in urban areas. In Wisconsin, Catholic voters in 1890 were successful in overturning the Bennett Law which had required that most of the instruction in private schools be given in the English language.[37]

Dissenters also utilized the court system to challenge anti-Catholic or anti-immigrant behaviors on the part of teachers and school systems. These forays into the legal domain resulted in both frustrations and victories. In 1854 the Maine Supreme Court upheld the right of the school authorities to expel Bridget Donahoe from school for her refusal to read the Protestant Bible. In 1884, the Iowa Supreme Court upheld a statute which forbade the exclusion of the Bible from the schools. Twenty years later the Kansas Supreme Court ruled unanimously that the use of Bible reading and the Lord's Prayer did not violate a state statute prohibiting religious worship and sectarian instruction in the schools.[38] Yet there were also occasions where protest was successful. In 1872 the Cincinnati Board of Education took a controversial step in forbidding Bible reading in schools, a decision which was upheld by the Ohio Supreme Court. In 1890, in response to Catholic petitioners, the Wisconsin Supreme Court ruled that the reading of the King James version of the Bible constituted sectarian instruction and hence it was unconstitutional. Similar rulings were handed down by the State Supreme Court in Nebraska (1902), Illinois (1910), and Louisiana (1915). Especially noteworthy is the Illinois case, People ex rel. Ring v. Board of Education, where the Court ruled in favor of the Catholic petitioners despite the fact that

20

the school excused children of those parents who objected to their participation in reading the King James version of the Bible, reciting the Lord's Prayer, and the singing of hymns.[39]

A comprehensive treatment of the literature of dissent from the Protestant consensus would also include the writings of philosophers and social workers such as Horace Kallen, John Dewey, and Jane Addams. For the sake of brevity only two points will be made at this time. Dissent was evident in John Dewey's attempts to root ethics in the scientific method. Central to Dewey's philosophy was an "emphasis on the virtues of the experimental scientific intelligence."[40] Consequently, Dewey moved to break the link between morality and religion. As Newman has pointed out, for Dewey, "morality was a secular concept ..., it flowed from social interaction, not divine will."[41] Dissent was also evident in the call for cultural pluralism as expressed by Horace Kallen and, supported to a large extent, by Jane Addams and John Dewey. Kallen rejected the notion that the establishment and preservation of a community could only be achieved through pouring all immigrants into one Anglo-Protestant mold. Citizenship, he argued, need not only be separated from religion; it could also be divorced from "language, cultured traditions, all that is called a race."[42]

On the balance sheet, the first three decades of the twentieth century dealt somewhat harshly with the dissenters. More in keeping with American popular thought was Josiah Strong's Our Country (1885), in which he combined Protestantism, Anglo-Saxon race theories, and evolutionary thought to justify his call for American and Christian expansion overseas.[43] Furthermore, World War I unleashed a drive for 100 percent Americanism which spilled over into the decade of the 1920s and culminated in the passage of the National Origins Act of 1924.

The drive for Americanization was aided by several school reforms. One was the drive to centralize the urban school systems; to replace the old ward system with one centralized school board. It was precisely the old decentralized ward system which the Irish had used in New York City to make the schools at least somewhat responsive to their fears and interests.[44] The other reform was compulsory education. Although all states, except for those in the South, had passed some form of compulsory school legislation in the nineteenth century, these were not enforced with any degree of regularity. This changed after 1900 as an embattled Anglo-Protestant community faced the immigrant. Voluntary assimilation in the schools now became coerced assimilation.[45]

The drive for assimilation was reflected in laws passed in several states. After 1913, 12 states and the District of Columbia enacted laws requiring daily Bible reading in the schools. North Dakota stipulated that the Ten Commandments must be posted in its public schools. When theories of evolution challenged older orthodox beliefs, Tennessee passed its anti-evolution law. Since foreignism was reflected not only in religion but also in language, and as the concept of a hyphenated American became increasingly unacceptable in World War I, numerous states forbade the teaching of German in public schools. Nebraska, however, went one step further. It sought to define Americanism and the American language not only for its public but also for its private schools. In 1919, the Nebraska Legislature enacted a law which stipulated that no child should be taught in a language other than English in the first eight grades. The Supreme Court, in the Meyer v. State of Nebraska case (1923) ruled that this law constituted an unreasonable infringement on the liberty guaranteed in the Fourteenth Amendment.[46]

It remained, however, for Oregon voters to demonstrate just how far a majority was willing to go to legislate conformity and orthodoxy in education. In 1922, Oregon voters passed an initiative petition, heavily lobbied by the Ku Klux Klan and seemingly supported by the state's public educators,

22

to require all children, ages 8 to 16, to attend
public schools. For the Klan leaders, the desire
to abolish religious pluralism was one motivating
factor, and the most visible target was the Roman
Catholic Church and its parochial schools. But in
defense of this bill, the Klan leadership also at-
tacked other church groups including the Episco-
palians, Seventh Day Adventists and Methodists —
all were portrayed as culprits who lit the torch to
the public school. Anglo-conformity, Protestantism,
and the public school were all wrapped in the
American flag. An embattled majority was ready to
safeguard the Republic by coercing a reluctant
minority. Again the plaintiffs sought redress in
the courts. In the <u>Pierce</u> v. <u>Society of Sisters</u>
case (1925) the Supreme Court ruled that the Act of
1922 constituted an unreasonable interference
> with the liberty of parents and
> guardians to direct the upbringing
> and education of children under
> their control.[47]

Conclusion

When the Americans ratified the First Amendment to the Constitution they had endorsed the
principle that one could separate citizenship from
religious sectarianism. Separation of Church and
State had been based on the assumption that people
of different religious affiliations could effectively cooperate in establishing and maintaining a
political community. The revivals of the early
nineteenth century had reinforced this assumption,
but with one important limitation. An American
community could only be maintained with the sanction of Protestant religion. It was this legacy
which the nineteenth century public school movement
inherited as it sought to transmit a common core of
values to all students in its attempt to create a
cohesive political and social community through
the school house.

The need for building a cohesive political and
social community became most urgent in times of

23

stress. At first this stress came from the rapidly growing urban and industrial centers, from the un-disciplined West, but in the end it came primarily from the immigrants, many of whom did not speak the English language or espouse the Protestant religion. In the desire to safeguard Americans from the divi-sive impact of ethnic and religious pluralism, schoolmen, politicians, and ministers fell back upon a pre-defined standard of Americanism, one which defined citizenship in relation to Protes-tantism. At first they called for voluntary par-ticipation, but when dissenters declined to conform they turned to compulsion. There were dissenters to the notion that a community could not be main-tained without the aid of a schoolhouse which linked morality and political orthodoxy to Protes-tantism and Anglo conformity. These cries of dissent, however, were drowned out whenever the embattled Protestant majority felt itself threat-ened. Beginning with voluntary suasion, schoolmen gradually turned to compulsion in their quest to safeguard the community. Just how far an embattled majority was willing to go to enforce conformity on a reluctant minority was revealed in the Nebraska and Oregon cases of the post World War I era.

Looking back at the nineteenth century consen-sus enables one to better understand the opposition of the religious fundamentalists to the Supreme Court's decisions of the 1960s relative to Bible reading and prayer in the schools. The public school was rarely religiously neutral, and religion was rarely divorced from morality. Yet piety or morality and not scholarship was what public schooling was all about. In this perspective education for a democratic society was rarely de-fined in pluralistic terms.

NOTES

1. David Tyack, "Onward Christian Soldiers: Religion and
   the American Common School," History and Education: The
   Educational Uses of the Past, ed. by Paul Nash (New
   York: Random House, 1970), p. 214.

2. Ibid., pp. 214-15. On the attempts by educators to use
   schooling and religion as tools for the creation of com-
   munity see Joseph Newman, "Morality, Religion, and the
   Public Schools' Quest for Community," Review Journal of
   Philosophy and Social Science, IV (Winter, 1979), 18-32;
   and R. Freeman Butts, Public Education in the United
   States: From Revolution to Reform (New York: Holt,
   Rinehart and Winston, 1978), ch. 5, 9, 10, 12.

3. Lawrence Cremin, American Education: The Colonial
   Experience, 1607-1878 (New York: Harper and Row, 1970),
   pp. 182-486, 494-99; James Axtell, The School Upon a
   Hill: Education and Society in Colonial New England
   (New Haven, Conn.: Yale Univ. Press, 1974), pp. 166-200.

4. Lawrence Byrnes, Religion and Public Education (New
   York: Harper and Row, 1975), p. 39; Daniel Boorstin,
   The Americans: The Colonial Experience, Vintage Bks.
   (New York: Random House, 1958), pp. 8, 138; Herbert
   Kliebard, ed., Religion and Education in America: A
   Documentary History (Scranton, Pa.: International
   Textbook Co., 1969), p. 2; and Anson P. Stokes and Leo
   Pfeffer, Church and State in the United States (Revised;
   New York: Harper and Row, 1964), pp. 4-7.

5. Roy Nichols, Religion and American Democracy (Baton
   Rouge: Louisiana State Univ. Press, 1959), pp. 3-49;
   Howard K. Beale, A History of Freedom of Teaching in
   American Schools: Report of the Commission of the
   Social Studies, Part IV (New York: Octagon Bks., 1966
   [1941]), p. 29.

6. Ronald D. Cohen, "Socialization in Colonial New England,"
   History of Education Quarterly, XIII (Spring, 1973),
   72-77; Richard Pratte, The Public School Movement: A
   Critical Study (New York: David McKay, 1973), p. 39;
   Beale, A History of Freedom of Teaching in Am. Schools,
   p. 29.

7. Butts, Public Education in the U.S., p. 7.

8. Barbara Finkelstein, "Pedagogy as Intrusion: Teaching Values in Popular Primary Schools in Nineteenth-Century America," reprinted in History, Education, and Public Policy, ed. by Donald Warren (Berkeley, Cal.: McCutchan, 1978), pp. 239-40; Axtell, The School Upon a Hill, p. 49.

9. Jonathan Messerli, Horace Mann: A Biography (New York: Alfred A. Knopf, 1972), p. 13; Robert L. Church and Michael W. Sedlak, Education in the United States: An Interpretive History (New York: Free Press, 1976), pp. 3-22; Ruther Miller Elson, Guardians of Tradition: American Schoolbooks of the Nineteenth Century (Lincoln, Neb.: Univ. of Neb., 1964), p. 5.

10. Stokes and Pfeffer, Church and State in the U.S., pp. 37, 72.

11. Ibid.

12. Cited in Butts, Public Education in the U.S., p. 29.

13. Timothy L. Smith, "Protestant Schooling and American Nationality," Journal of American History, LIII (March, 1967), 679; Butts, Public Education in the U.S., pp. 26-37; Nichols, Religion and Am. Democracy, pp. 39-41.

14. Cited in Harvey Neufeldt, "The American Tract Society, 1825-1865: An Examination of its Religious, Economic, Social, and Political Ideas" (Unpublished Ph.D. Dissertation, Michigan State University, 1971), p. 199.

15. Cited in Neufeldt, "The American Tract Society", p. 228.

16. Ibid., pp. 8-9, 106-107; David B. Potts, "American Colleges in the Nineteenth Century: From Localism to Denominationalism," History of Education Quarterly, XI (Winter, 1971), 363-80; David Tyack, "The Kingdom of God and the Common School: Protestant Ministers and the Educational Awakening in the West," Harvard Educational Review, XXXVI (Fall, 1966), 447-69.

17. The conservative nature of evangelical Protestantism and the attempt of the managers of benevolent organizations to use religion as an instrument for controlling the direction of social change in Jacksonian America is emphasized in C. S. Griffin, Their Brothers' Keepers: Moral Stewardship in the United States, 1800-1865 (New Brunswick, N.J.: Rutgers Univ., 1960).

18. Tyack, "Onward Christian Soldiers," pp. 214-15.

26

19. Church and Sedlak, Education in the U.S., pp. 70-72.

20. Cited in Neufeldt, "The American Tract Society," p. 470.

21. Ibid., p. 473.

22. Rush Welter, "The Frontier West as Image of American Society: Conservative Attitudes Before the Civil War," Mississippi Valley Historical Review, XLVI (March, 1960), 593-614; Tyack, "The Kingdom of God and the Common Schools," pp. 447-69.

23. Smith, "Protestant Schooling and Am. Nationality," p. 680.

24. Neufeldt, "The American Tract Society," p. 415.

25. Lawrence Cremin, ed., The Republic and the School: Horace Mann on the Education of Free Men (New York: Teachers College, 1957), p. 91.

26. Ibid., pp. 100-101; Kliebard, Religion and Education in Am., p. 6.

27. Church and Sedlak, Education in the U.S., p. 90; Kliebard, Religion and Education in Am., p. 6.

28. Church and Sedlak, Education in the U.S., pp. 86-93; Finkelstein, "Pedagogy as Intrusion," p. 245; Michael Katz, The Irony of Early School Reform: Educational Innovation in Mid-Nineteenth Century Massachusetts (Boston: Beacon, 1968), pp. 141-45.

29. Messerli, Horace Mann, pp. 310-11.

30. Diane Ravitch, The Great School Wars: New York City, 1805-1973: A History of the Public Schools as Battle-field of Social Change (New York: Basic Bks., 1974), pp. 18-26.

31. Ibid., pp. 33-104; Smith, "Protestant Schooling and Am. Nationality," p. 687; Church and Sedlak, Education in the U.S., pp. 157-67.

32. Elson, Guardians of Tradition, pp. 15-54, 226-28, 251.

33. Marvin Lazerson, Origins of the Urban School: Public Education in Massachusetts, 1870-1915 (Cambridge, Mass.: Harvard Univ., 1971), p. 204.

34. Quotations cited in Tyack, "Onward Christian Soldiers," pp. 221-26.

35. Ibid., pp. 241-42.

36. Smith, "Protestant Schooling and Am. Nationality,"
    pp. 534-35, 539, 542; Robert D. Cross, "Origins of the
    Catholic Parochial School" reprinted in The American
    Experience in Education ed. by John Barnard and David
    Bruner (New York: New Viewpoints, 1975), pp. 168-82;
    Tyack, "Onward Christian Soldiers," p. 243; and David
    Tyack, The One Best System: A History of American
    Urban Education (Cambridge, Mass.: Harvard Univ.,
    1974), pp. 84-86.

37. Tyack, The One Best System, pp. 94-95, 109.

38. Donahoe v. Richard et al., 38 Maine 407, 409 (1854);
    Moore v. Monroe, 64 Iowa 367 (1884); Billiard v. Board
    of Education of Topeka, 69 Kansas 53 (1904), all dis-
    cussed in Beale, A History of Freedom of Teaching in
    Am. Schools, pp. 102-103, 213.

39. Beale, A History of Freedom of Teaching in Am. Schools,
    pp. 216-17; Philip B. Kurland, "The Regents' Prayer
    Case: 'Full of Sound and Fury, Signifying ...'" in
    Church and State: The Supreme Court and the First
    Amendment ed. by Philip Kurland (Chicago: Univ. of
    Chicago, 1962), pp. 18-19.

40. Paul F. Bourke, "Philosophy and Social Criticism:
    John Dewey, 1910-1920," History of Education Quarterly,
    XV (Spring, 1975), 12.

41. Newman, "Morality, Religion, and the Public Schools'
    Quest for Community," p. 26.

42. Cited in J. Christopher Eisele, "John Dewey and the
    Immigrants," History of Education Quarterly, XV (Spring,
    1975), 74. See also Butts, Public Education in the
    U.S., pp. 380-81.

43. Richard Hofstadter, Social Darwinism in American Thought
    (Revised ed.; Boston: Beacon, 1955), pp. 178-79.

44. On the drive for political reforms in urban schools see
    Tyack, The One Best System, pp. 126-76.

45. Michael S. Katz, A History of Compulsory Education Laws,
    Fastback No. 75 (Bloomington, Ind.: Phi Delta Kappa,
    1976).

46. Kliebard, Religion and Education in Am., pp. 115-20.

47. Cited in <u>Ibid.</u>, p. 125. On the <u>Pierce</u> Case see also David Tyack, "The Perils of Pluralism: The Background of the Pierce Case," <u>American Historical Review</u>, LXXIV (October, 1968), 74-98; Church and Sedlak, <u>Education in the U.S.</u>, p. 185.

Schools, the State, and the First Amendment

James F. Herndon

The First Amendment to the United States Constitution requires that "Congress shall make no law
respecting an establishment of religion, or prohibiting the free exercise thereof." These pro-
hibitions appear to be absolute, and so they may
have been intended, but they are not; governments
in the United States have customarily maintained
close relationships with organized religion and
have supported a variety of religious traditions.
Nor has government refrained from regulating some
kinds of conduct merely because that conduct is
part of a religious exercise. The First Amendment
should be seen, then, not as a set of absolute commands but as a guide to what actions of government
are permissible as public authority tries both to
accommodate itself to religious interest and to set
the terms by which religious exercise is accommodated to the public interest. Viewed in this way,
the First Amendment is necessarily ambiguous. It
allows many interpretations, some in conflict with
each other. American political and constitutional
practice directs that such ambiguities, and the
conflicts that result, are to be resolved by
courts. Since the Supreme Court of the United
States speaks in some ultimate sense to these
questions, it is customary to look to that court's
opinions to learn what constitutional restrictions
actually permit and proscribe. We shall follow
that custom here.

Since the Supreme Court's decisions regarding
the free exercise clause, as applied to religion
and schooling, are somewhat more straightforward
than those involving the establishment of religion,
we shall consider that prohibition first. Later
we will examine the Court's ruling on the establishment clause as a restriction on religious practice in the public schools and as a restriction on
public aid to religious schools. We shall conclude
with a discussion of ways in which each of the two
clauses defines permissible state action under the

other. It will be good to bear in mind throughout that the First Amendment is neither self-enforcing nor self-interpreting, that whatever meanings have been given to the religion clauses are subject to intense disagreement, and that these meanings may well change in the future.

In interpreting the free exercise clause the Supreme Court has generally balanced an interest in religious freedom against the purportedly greater social interest represented by the public policy at issue. The process was set in motion by Reynold v. U.S. (1878), [1] a case presenting a challenge by Mormons to a federal statute making bigamy a crime. Despite the claim that polygamous marriage for Mormons was justified by religious belief, the Court upheld the statute arguing that while Congress was forbidden by the First Amendment to legislate in matters of opinion, no such impediment prevented Congress from concerning itself with actions "in violation of social duties or subversive of good order."[2] A few years after Reynolds, in Davis v. Beason (1890),[3] the Court permitted disenfranchisement of Mormons on similar grounds. Free exercise of religion was protected by the First Amendment, to be sure, but only so long as "the laws of society ... and the morals of its people, are not interfered with."[4]

These cases had little relevance to education, but they made the point that there are limits on what the free exercise clause permits and that the state is not without legal authority to regulate or even to forbid actions associated with religious belief which are contrary to some higher interest of the state. The Supreme Court did not link religious freedom and education until well into the twentieth century and then through the agency of the Fourteenth rather than the First Amendment. In Permioli v. Municipality of New Orleans (1845),[5] the Court had held that the First Amendment was not applicable to the states, a position from which the Court departed only in 1940, in Cantwell v.

Connecticut.[6] From adoption of the Fourteenth
Amendment in 1868 it was that amendment's guarantee
of liberty to all persons that was used to protect
religious exercise against state action. The first
case raising a religious issue on Fourteenth Amendment grounds was Meyer v. Nebraska,[7] decided in
1923. Here the state contended that its interest
in the education of children permitted it to forbid
teaching in a foreign language, even in Lutheran
schools where Bible stories were read in German.
The Court disagreed, finding Nebraska's laws to be
an unreasonable deprivation of the liberty protected by the Fourteenth Amendment. A more direct
threat to religious schools was turned back by the
Supreme Court in Pierce v. Society of Sisters
(1925),[8] a case involving an Oregon statute that
denied accreditation to any but public schools. A
Roman Catholic order of nuns challenged the statute
on grounds that enforcement of the law, coupled
with active administration of the state's truancy
laws, would have meant the demise of parochial
schools. The Court agreed, finding that though the
state could regulate all schools and require that
every child attend some school and that teachers
"be of good moral character and patriotic disposition,"[9] the state was made powerless by the Fourteenth Amendment to "standardize its children by
forcing them to accept instruction from public
teachers only."[10]

In the first case applying the First Amendment's protection of religious liberty to school
children, the Court was not so generous. In
Minersville v. Gobitis (1940)[11] the Court upheld a
Pennsylvania requirement that public school pupils
recite the Pledge of Allegiance despite objections
by Jehovah's Witnesses that the Pledge was a form
of idolatry forbidden by their religion. A
majority of the Court held that the state's interest in fostering patriotism had greater legal
weight than the religious interest represented by
those to whom the Pledge was offensive. Later,
however, in West Virginia State Board of Education
v. Barnette (1943),[12] the Court found the state's
requirement of the Pledge of Allegiance, when

33

applied to Jehovah's Witnesses, to be an act of un-constitutional hostility to religion. Such hos-tility, the Court said, was not permitted by the First Amendment's guarantee of free exercise.[13]

Three other claims to freedom from state com-pulsion in educational matters have been made on First Amendment grounds. The first of these con-cerns the simple questions of attendance. In Pierce the Court said that the state could legitimately "require that all children of proper age attend some school."[14] That position was re-affirmed in Donner v. New York (1951),[15] a case in which the Supreme Court summarily affirmed the decision of a state court upholding a compulsory attendance statute as applied to elementary school children despite a claim that enforcement of the law compromised religious belief. But in Wisconsin v. Yoder (1972),[16] the Court found that the state's interest in education could not support compulsory attendance beyond the eighth grade in the face of religious objections made by two Amish sects. Ac-commodating these objections, the Court held, would result in the loss of only one or two addi-tional years of schooling and would not therefore "impair the physical or mental health of the child, or result in an inability to be self-supporting or to discharge the duties and responsibilities of citizenship, or in any other way to detract from the welfare of society."[17] The state's interest in these matters was not enough to justify what the Amish regarded as a threat to religious values posed by a public high school.

Religious values have not been sufficient, however, to protect a private school in its appli-cation of racially discriminatory admissions policies. In Dade Christian Schools v. Brown (1978),[18] the Court summarily affirmed a lower court decision holding that the free exercise clause cannot be used to support racial bias and thereby to set aside the state's interest in equality of educational opportunity. The last re-maining area in which objections have been made to state action on religious grounds concerned an attempt by the National Labor Relations Board to regulate relationships between teachers and administrators of religious schools.[19] This effort, the Court said, "would give rise to serious constitutional questions,"[20] questions the Court chose not to answer after finding that Congress had never authorized any such effort by the statute relied on by the NLRB.

A claim to religious belief, then, does not justify full exemption from state concern for any and all actions that may stem from that belief. The state has a legitimate interest in requiring attendance, at least at elementary schools, and it may protect its citizens from racial discrimination. Yet the state interest in education is not absolute. It may not compel attendance of high school students whose religious beliefs are threatened by the school's environment, nor may it require participation in patriotic exercises by those for whom such rituals are a form of idolatry. And as the earliest cases showed, the state's interest does not extend lawfully to the monopolization of schooling or to the forbidding of foreign language instruction in religious schools. Deriving a principle from these cases is not so simple, both because there are so few cases and because the Court has not always spoken with a single voice. The Court seems disposed to favor freedom of religious exercise when it could while recognizing that the state retains a bedrock interest in education that religious claims cannot dislodge. Perhaps the most direct statement of the Court's view of the underlying principle is that given by Chief Justice Burger in Yoder: "Only those interests of the highest order not otherwise served can overbalance legitimate claims to the free exercise of religion."[21]

The issues that have arisen in the establishment cases are of two kinds. The first concerns religion in the public schools, the second public aid in support of religious schools. As in the free exercise cases, it is possible to identify both permissible and impermissible action by the state, and it is possible (though somewhat more difficult) to state the principles that distinguish one from the other.

The earliest case involving religion in the public schools, McCollum v. Board of Education (1948),[22] had to do with arrangements an Illinois school board had made for sectarian teachers to offer religious instruction once a week in public schools. Children of a particular faith were to attend classes led by a representative of that faith, while those who professed no faith or those whose parents wished them not to attend religion classes were sent to study halls. The religious teachers were approved and supervised by the school superintendent, and the school's regular faculty were to keep attendance records to make certain that the children were where they belonged. Finding that these arrangements were "a utilization of the tax-established and tax-supported public school system to aid religious groups to spread their faith,"[23] the Court struck down the Illinois program as a clear violation of the First Amendment.

A short time later, in Zorach v. Clauson (1952),[24] the Court upheld a New York program similar in all material respects to the Illinois plan, save one. The difference was that in New York the instruction by religious teachers took place off school grounds. The regular teachers maintained attendance records, and children who did not attend religious classes were to stay in school and attend to their regular studies. Though the machinery of the public school system was implicated in the conduct of religious studies, the Court felt that the conduct of those studies away from the public school building was enough to render the New York practice constitutional. The public schools had not made an establishment of religion but had only accommodated the school schedule to religious interest. While the First Amendment forbids mutual dependence of church and state, it does not impose separation of church and state "in every and all respects."[25] Any other reading, the Court said, would make church and state "aliens to each other--

hostile, suspicious and even unfriendly."[26] The First Amendment made the state powerless to offer direct and substantial aid to religion at the same time that it forbade the state to adopt a posture of hostility to religion, which its refusal to practice simple accommodation of interest would be.

Something more than accommodation takes place when public school facilities are used to promote religious exercises. Holding that governments have no authority to write a prayer and mandate its use in public schools, the Supreme Court struck down the practice of daily recital in New York schools of a prayer composed by the state Board of Regents in Engel v. Vitale (1962).[27] That the prayer was written in a way that the Board felt would offend no particular sect, and that children who wished not to pray could be excused, made little impression on the Court. The practice amounted to an establishment of religion and was forbidden by the First Amendment.[28]

A similar finding was made a year later in Abington School District v. Schempp (1963),[29] a case involving Pennsylvania's requirement that Bible verses be read at the start of the school day. Though the reading was to be done without comment, and children were to be excused on the request of a parent or guardian, the Court saw Pennsylvania's action as an unconstitutional establishment of religion. After noting that "our national life reflects a religious people,"[30] the Court wrote that religious freedom is just "as strongly embedded in our public and private life."[31] The joining of church and state threatens that freedom, the Court said, and led to its earlier decisions prescribing a "wholesome neutrality" between church and state. If neutrality is to be maintained, any state action must have "a secular legislative purpose and a primary effect that neither advances nor inhibits religion."[32] Since Bible reading in Pennsylvania schools had the effect of advancing religion, and since the purpose of the practice was other than secular, the state's action necessarily contravened the First Amendment.[33]

37

The next major issue involving religious practice in public schools concerned the efforts of fundamentalists to rid high school biology classes of the Darwinian theory of evolution. An Arkansas statute had forbidden instruction in Darwinian theory, an action the Court found unconstitutional in Epperson v. Arkansas (1968).[34] Since the statute had the effect of lending support to sectarian doctrines regarding the origin of humanity, the state's action amounted to an unlawful establishment of religion.

In this set of establishment cases, religion appears not to have fared so well as it did in the free exercise cases. The public schools may cooperate in providing off-the-premises religious instruction, but they may not be used for sectarian teaching or for religious exercises. Accommodation of schedule is permitted, but little else. The schools may not adopt a posture of hostility to religion, but neither may they be so friendly that they become the means for the support of religious doctrine. The principle that divides permissible state action from the impermissible is the one enunciated in Schempp: for a state practice to fall within what the First Amendment allows, the practice must have "a secular legislative purpose and a primary effect that neither advances nor inhibits religion."[35]

This same principle was eventually used to dispose of issues in a second set of establishment cases, to which we turn now. Whereas the first set of cases involved religion in the public schools, this second group concerns public aid to religious schools. Though having little to do with education, the Court's decision in Bradfield v. Roberts (1899)[36] set a rule it was to follow later as it dealt more specifically with the limits to aid government could furnish to sectarian schools. In this case, the question was whether the national government could constitutionally provide financial help to a hospital administered by a religious order. Since federal aid was designed to serve medical and not religious purposes, the Supreme

Court saw no impediment in the First Amendment to this use of money.

A similar argument led to the Court's approval of textbook loans to Louisiana parochial school children in Cochran v. Louisiana (1930).[37] Since the First Amendment had not yet been made applicable to the states, the Court did not address the establishment question in this case, relying instead for disposition on the Fourteenth Amendment. The Court nevertheless developed a principle here, very much like the one it set out in Bradfield, that it was to use when later it met the establishment issue head on. Against a claim that Louisiana's action constituted an unequal use of property for private rather than public purposes (a use that the Fourteenth Amendemnt did not permit), the Court found that action conferred a benefit not on the private schools but on the children attending them. The state's power to tax was therefore used not for private gain but for a public purpose and so fell within what the Fourteenth Amendment allowed.

The Court's first encounter with a claim that public aid to religious schools was an establishment of religion, and therefore forbidden by the First Amendment, occurred in Everson v. Board of Education (1947).[38] Here the issue was whether a New Jersey school board could lawfully reimburse parents for the costs of transporting their children to and from parochial schools. Certainly, the Court said, this policy helps children get to church schools, and it may even help some attend who would not do so otherwise. To the extent that these effects are present, the board's policy is an aid to religion. But is it an establishment of religion? The Court thought not, arguing that in maintaining the barriers against religious establishment the Supreme Court must not interfere with the state's ability to offer its benefits to all regardless of religious faith. Since the board's spending of public money to transport parochial school children was part of a broader program benefitting all school children, that action was

39

not offensive to the First Amendment. As in
Bradfield and Cochran, public aid was designed to
serve other than religious purposes and so was
constitutional.[39]

Following Everson, the Court was presented
with a great variety of efforts by local and state
governments to aid religion. One of the first of
these was a New York requirement that local school
boards lend non-sectarian textbooks to children in
private high schools. In Board of Education v.
Allen (1968),[40] the Court had little difficulty ap-
proving New York's action on the "child benefit"
theory it had followed in Cochran and Everson.
This theory, along with the "secular legislative
purpose" and "primary effect" test given in Schempp,
might well have permitted the Court to dispose of
subsequent cases with equal ease. But in another
of those cases that had no immediate bearing on
education, the Court developed a third test. This
case, Walz v. Tax Commission (1970),[41] arose as a
challenge of the New York City Tax Commission's
practice of giving religious organizations tax
exemptions on holdings used only for religious purposes. The argument against such tax exemptions
was that they amounted to an establishment of religion, a claim the Court found to have no merit.
Since the Commission's action was part of a more
general program of tax exemptions for nonprofit
organizations, the purpose of the program was not
to establish, sponsor, or support religion and was
therefore permitted by the Constitution.

That much might have been enough to decide the
case, but the Court went further. In Chief Justice
Burger's words: "Determining that the legislative
purpose of tax exemption is not aimed at establishing ... religion does not end that inquiry ....
We must also be sure that the end result -- the
effect -- is not an excessive entanglement with
religion."[42] Now, as the Court approached later
cases, it had three separate tests of the legitimacy of state action in aid of religious schools:
(1) does the aid have a secular purpose, that is,
does the aid benefit children primarily, or does it

benefit the school (and indirectly the church) they attend? (2) does the aid have a primary effect of advancing or inhibiting religion? (3) does the aid constitute an excessive entanglement of church and state?

In Lemon v. Kurtzman (1971),[43] and the two companion cases decided the same day,[44] the Court had its first opportunity to apply its newest test. At issue was a Pennsylvania law to reimburse private schools for costs of teachers' salaries, texts, and related materials in certain secular subjects, and in the companion cases a Rhode Island statute authorizing payment of up to 15 percent in annual salary supplements to private school teachers of secular subjects. In both states, the schools kept records for the state to audit before payment. In Rhode Island, the teachers were required to teach only those subjects taught in public schools and had to agree in writing that they would not teach religion. Administering these laws, the Court found, would require a great degree of surveillance by the state of the schools' activities and would so lead to the "excessive entanglement" that was found in Walz to have been forbidden by the First Amendment. The Court also suggested that the annual appropriations process would likely lead to the very political divisiveness that constitutional separation of church and state was designed to forestall.[45]

Three cases decided on the same day in 1973 further defined what forms of aid to religious schools the Court would and would not permit. In PEARL v. Nyquist[46] the Court struck down a New York statute providing maintenance grants and an option of tax credits or tuition reimbursements to parents of parochial school children. Here the Court found that though the legislative purpose of the law was secular, its primary effect was to advance religion and was therefore in violation of the First Amendment. In Levitt v. PEARL[47] the Court invalidated a New York law offering reimbursements to sectarian schools for costs incurred in carrying out state mandated testing and record-keeping. The difficulty

41

for the Court in this case was its finding that the
state would have to examine questions asked on
tests given in religious schools to insure that
only secular materials were being covered. Such
examination would necessarily entangle the state
excessively in the affairs of religious schools and
could not therefore withstand a First Amendment
challenge. In Sloan v. Lemon[48] the Court held a
Pennsylvania plan for tuition reimbursement unconstitutional on the same grounds as those set out in
Nyquist.[49]

Portions of another Pennsylvania law were
found wanting in Meek v. Pittenger (1975).[50]
Though it upheld the loan of secular texts to sectarian school pupils on the "child benefit" theory
followed in earlier cases, the Court disallowed the
loan of instructional materials and the provision
of auxiliary services such as counseling and
testing. Unlike textbooks, which students used at
home, instructional materials (films, records,
maps, and the like) were used in the schools. For
the state to be certain that these things were used
only for secular purposes, public authority would
become excessively entangled in sectarian instruction. The same result would occur were the state
to meet its responsibility to see that the auxiliary services the state offered would not be put
to sectarian use. The Court also held that both
the loan of materials and the provision of services
failed its "primary effect" test because of the
"predominantly religious character of the schools"[51]
in which services and materials would be employed.
As the Court said, "substantial aid to the educational functions of such schools necessarily results in aid to the sectarian enterprise as a
whole."[52]

In a later case involving several forms of
public aid to religious schools, Wolman v. Walter
(1977),[53] the Supreme Court upheld Ohio's textbook
loans, the state's funding of standardized testing,
and state-supported diagnostic and off-the-premises
therapeutic services. Textbook loans were allowed
on "child-benefit" grounds, and testing was approved

42

on the Court's finding that the schools could not
control the content of standardized tests and so
required no surveillance to insure the absence of
sectarian influence. Diagnostic services were permitted because they had no educational content and
because the diagnostician would be a public em-
ployee having little contact with the children.
Therapeutic services, offered away from school
grounds, would avoid the constitutional problem
since "it can hardly be said that the supervision
of public employees performing public functions on
public property creates an excessive entanglement
between church and state."[54] The Court also held
that these programs were designed to achieve a
secular purpose and that they did not have a primary effect of advancing religion.

The Court was not so generous in its view of
the state's loan of equipment and instructional
materials or in its concern with the public funding
of transportation for field trips. The loans were
invalidated because "in view of the impossibility
of separating the secular education function from
the sectarian, the state aid inevitably flows in
part in support of the religious role of the
schools."[55] The state's financing of field trips
set "an unacceptable risk of fostering religion as
an inevitable by-product"[56] because the sectarian
teacher would decide where the children went and
how the trip would relate to other segments of
their education. To minimize the "unacceptable
risk," would involve the state in supervision to a
degree that would amount to excessive entanglement.

A New York statute ordering payment to sectarian schools for testing and record-keeping was
at issue in the most recent state-aid case to reach
the Supreme Court, Committee for Public Education
and Religious Liberty v. Regan (1980).[57] Finding
that tests prepared by public authority (though administered by private school employees) prevented
sectarian control over the content and outcomes of
the tests, the Court concluded that the testing
program posed no substantial risk that the tests
would be used for religious purposes. The record-

43

keeping requirements were similarly straightforward, were not part of the teaching process, and were not therefore capable of being bent to some religious purpose. In sum, the Court saw the New York practice as having a secular purpose, as having no effect that advanced or inhibited religion, and as offering no possibility of excessive entanglement. State payments, the Court said, "would serve the State's legitimate secular ends without any appreciable risk of being used to transmit or teach religious views."[58]

These latter cases show reasonably well what aid the First Amendment lets the state offer religious schools as well as what aid is forbidden. Statutes whose purpose is some fairly direct support for religious education or whose effect is to entangle the state in the affairs of sectarian schools are likely to be struck down. Payment of teachers' salaries, maintenance grants, tuition reimbursements or tax credits, support for testing whose content the parochial school controls, loans of instructional materials, and money for field trips and some auxiliary services have been held unconstitutional on either or both of these grounds. But government may lawfully loan textbooks, and supply transportation, standardized testing, and diagnostic and therapeutic services. These forms of aid are aimed primarily at children (for whose welfare the state has a legitimate concern regardless of where they go to school), convey only an indirect benefit to school or church, and do not involve the state excessively in private matters.

But just as there is a limit to what the state may do, there is a limit to its discretion in refusing aid. As Justice Douglas observed in Zorach, the Bill of Rights is not to be read in support of a "philosophy of hostility to religion."[59] And as the Court had written earlier in Everson, "state power is no more to be used so as to handicap religions than it is to favor them."[60] State action cannot be used to support religious activities or institutions, but in avoiding that result the state must not penalize religious institutions for the fact that they are religious. The free exercise clause of the First Amendment, or at least the interest that clause is intended to secure, operates as a constraint on government as it tries to live within the strictures of the establishment clause. No direct aid to sectarian schools for specifically religious purposes is allowed, but in denying help the state must not hinder religious institutions in their exercise of religious liberty.

Similarly, in accommodating religious interests within its own institutions, an accommodation the free exercise cases require, the state must be careful to avoid establishment. Adjustments of schedule, relaxing of attendance requirements, and excusing students from patriotic rituals are permitted, but religious exercises in the schools are not. Just as the free exercise clause limits what the state may do in obeying the commands of the establishment clause, so does that clause constrain the state in those of its actions taken to avoid interference with free exercise. The two clauses complement one another, each placing a constraint on government as it tries to avoid constitutional problems with the other. Government is to refrain from interfering with most expressions of free exercise but in doing so it is bound by the establishment clause not to promote or foster religion. In resisting establishment pressures government is required by the free exercise clause not to handicap or penalize religious institutions.

Only compelling interests of the state not otherwise attainable can justify any interference with religious freedom, as the Court held in Yoder. In steering clear of such interference, that is, in accommodating religious interests within its own or in private institutions, the state must insure that its efforts have a secular legislative end and that they neither advance nor impede religion, as the Court insisted in Schempp. But in whatever steps it takes to be certain that its policies do not advance or inhibit religion, the state must avoid the excessive entanglement with religion the Court found in Walz to threaten the free exercise of religion.

45

But just as the First Amendment is no pairing of absolute commands and constraints, neither are the Yoder, Schempp, and Walz tests more than guideposts to what is allowed and forbidden in relations between church and state. The facts and holdings in specific cases help to define the guideposts more clearly, but the underlying principle remains indistinct, flexible, and open in meaning and application. In Regan, the Supreme Court may have said as much itself in a rare confession of its perplexity in interpreting the establishment clause and of the evolutionary course its decisions follow. The Court's remarks about the establishment clause in that case could well be extended to the First Amendment as a whole:

> ... our decisions have tended to avoid categorical imperatives and absolutist approaches to either end of the range of possible outcomes. This course sacrifices clarity and predictability for flexibility, but this promises to be the case until the continuing interaction between the courts and the States -- the former charged with interpreting and upholding the Constitution and the latter seeking to provide education for their youth -- produces a single, more encompassing construction of the Establishment Clause.[61]

NOTES

1. 98 US 156.   2. *Ibid.*, at 164.   3. 133 US 333.

4. *Ibid.*, at 342. See also *Pack* v. *Tennessee*, 424 US 954 (1976).

5. 3 How. 589.   6. 310 US 296.   7. 262 US 390.

8. 268 US 510.   9. *Ibid.*, at 534.   10. *Ibid.*, at 535.

11. 310 US 586.   12. 319 US 624.

13. Teachers who are Jehovah's Witnesses do not, it appears, have the same right to refuse to lead a class in reciting the Pledge that students have in refusing to follow. The Court has recently let stand a lower court decision upholding a school board's dismissal of a Jehovah's Witness, who, as a teacher in a public school, declined on religious grounds to teach the Pledge of Allegiance. The lower court held that the state had a compelling interest in curriculum that overrode the teacher's profession of religious faith. Allowing the teacher's beliefs to take precedence over that interest would deprive students of the opportunity to learn what the state had legitimately decided they should learn. See *Palmer* v. *Chicago Board of Education*, 48 LW 2180, 3422, 3436 (1980).

14. 268 US 510, at 534.   15. 342 US 884.   16. 406 US 205.

17. *Ibid.*, at 234.

18. 434 US 1063 (1978). Cf. *Gilmore* v. *Montgomery*, 417 US 556 (1974); *Norwood* v. *Harrison*, 413 US 455 (1973); and *Runyon* v. *McCrary*, 427 US 160 (1976).

19. *NLRB* v. *Catholic Bishop of Chicago*, 440 US 490 (1979).

20. *Ibid.*, at 501.   21. 406 US 205, at 214.

22. 333 US 203.   23. *Ibid.*, at 210.   24. 343 US 306.

25. *Ibid.*, at 312.   26. *Ibid.*   27. 370 US 421.

28. It must be noted that Engel does not prevent prayer in schools, a legal and physical impossibility in any case. What Engel does is to forbid use of state property and personnel to sponsor and carry out a religious exercise.

29. 374 US 203.   30. *Ibid.*, at 213.   31. *Ibid.*, at 214.

32. Ibid., at 222.

33. Following Engel and Schempp the Supreme Court refused to hear (and therefore let stand) a number of state and lower federal court decisions that invalidated a variety of attempts to retain prayer and devotional Bible study or reading in public schools. See Chamberlin v. Dade County, 377 US 402 (1964); Stein v. Olshinsky, 382 US 957 (1965); DeKalb School District v. DeSpain, 390 US 906 (1967); Board of Education v. Netcong, 401 US 1013 (1971); State Commissioner of Education v. School Committee, 404 US 849 (1971); and Johnson v. Huntington Beach, 434 US 877 (1977).

34. 393 US 97. See also Brown v. Houston, 417 US 969 (1973) and Cf. Joseph Burstyn, Inc. v. Wilson, 343 US 496 (1952).

35. 374 US 203, at 222.   36. 175 US 291.   37. 281 US 370.

38. 330 US 1.

39. While states may supply transportation to parochial schools, they are not required to do so. See Luetke-meyer v. Kaufman, 419 US 888 (1974). For other services to sectarian schools which the First Amendment may permit but not require, see Brusca v. State Board of Education, 405 US 1050 (1972); Wheeler v. Barrera, 417 US 402 (1974); and Reynolds v. Paster, 419 US 1111 (1975).

40. 392 US 236.   41. 397 US 664.   42. Ibid., at 674.

43. 403 US 602.

44. Earley v. DiCenso and Robinson v. DiCenso, 403 US 602 (1971).

45. Questions about the legitimacy of reimbursing parochial schools for expenses incurred before the statutes at issue were held unconstitutional occupied the Court in Lemon v. Kurtzman, 411 US 192 (1973); and New York v. Cathedral Academy, 434 US 125 (1977). See also Sanders v. Johnson, 403 US 955 (1971).

46. 413 US 756.   47. 413 US 472.   48. 413 US 472.

49. Later cases in which the Supreme Court affirmed lower court rulings that tax credits and tuition reimbursements were unconstitutional included Grit v. Wolman,

48

413 US 901 (1973); Marburger v. Public Funds, 417 US
961 (1974); Franchise Tax Board v. United Americans for
Public Schools, 419 US 890 (1974); and Minnesota v.
Minnesota CLU, 421 US 988 (1975).

50. 421 US 349.   51. Ibid., at 363.   52. Ibid., at 366.

53. 433 US 229. See also Essex v. Wolman, 409 US 808 (1972)
and Wolman v. Essex, 421 US 982 (1975).

54. 433 US 229, at 248.   55. Ibid., at 250.

56. Ibid., at 254.   57. 444 US 646.   58. Ibid., at 662.

59. 343 US 306, at 315.   60. 330 US 1, at 18.

61. 444 US 646, at 662.

SECTION TWO

CHURCH-AFFILIATED SCHOOLS TODAY

Catholic Schools in a
Changing Church

Thomas F. Sullivan

In 1884 the Roman Catholic bishops of the
United States assembled in the Fourth Plenary Council of Baltimore to confront the problems of the
Church in this country. In what is their most historically important pronouncement they said, "We
not only exhort Catholic parents with paternal love
but also command them with all the authority in our
power to procure for their beloved offspring ... a
truly Christian and Catholic education."[1] They
added that "near each church, where it does not
exist, a parochial school is to be erected within
two years from the promulgation of this council,
and is to be maintained in perpetuum unless the
bishop, on account of grave difficulties, judges
that a postponment be allowed."[2]

This was not the first time the bishops had
urged the foundation of a widespread Catholic
school system, but it was their strongest plea.
As early as 1829 the First Council of Baltimore
had urged Catholics to erect their own schools, and
subsequent councils had repeated the exhortation.
The early call for a separate school system was
prompted by two considerations. First, the public
schools of the first part of the nineteenth century
were perceived as Protestant schools. For example,
in New York during the 1830's the King James version of the Bible was read daily in public schools,
and regular prayers, hymn singing, religious instruction and ecclesiastical history were part of
the curriculum. In 1840 when Catholics under the
leadership of New York's stormy Bishop John Hughes
protested the sectarianism of the schools and demanded that Catholic children be allowed to use the
approved Catholic version of the Bible, a long and
bitter controversy ensued. Finally, a public debate was arranged by the Common Council of New
York, the agency responsible for deciding which
schools could share in the city's educational
funds. Not one to spare words, Hughes spoke

53

animatedly for three hours before the crowded hall.
Protestant speakers continued their rebuttal of his
charges for two whole days with responses which
consisted largely of attacks on Catholicism as an
anti-biblical religion. The final result of the
debate was the complete rejection of the Catholic
claims by the council.[3]

A second reason for the uneasiness of Catholic
authorities was the overtly anti-Catholic tone of
some of the textbooks used in the public schools.
One history text, for example, emphasized the cor-
ruptions of Catholicism and claimed that biblical
prophecy had foretold the overthrow of the pope,
"the man of sin, mystery of iniquity, son of per-
dition."[4] Other textbooks emphasized that people
in Catholic countries like Ireland, Italy and Spain
were not only ignorant and superstitious, but were
also forbidden to read the Bible. By contrast,
people in England and the Protestant parts of
Germany were portrayed as progressive, educated and
inveterate Bible readers.[5]

Catholic suspicion of the denominational bias
of public education lingered for many years, but by
1880 concern had shifted to fear of the secularized
nature of public schools, a development which was
deemed no less harmful to the religious development
of young Catholics.

Before 1884 Church authorities had merely
urged the establishment of Catholic schools. Now
they commanded that each parish set up a school in
two crises of the times, namely the influx into the
country of unprecedented numbers of European immigrants, many of them from the Catholic sections
of the old world. It is estimated that by 1880
there were over 6,000,000 foreign born Catholics in
the United States.[6]

Most of the immigrants were poor and unedu-
cated. Except for the Irish, they spoke languages
other than English. Their religious and ethnic
practices were judged not only different from those
of mainstream America, but a threat to the unity of

54

the national ethos. On the political front
nativist organizations fought to have them excluded
from gaining political power by tightening up the
naturalization laws. On the educational front the
public schools were seen as a natural melting pot
in which the children of the immigrants could be
purified of their alien ways and transformed into
authentic Americans.

Roman Directives

Another impetus to the bishops' decisive pronouncement can be traced indirectly to the writings
of John McMaster, the militantly Catholic lay
editor of the Freeman's Journal. McMaster not only
inveighed against the "godlessness" of the public
schools, but he also excoriated bishops and priests
who allowed Catholic children to attend these
schools. Impatient with the slow movement of local
ecclesiastical authorities, he petitioned the Holy
See in 1874 to clarify the Church's law concerning
Catholics attending public schools. Two years
later the Congregation of the Inquisition (now more
felicitously named the Congregation for the Doctrine of the Faith) sent a letter to the U.S.
bishops declaring that public school education "has
appeared intrinsically dangerous and absolutely
contrary to Catholicism" because children "from
their formative age grow up without any sense of
religion."[7] The letter added:
> The fact that in these schools, or at
> least in the majority of them, adoles-
> cents of both sexes are grouped to-
> gether in the same classrooms to attend
> lessons, and boys and girls must sit
> together on the same benches, exposing
> them to corruption to a certain extent.
> The result of all this is that youth
> is in danger of losing its faith while
> its morals are threatened.[8]
What nefarious behavior might be anticipated from
boys and girls who sat on the same benches was not
spelled out. But evidently the threat to faith and
morals was considered sufficiently serious for the

Congregation to say that "it is absolutely necessary that all bishops make every effort to see to
it that the flock entrusted to them avoid every
contact with public schools" and "in all places
Catholics should have their own schools." The
letter added a warning that parents who persisted
in sending their children to public schools could
not receive the sacraments of the Church.

There can be little doubt that the Baltimore
Council's legislation on parochial schools was influenced by this document. But in preparing their
legislation the American bishops did not follow the
Roman directives uncritically. In regard to the
exclusion of parents from the sacraments for
sending their offspring to public schools, the
bishops said: "We strictly enjoin that no one,
whether bishop or priest, should dare to repel such
parents from the sacraments as unworthy."[9]

The ideal of every Catholic child in a
Catholic school was motivated by the desire to preserve the faith of an immigrant people in a hostile
environment. But this ideal also served to preserve the cultural heritage of the various ethnic
groups. It is no accident that the proliferation
of Catholic schools coincided historically with the
huge ingress into the nation of European immigrants
of many different languages and customs. For these
groups Catholic schools preserved not only the
faith but the cultures in which that faith was
rooted. There is little exaggeration to the observation that prior to World War II there were no
Catholic schools in this country but only Polish
Catholic schools, Irish Catholic schools, Italian
Catholic schools and so forth. Not uncommon in
large Catholic urban areas was the situation in the
neighborhood of the late Mayor Daley of Chicago.
Here in one square mile were ten parochial schools,
each originally serving a different ethnic group.

The massive effort to provide Catholic schools
initiated in 1884 continued unabated well into the
1960's. The ideal of a Catholic education for
every child has become part of the conventional

wisdom of Church members at every level. In many places it was customary that when new parishes were founded, the first building to be erected was the school. Construction of the church, rectory and convent could all wait until the school was operating and its debt at least partially retired. By 1964 over five and a half million students were enrolled in the Church's 13,920 elementary and secondary schools.[10]

The first systematic study of the effectiveness of Catholic education concluded optimistically that "there can be no doubt that those who have had a comprehensive education in a religious system will be notably different both in religious behavior and social attitudes from those who did not have such schooling."[11] While such scientifically based reassurances were welcome in Catholic circles, they hardly came as a surprise. For generations Catholic parents were reasonably confident that if they sent their children to Catholic schools, the children would grow up very much like themselves with the same religious values and loyalties. The urban neighborhoods where most Catholics lived strongly supported traditional religious values. Frequently children, parents, grandparents and other relatives lived in the same stable neighborhood. The parish, the school and the neighborhood all shared the same basic view of life, and a common ethnic background added cultural reinforcement to that view.

For the Church and its schools the future looked bright indeed in the early sixties. A Catholic, John F. Kennedy, had been elected president. Vatican Council II, which began in 1962, appeared to Catholics and others as well as a dramatic effort to do away with the Catholic Church's traditional rigidity and intransigence toward modern society. John XXIII was the pope, and his warm personality did much to dispel popular antipathy toward the papacy and the Church in general.

The Gathering Storm

The period of Vatican Council II (1962-1965)
and the years immediately following were a time of
unparalleled exhilaration in much of the Catholic
world. A church which for so long appeared to be
impervious to change, was changing in ways which a
few years earlier would have been utterly unthinkable. At a time when so many traditional Catholic
beliefs and practices were undergoing reexamination,
it is not surprising that the long cherished ideal
of Catholic education was also subject to critical
scrutiny. A growing number of liberal writers
began to question whether separate schools were the
appropriate vehicle for educating young Catholics
who would be living in a pluralistic society. A
very important contribution to the discussion was
Mary Perkins Ryan's Are Parochial Schools the
Answer? which suggested that the schools were not
only ineffective but that the investment of so much
money and personnel in child centered programs prevented the Church from concentrating on such important tasks as adult education and liturgical
celebration which for centuries had been the main-
stay of its educational mission.[12]

The interest of many in the civil rights
movement of the sixties led to another complaint
against Catholic schools. Critics pointed out that
the attitude of the products of Catholic education
toward racial justice was no better than that of
the population at large. One widely publicized
salvo came from a most unlikely source, the director of the Department of Education at the United
States Catholic Conference (the executive agency of
the National Conference of Catholic Bishops).
Monsignor James Donohoe charged that Catholic
schools were not providing leadership in the area
of social justice.[13] Researchers Greeley and Rossi
were probably closest to the truth when they observed, "It is not that education for racial justice was tried and found wanting, but that it was
found hard and not tried at least while our respondents were in school."[14]

It is ironic that while liberals were chastising the schools for their failure in social concern, conservatives began to attack the schools for their attempts to confront problems of social injustice. Prior to 1960 most of the religious education textbooks used in Catholic schools preached a rather individualistic ethic. They tried to inspire students to lead personally blameless lives but gave little attention to the social implications of the gospel. Some diocesan school systems still used the Baltimore Catechism (written in 1885 and last revised in 1940) as the basic text while others had turned to more contemporary graded texts. But in both cases the basic thrust of moral education was more individualistic than social in emphasis.

In 1966 a new elementary religion series, Word and Worship, was introduced into the schools of a number of dioceses around the country.[15] The Archdiocese of Chicago, which had the largest school system of any diocese, adopted the sixth, seventh and eighth grade books of this series for its schools. While all three books had a distinct social justice orientation, none of them sparked any immediate objections from parents. A short time later four schools in Chicago received permission to use the primary grade texts of Word and Worship on a pilot basis while these texts were being evaluated for possible adoption throughout the archdiocese. The third grade book contained a lesson on racial justice and included two photographs of Dr. Martin Luther King who, the text said, was like Jesus. Some white parents were offended, and word spread quickly around the city. Hundreds of letters poured into the archdiocesan school office, most of them heatedly objecting to the use of this religion series in the schools. Meetings were called by disgruntled parents in different parts of the city to protest the books. It is safe to say that most of the protesters were unaware that the book they objected to was being used in only four of the more than 400 elementary schools of the Archdiocese of Chicago. The controversy continued and dissident groups began to sound the call for a

59

return to the basics and away from what they termed "sociological religion."

Religion textbooks by other publishers of the time also addressed issues of social justice, and soon the controversy had spread to every large diocesan school system in the country. Almost immediately another ingredient was added to the bubbling cauldron. Some conservative Catholic groups circulated evaluations of the most popular religion series and claimed that they were objectionable either because they omitted certain doctrinal basics or because they positively distorted the teaching of the Church and were, therefore, theologically unorthodox.

While the charges of doctrinal deficiency and heterodoxy had little to commend them by way of theological scholarship, the bitterness of the protests and the attendant publicity alarmed some Church leaders. In 1969 the National Catholic Educational Association called a meeting of diocesan directors of religious education at Metarie, Louisiana, to discuss the textbook problem. At the end of the meeting the directors issued a statement affirming their support of the books under attack and certifying the orthodoxy of their contents.[16]

Another effort to resolve the controversy was undertaken shortly after this when the United States Catholic Conference conducted an ambitious project of evaluating all the commonly used religion textbooks on the market.[17] Each religion series was examined by at least two independent committees composed of catechetical specialists and some representative lay persons. The religion series which had been under attack were all given generally favorable reviews in the final, published evaluation.

Nonetheless complaints continued to be raised that children were not learning the basics of the faith. In response the National Conference of Catholic Bishops prepared a 35 page booklet entitled Basic Teachings for Catholic Religious

Education which listed the fundamental teachings
that were to be incorporated in all religion curricula.[18] "It is necessary," the bishops said,
"that these basic teachings be central in all
Catholic religious instruction, be never overlooked
or minimized, and be given adequate and frequent
emphasis."[19]

Polarization in the Church

The above efforts were at best only partially
successful in quelling the ongoing debate. Brush
fires of controversy continued to spring up throughout the country. One reason ecclesiastical leaders
were unable to bring lasting peace to the religious
education scene was that the charges and counter-
charges of this debate were only symptomatic of a
larger malaise which had afflicted the American
Church since the time of Vatican Council II.

One of the fundamental aims of this council as
envisioned by Pope John XXIII was the modernization
of the Church. The council sought to identify the
distinctive traits of our times and to indicate how
an updating of the Church could be accomplished
without harm to its essential mission. In this the
council was influenced by many progressive theologians who had been attempting for some time to re-
interpret the Christian message and the consequent
tasks of the Church in our day. But change did not
come without serious resistance from more traditionally minded bishops and theologians at the
council. As a result many of the council's final
documents were compromises which tried to accommodate contrasting theological views without resolving the practical ramifications of the interaction of the differing positions. Differences
were thus papered over rather than definitively
resolved.

Since the council, progressive theologians
have sought to press for the reforms explicitly
authorized by Vatican II and even to go beyond the
letter of the council in updating the Church.

Conservatives, by contrast, became ever more
fearful that the updating process advocated by the
progressives would lead to a loss of Catholic identity.[20] Their fears deepened when some moderate
liberals became radicalized at the time of the
university riots and anti-war demonstrations of the
late sixties.

Another major cause of division in the
Catholic community was the issuance of the papal
encyclical on birth control, Humanae Vitae, in 1968.
At the request of Pope Paul VI, Vatican Council II
did not explicitly take up the question of contra-
ception. However, the council did teach that
married couples themselves have the right and obligation for deciding how many children they should
have.[21] The fact that a special 52 member papal
commission had been reexamining Catholic teaching on
family limitation lent credence to rumors that the
pope would certainly change or at least modify the
absoluteness of Catholic teaching in this sensitive
area.

Publication of the encyclical with its un-
compromising rejection of all forms of contracep-
tion was greeted with an outburst of dissent
unprecedented in the history of American Catholicism. Numerous theologians and clergy publicly
opposed or questioned the teaching of the pope.
Nor were the laity unaffected. Andrew Greeley and
his colleagues have documented a widespread dissatisfaction of Catholics with their Church in the
decade 1964-1974. Their study persuasively argues
that the encyclical Humanae Vitae was the chief
cause for the decline in Catholic practice during
those years.[22]

Declining Enrollment

Catholic schools found themselves in the
crossfire between opposing ideological forces
within the Church. But ideological conflicts were
not the only problems facing school administrators
and superintendents. The late sixties witnessed a

precipitous decline in enrollment in both elementary and secondary Catholic schools. In the decade 1964-1974 enrollment slipped from 5,590,000 to 3,786,000. During the same decade the number of Catholic schools shrunk from 12,205 to 10,534. Greeley et al. say that their data clearly shows that the chief cause in the overall drop in attendance was the unavailability of Catholic schools in new suburban areas.[23] Like many other Americans Catholics had been moving to the suburbs for some years. In 1964 the number of Catholic children living in the suburbs was about the same as the number living in the cities. By 1974, however, there were twice as many Catholic school age children living in the suburbs as in the cities. The chief cause of the decline was the failure of ecclesiastical authorities to build schools in the new or expanding suburbs.[24]

The authorities had good reasons for hesitating to build new schools. As the costs of education in general increased, the costs of Catholic education increased proportionately. The financial woes of the Catholic schools were augmented by another development of the post-Vatican II era. From the very beginning these schools had been staffed by members of the various religious orders of the Church. The years immediately following Vatican II saw the exodus of a large number of priests, brothers and sisters from the active ministry. The result was that the religious orders who had traditionally run the schools found themselves perilously short of personnel. More and more lay teachers had to be hired. In 1964 religious sisters made up two-thirds of the faculties of Catholic elementary schools. Ten years later two-thirds of these faculties were lay teachers who could not be expected to live on the modest stipends usually allotted to the sisters.[25]

Financial constraints were not the only reason new schools were not started. Formerly when a bishop wished to establish a school, he turned to one of the religious orders for a principal and the core of a faculty. But now the religious orders were already overextended and could not take on the staffing of any additional schools. The only alternative would have been to found schools with completely lay faculties. The cost of such a venture coupled with the fear that parents might not support all-lay schools seemed insuperable obstacles to most Church authorities.

By the mid-sixties the winds of change were swirling across the once peaceful Catholic landscape with unaccustomed ferocity. In the atmosphere of the time no Catholic practice or institution was immune to critical questioning. Did it make sense for Catholics to continue to have their own schools? They were no longer a scorned minority but had edged themselves steadily into the mainstream of American life. While in past times critics outside the Church accused Catholic schools of being divisive, now some within the Church began to decry the ghetto mentality allegedly fostered by parochial schools. Public schools could hardly be accused of being anti-Catholic or of trying to undermine the faith of Catholic children. Liberals complained of the social insensitivity of graduates of Catholic education, and conservatives charged that the schools were neglecting the basics of the faith and watering down Catholic belief. Enrollment was plummeting while costs were skyrocketing.[26]

In an atmosphere of declining confidence superintendents, bishops and pastors found themselves increasingly asked to justify the continued existence of Catholic schools. To some the request to defend the right of the schools to stay open seemed like being asked to throw light on the sun. More perceptive minds noted, however, that the United States of 1970 was a far different nation than that in which the Catholic school movement took root. Furthermore the Church itself had undergone more widespread and radical change in the years since Vatican Council II than in the 400 years which preceded that council. A new articulation of the meaning of Catholic education was indeed imperative.

A Changing Church

Rivulets of thought began to gather independently in various parts of the country and flowed eventually into a number of official Church documents which addressed the problems of religious education. Publication of these documents by the Holy See or by the American bishops was usually preceded by varying degrees of consultation with theologians, catechetical specialists, educators and, in one case, with the Catholic community at large. As a result most of the insights generated at the grassroots are reflected in the official documents.[27] One of these pronouncements, Sharing the Light of Faith, was prepared in final form only after extensive and repeated consultations over a six year period.[28]

It would be naive to imagine that the issuance of one or many official pronouncements could settle all controversies once and for all. Nonetheless it is possible to distill from these documents a basic understanding of the nature and purpose of the Catholic school with which bishops, parents and educators can agree even though they might give greater or lesser prominence to one or other components of this understanding.

Before proceeding to sketch the contemporary Catholic school, I would call attention to one theological development which is largely responsible for new thinking concerning the nature of Catholic education.

Catholic schools exist to initiate students into the life of the Church. Therefore one's understanding of the nature of the school must depend on one's understanding of the nature of the Church. What is the Church? Since at least the second half of the nineteenth century, the theological view that dominated Catholic theology was that of the Church as a hierarchically stratified and highly authoritarian institution. This theology reached its zenith in 1870 when Vatican Council I solemnly defined papal primacy and papal infallibility. The council had planned to elaborate further on the reciprocal relationship between the papacy and other segments of the Church, but the Franco-Prussian war broke out and forced a sudden and untimely end to its deliberations.

The failure of this council to address the roles of bishops, clergy and laity in the Church led to an excessively monarchical view of the Church in which all members were to accept official teaching — and especially papal teaching — without question. While, in fact, papal infallibility has been exercised only once in the 110 years since Vatican I, for most of this century declarations by popes or even Roman Congregations have been received in the Church as though they were for all practical purposes infallible. In the area of moral living, faithful observance of Church laws and loyal obedience to official moral teaching were hallmarks of Catholics who took their religion seriously.

It was left to Vatican Council II to try to correct this imbalance. Without repudiating any essential teaching of its predecessor, Vatican II sought to return to a more scripturally based understanding of the Church and envisioned the Church in a much broader context. In what is probably this council's most important document, it took as its controlling theme the idea of the Church as the People of God, that is the Church as a community of believers.[29] Richard McBrien sums it up well when he says, "The Church is, first of all, a community. It is people. It is not in the first instance an organization or a means of salvation. It is not the hierarchy or the clergy. The Church is a community."[30]

When the Church is seen primarily as a community rather than as a hierarchical pyramid, its various elements can be seen in a new light. In this community all are essentially equal.[31] Pope and bishops are not king and overlords but servants of the community and symbols of its unity and commonality of purpose. All members of the community

66

and not just its ordained officials share a responsibility for the ongoing direction and work of the
Church. The sometimes erratic postconciliar proliferation of parish councils, education boards,
diocesan synods and other structures for shared decision making all emanate from the council's vision
of the Church as a faith community.

The Church as described in Vatican II was to
divest itself of its defensive mentality.
Catholics were told to "joyfully acknowledge and
esteem the truly Christian endowments from our
common heritage which are found among our separated
brethren."[32] In addition the Church was to have an
appreciation of non-Christian religions such as
Jews and Moslems, who too shared a belief in God.
Openness was to be demonstrated not only in the
religious sphere but in the secular as well. The
suspicion and distrust of the modern world which
characterized much of Catholicism since the time of
the French Revolution were finally laid to rest.[33]
Catholics had a responsibility to participate in
the search for solutions of the problems of the
modern world.

A final point of major emphasis by Vatican II
deserves mention. The highly juridic understanding
of ecclesiastical authority which predominated from
the time of Vatican I left little room for the independent exercise of individual conscience. In
theory, of course, the supremacy of conscience was
recognized in the standard works of moral theology.
In practice, however, the heavy stress on the
binding force of official teaching made conscientious disagreement by an individual Catholic almost
unthinkable.

A quite different spirit prevailed at Vatican
II. Its Declaration on Religious Liberty taught
that in religious matters all persons should be
immune from coercion and that "the right to religious freedom is based on the very dignity of the
human person."[34] Elsewhere the council stated that
in the Church "both clergy and laity should be ac-
corded a lawful freedom of inquiry of thought and

67

of expression."[35] It said that "children and young people have a right to be encouraged to weigh moral values with an upright conscience and to embrace them by personal choice."[36]

Catholic Schools Today

Catholic schools exist to "lead both communities and individual members of the faithful to maturity of faith."[37] Religious education is a process through which persons are aided to grow in faith. Growth in faith is not the same thing as growth in knowledge. Rather it means the person's ongoing turning or conversion to God. Pope John Paul II writes that religious education materials "must really aim to give those who use them a better knowledge of the mysteries of Christ, aimed at true conversion and a life in conformity to God's will."[38] The goal of religious education in the Catholic school is not merely the transmission of knowledge but ever deepening personal conversion.

Six tasks can be identified which are essential to the process of Catholic education. One essential task in promoting the faith is the proclamation of the Christian message as it is received in the Roman Catholic tradition. All the official documents insist on a systematic presentation of the whole of the message, and three of them give detailed listings of the concepts to be taught.[39] The strong and repeated emphasis on teaching the entire message is doubtlessly a response to the lay and clerical critics who feared that contemporary religion programs were omitting or underplaying certain teachings in the quest to be relevant to students' interests. I suspect, too, that the repeated stress on the whole of the message is motivated by a desire to reduce the incidence of "a la carte" Catholicism, a tendency by some Catholics to pick and choose from the Church's teachings on the basis of personal taste.

Second, no less important than what is taught is the setting in which it is taught. If the

68

Church is viewed theologically as a community, the school too must be a faith community in which students are loved and respected as unique persons. "Building and living community must be prime, explicit goals of the contemporary Catholic school."[40] The school must, of course, instruct students in the usual subject fields and hand on the Catholic, Christian heritage. But the idea of the school as a community suggests that it must do much more, namely, provide students with an actual experience of lived Christianity. Religious learning and formation are not restricted to the formal religion class. The structures of the school, its environment and, above all, the quality of human relationships students experience with teachers and each other contribute to the effectiveness and indeed the credibility of the religion class. The formal religion lesson is to be the explicitation in structured, thematic form of what the child experiences in many informal ways in the total school setting.

For example, a unit on the nature of the Church will have little impact unless the child has a personal sense of belonging to a caring community. Without such an experiential base, the child's religious learning will be at best a sterile cognitive exercise. Children must experience Christianity before they learn the religious labels that are put on that experience.

Third, integral to experiential learning in a faith community are the ritual celebrations by which the community expresses its identity. "Faith brings the community together to worship; and in worship faith is renewed."[41] Instruction prepares for participation in liturgy, and participation in liturgy provides a basis for ongoing reflection on the community's experiences of worship and tries to relate them to daily life situations.[42] In the school sacramental celebrations as well as more informal prayer exercises can be adapted and modified according to the age and needs of different student groups.

Fourth, if the school is to be a genuine community of faith, an attitude of respect for the religious freedom of students must be a high priority. Educators are exhorted "never to forget that faith is a free response" and acceptance of the Christian message "is a fruit of grace and freedom."[43] Students can be manipulated into acting in morally desirable ways through coercion or the use of fear inducing techniques, but such techniques do not promote authentic moral growth. Ultimately all persons must personally choose whether they want to be Christians. All schemes, no matter how well intentioned, to compel fidelity to religious practice, are not only short sighted but in the long run doomed to failure.

Fifth, a particularly crucial consequence of the idea of the school as faith community has to do with the faculty. The school will be a genuine community of believers to the extent that the teachers are striving to form community among themselves. This means that they must not only be convinced of the religious purpose of the school, but that they pray together, share together and become genuinely concerned about each other as persons. "It is the human and Christian qualities of catechists [religious teachers] more than their methods and tools upon which the success of their work depends."[44] In a Catholic school all teachers are religion teachers whether they teach a formal religion class or not. Often enough the implicitly religious attitudes of a science teacher or a physical education instructor can have a greater impact on an individual child than anything that is said or done in the religion class.

Sixth, if a school is to be a Christian community, it must be an outgoing community. Religious education must be ecumenical in outlook and should present information about other religions "honestly and accurately, avoiding words, judgments and actions which misrepresent their beliefs and practices."[45] Students are to be prepared "for living with non-Catholics, affirming their Catholic identity while respecting the faith of others."[46]

The Church, and therefore the school, must not only be concerned with other religions but must also look beyond itself to the modern world and its institutions. "Actions on behalf of justice and participation in the transformation of the world fully appear to us as a constitutive dimension of the preaching of the gospel or, in other words, of the Church's mission."[47] Sharing the Light of Faith emphasizes the importance of education in social justice by devoting an entire chapter to that subject. Without reservation it insists that "each Catholic has a responsibility for social action."[48] Those who favor a return to the more individualistic ethic of yesteryear will derive little comfort from the official directives on education in social justice.

Students are not only to study about social injustice as part of their religious education, they are also to do something about the problems and inequities of our society. The performance of Christian service is an essential part of the religious education process. "Service is itself an efficacious means of teaching Christian doctrine, and thus programs should include opportunities for service as part of the educational experience."[49]

When children are old enough, they are expected to take part in such activities as visiting the aged and shut-ins, assisting at programs for the handicapped, and working with community action programs.[50] Through such service projects students can develop the attitudes and skills necessary for later, more mature contributions to society.

Religion and Life

In American society education is a central value. For children and adolescents attendance at school is one of the most significant experiences of their lives. What Catholic education ultimately aims at is the integration of religion and life. There is no dichotomy between the sacred and the secular, for the secular when seen in its true

71

depth is sacred. Students are to be taught their faith, but in the context of a caring community which is the school. They are to be helped to see religion not as a set of abstract concepts and principles, but as a way of life. Prayer and liturgical celebration are part of this way of life, but so are Christian service and concern for the complex problems of the wider human family.

The integration of religion and life is brought about most importantly by the presence of teachers who express an integrated approach to learning and living in their private and professional lives.[51] Integration of religion and life is also effected by an interdisciplinary curriculum in which religion is not excluded from any subject area. This does not mean that the autonomy of the various disciplines should be violated or that science or the humanities ought to be artificially baptised and used as occasions for moralizing. However religion often adds a depth to consideration of matters which are not explicitly theological. For example, a science lesson on ecology takes on a new dimension when all creation is viewed as the gift of a loving God to whom we are responsible for our stewardship. Integration of religion and life seems particularly important in a secularized culture where religion is too often privatized and sealed off from the central issues of life.

Today children grow up in a world which is politically, culturally and religiously pluralistic. The omnipresence of the television set makes it certain that children will be exposed to multiple ideological currents of thought. It is neither possible nor desirable to try to shield them from their pluralistic environment. Neither parents nor educators can compel children to accept certain beliefs and values. What they can do is to provide an atmosphere of example, love and freedom in which children can eventually choose for themselves the values by which they will live. For many Catholic parents such an atmosphere can best be supplied when both home and school share a common and explicitly religious understanding of the meaning of life.

NOTES

1. Text as quoted in Theodore Maynard, The Story of American Catholicism (New York: Macmillan Book Company, 1941), p. 465.

2. Ibid.

3. For details see Ray Allen Billington, The Protestant Crusade 1800-1860 (New York: Macmillan Company, 1938), pp. 145-148.

4. Ibid., pp. 144-145.   5. Ibid., p. 145

6. See Joseph McSorley, An Outline History of the Church by Centuries (St. Louis: B. Herder Book Company, 1947), p. 850.

7. The English translation of this document can be found in Benedictine Monks of Solesmes (eds.), Papal Teachings: Education (Boston: Daughters of St. Paul, 1960), pp. 66-70. A discussion of McMaster's part in influencing Rome is contained in Thomas T. McAvoy, A History of the Catholic Church in the United States (Notre Dame, IN: University of Notre Dame Press, 1969), pp. 178-230.

8. Papal Teachings: Education, p. 67.

9. Quoted in Maynard, The Story of American Catholicism, p. 465.

10. H. Buetow, "Catholic Education," New Catholic Encyclopedia, vol. 16, p. 60.

11. Andrew Greeley and Peter H. Rossi, The Education of Catholic Americans (New York: Doubleday and Company, 1966), p. 237.

12. M. P. Ryan, Are Parochial Schools the Answer? (New York: Guild Press, 1968).

13. J. C. Donohoe, "Catholic Education in Contemporary American Society," National Catholic Education Association Bulletin (August 1967), pp. 13-17.

14. Greeley and Rossi, The Education of Catholic Americans, p. 127.

15. Gerard Weber, James Killgallon and M. Michael O'Shaughnessy, (eds.), The World and Worship Program of Religious Education (New York: Benziger Brothers, 1966).

16. The National Catholic Reporter, 19 November, 1969.

17. U.S. Catholic Conference Department of Education, Evaluative Reviews of Religion Textbooks (Washington: U.S.C.C. Publications, 1971). In addition to Word and Worship the most widely used and heavily criticized texts were E. Fowkes, J. Cohan and A. Boyer, Bible Life and Worship (Rockleigh, NJ: Allyn and Bacon, 1959); Marie Venard et al., Our Life with God (New York: William Sadlier, Inc., 1966) and Come to the Father (New York: Paulist Press, 1966).

18. National Conference of Catholic Bishops, Basic Teachings for Catholic Religious Education (Washington: U.S.C.C. Publications, 1973).

19. Ibid., p. 1.

20. For background see Avery Dulles, The Resilient Church (Garden City, NY: Doubleday and Company, 1977), especially pp. 29-44.

21. Pastoral Constitution on the Church in the Modern World, no. 50 in W. M. Abbot (ed.), The Documents of Vatican II (New York: America Press, 1966), p. 254.

22. Andrew Greeley, William McCready and Kathleen McCourt, Catholic Schools in a Declining Church (Kansas City: Sheed and Ward, 1976), pp. 103-154.

23. Ibid., pp. 234-240.   24. Ibid., pp. 36-38 and 228-237.

25. H. Buetow, "Catholic Education," New Catholic Encyclopedia, vol. 16, p. 60.

26. Greeley et al. later showed that 89% of Catholics at this time supported the idea of Catholic schools, but unfortunately this knowledge was not available to superintendents in the dark days of the late sixties. See Catholic Schools in a Declining Church, pp. 220-243.

27. The following are the official documents: Sacred Congregation for the Clergy, General Catechetical Directory (Washington: U.S.C.C. Publications, 1971); National Conference of Catholic Bishops, Basic Teachings for Catholic Religious Education, 1973; National Conference of Catholic Bishops, To Teach as Jesus Did (Washington: U.S.C.C. Publications, 1972); Sharing the Light of Faith: National Catechetical Directory for Catholics of the United States (Washington: U.S.C.C. Publications,

1979); and John Paul II, <u>Apostolic Exhortation on Catechesis</u> (Washington: U.S.C.C. Publications, 1980).

28. For a description of the process of consultation see Mariella Frye, "Sharing the Light of Faith: The Process," <u>The Living Light</u> 16 (Summer, 1979), pp. 150-154.

29. <u>Dogmatic Constitution on the Church</u>, nos. 9-17, in Abbott, <u>The Documents of Vatican II</u>, pp. 24-37.

30. R. McBrien, "The Church," <u>An American Catholic Catechism</u>, G. Dyer (ed.) (New York: Seabury Press, 1975), p. 17.

31. <u>Dogmatic Constitution on the Church</u>, no. 32, in Abbott, <u>The Documents of Vatican II</u>, p. 58.

32. <u>Decree on Ecumenism</u>, no. 4, in Abbott, p. 347.

33. <u>Pastoral Constitution on the Church in the Modern World</u>, nos. 63-93, in Abbott, p. 271-308.

34. <u>Declaration on Religious Liberty</u>, no. 2, in Abbott, p. 679.

35. <u>Pastoral Constitution on the Church in the Modern World</u>, no. 62, in Abbott, p. 270.

36. <u>Declaration on Christian Education</u>, no. 1, in Abbott, p. 639.

37. <u>General Catechetical Directory</u>, no. 21.

38. John Paul II, <u>Apostolic Exhortation on Catechesis</u>, no. 49, <u>The Living Light</u> 17 (Spring, 1980), p. 72.

39. <u>The General Catechetical Directory</u>, nos. 47-69; <u>Basic Teachings For Catholic Religious Education</u> and <u>Sharing the Light of Faith</u>, nos. 83-111.

40. <u>Sharing the Light of Faith</u>, no. 232 and <u>To Teach as Jesus Did</u>, no. 108.

41. <u>Sharing the Light of Faith</u>, no. 112.

42. See <u>Ibid.</u>, no. 113 and 232.

43. <u>Sharing the Light of Faith</u>, no. 58 and <u>General Catechetical Directory</u>, no. 71.

44. <u>Sharing the Light of Faith</u>, no. 205.

45. <u>Ibid.</u>, no. 76.

46. <u>Apostolic Exhortation on Catechesis</u>, no. 32.
47. <u>Sharing the Light of Faith</u>, no. 160.
48. <u>Ibid.</u>, no. 170.
49. <u>To Teach as Jesus Did</u>, no. 89.
50. <u>Sharing the Light of Faith</u>, no. 232.
51. <u>To Teach as Jesus Did</u>, no. 104.

The Christian Day School in the
American Social Order, 1960-1980

James C. Carper

For almost two decades American society has
been in the throes of a fundamental reorientation
of its system of belief or civil religion and institutional structure. Although it is too early to
assess the total impact of these years of profound
disenchantment and uncertainty, it is apparent that
there has been a collapse of consensus concerning
the basic nature and function of our institutions
and the values, traditions, and purposes undergirding them. As national cohesiveness has
evanesced, alternative modes of believing, valuing,
and behaving have emerged. These options and accompanying tendencies such as the apotheosis of
self, a decline of belief in all forms of obligation and authority, the rejection of the past, and
confusion about the meaning of progress, justice,
equality, morality, and community suggest a "water-
shed" in American history.[1] As noted historian
Henry Steele Commager has astutely observed:
"Perhaps the 60s and 70s are a great divide — the
divide of disillusionment."[2]

This disillusionment and collapse of consensus
has been reflected clearly in Americans' dissatisfaction with public education. While systematic
schooling has been the object of much acrimonious
discussion since its inception during the middle
decades of the nineteenth century, never before has
the criticism been so caustic. The lay public,
commentators of all socio-political persuasions,
and many professional educators have scrutinized
the schools and found them wanting. Evincing the
fragmented state of the social order and bewilder-
ment concerning the purposes and outcomes of
schooling, charges leveled at public education have
been legion and often contradictory. It has been
characterized as racist, permissive, authoritarian,
trendy, irreligious, oppressive, too liberal, too
conservative, too involved in social change, an
instrument for perpetuating the status quo, and

generally unresponsive to both individual and public needs.[3]

Solutions to the school crisis have also been many and varied. Some critics have proposed reforms of the curriculum, while others have advocated changes in school governance patterns, teacher education, and methods of school finance. Eschewing reform altogether, several have argued for the abolition of public schooling.[4]

Of all the proposed remedies, one of the most discussed has been the free school movement which emanated originally from the socio-political left. Dedicated to a more "humane" and "liberating" education and opposed standardization and authoritarian institutions, as many as five hundred of these institutions were established independently of the public school system during the late 1960s and early 1970s. Variations of the free school movement were eventually incorporated within the public system in the form of alternative schools, open campuses, "relevant" curricula, and community control. While much has been written about the successes and failures of the free school and related alternative education schemes, one option, the Christian day school, has received scant attention outside the religious press.[5]

Since the mid-1960s evangelical Protestants have been establishing Christian schools, many of which are interdenominationally sponsored and attended, at a phenomenal rate.[6] Not only do these institutions currently constitute the most rapidly expanding segment of formal education in the United States, but they also represent the first widespread secession from the public school pattern since the establishment of Catholic schools in the nineteenth century.

Protestant-sponsored weekday education is not a contemporary development. Since the nineteenth century most denominations have experimented with parochial schooling as an alternative to public education. Yet, until recently, the vast majority of Protestants have shown little interest in such an educational arrangement. Only certain Lutheran bodies, the Seventh Day Adventists, and the Christian Reformed Church have maintained a significant number of weekday schools.[7]

Most Protestants have supported public schooling since its inception. They approved of early public education because it reflected the Protestant belief-value system of the society and was viewed as an integral part of the crusade to establish a Christian America. According to church historian Robert T. Handy, elementary schools did not need to be under the control of particular denominations because "their role was to prepare young Americans for participation in the broadly Christian civilization toward which all evangelicals were working."[8] While the public school by means of Bible reading, prayers, and the ubiquitous McGuffey readers emphasized nondenominational evangelical Protestantism, which was tantamount to the American civil faith for the better part of the nineteenth century, the Sunday school stressed the particular tenets of the various denominations. To most evangelical Protestants this "parallel institutions" educational arrangement was very satisfactory. As William B. Kennedy, an authority on Protestant education, has argued:

> By 1860 there had emerged a general consensus in American Protestantism that the combination of public and Sunday school teaching would largely take care of the needed religious teaching of the young. In that pattern the public school was primary; the Sunday school was adjunct to it, providing specific religious teaching it could not include.[9]

Much has changed in America since the establishment of this dualistic educational strategy. No longer does evangelical Protestantism influence the society and the public schools as it did in the nineteenth century. The past six decades have witnessed its rapid decline as the moving force behind cultural and behavioral patterns. By the 1960s the

81

once dominant evangelical strain in American civil religion had been superseded by the Enlightenment theme.[10]

Despite this radical alteration of the character of American culture, most Protestants have clung to the myth of the "parallel institutions" educational strategy. The growth of the number of Christian day schools during the past fifteen years suggests, however, that an increasing number of evangelicals are not only wrestling with the consequences of the collapse of Protestantism as a social foundation but also questioning their historical commitment to public schooling and the dualistic pattern of education.

The term Christian day school has been used recently to describe those weekday educational institutions, many of which are of an interdenominational character, founded by evangelical Protestants during the past fifteen to twenty years.[11] These schools are quite diverse in several respects. Facilities, for example, range from poorly equipped church basements to modern multibuilding campuses. While a majority are elementary schools, an increasing number are offering secondary education as well. Though the average per school is probably around 200, enrollments vary from less than 50 to over 2000. Programs of study differ considerably from the most rudimentary to the most comprehensive available anywhere. Most schools follow traditional teaching practices while others utilize, for economic as well as pedagogic reasons, individualized instruction schemes. Some mix healthy doses of pre-1960 "Americanism" with religious education while others shun this questionable practice. Some Christian day schools are attended by whites only, sometimes, regrettably, because of segregative intent while many are integrated. A militant rejection of any formal state regulation or licensing characterizes some institutions while others cooperate to varying degress with state education agencies.[12]

Although these institutions are diverse in

82

many ways, they all profess the centrality of Jesus
Christ and the Bible in their educational endeavors.
Regardless of the subject matter, a conservative
Christian perspective is employed. History, for
example, is generally viewed as the record of God's
involvement in human affairs. Though the theory
of evolution receives some attention, science is
usually taught from a creationist perspective.
Moral education, an important aspect of the instructional program, is also biblically based.
Students are instructed to search the Scriptures as
the final authority for value judgments. Summing
up the differences between the ethos of the Christian school and that of public education, Paul A.
Kienel, Executive Director of the recently formed
Association of Christian Schools International, has
maintained:

> ... Christian schools are Christian
> institutions where Jesus Christ and the
> Bible are central in the school curricu-
> lum and in the lives of the teachers and
> administrators. This distinction re-
> moves us from direct competition with
> public schools. Although we often com-
> pare ourselves academically, we are
> educational institutions operating on
> separate philosophical tracks. Ours is
> Christ-centered education, presented in
> the Christian context. Theirs is man-
> centered education presented within the
> context of the supremacy of man as op-
> posed to the supremacy of God. Their
> position is known as secular humanism.[13]

While there is no doubt that the number of
Christian day schools has multiplied, particularly
since the late 1960s, it is difficult to determine
precisely their number and student population.[14]
The very character of the Christian school movement
prohibits an accurate accounting. Many schools are
of such a separatist persuasion that they refuse to
report enrollment and related figures to state and
federal education agencies. For similar reasons
some do not affiliate with one of the many state,
regional, and national associations of Christian

schools which are currently the primary sources of
data. Furthermore, the rapid growth of these
schools is so unorganized that exact figures are
difficult to obtain.

The variation in estimates of the number of
Christian day schools and their enrollment illustrates these problems. Calculations of the number
of these schools founded since the early 1960s
range from 4,000 to as many as 10,000. Enrollment
figures for these schools range from 250,000 to
over 1,200,000. Based on the best data available,
an estimate of between 5,000 and 6,000 schools
established during the past fifteen to twenty years
with a student enrollment of approximately 950,000
seems reasonable.[15]

Perhaps the most concrete evidence of the
burgeoning Christian day school movement can be
seen in the figures of several associations. The
Western Association of Christian Schools, which in
1978 merged with two smaller groups, the National
Christian School Education Association and Ohio
Association of Christian Schools, to form the Association of Christian Schools International, claimed
a membership of 102 schools with an enrollment of
14,659 in 1967. By 1973 the figures were 308 and
39,360 respectively, and in 1979 approximately
1,350 and 200,000. The American Association of
Christian Schools, a rival organization of a more
separatist nature, was founded in 1972 with 80
schools enrolling 16,000 students. In 1979 the
association claimed 876 schools with a student
population in excess of 135,000. Despite the fact
that a few schools probably hold dual memberships
and some were founded long before they affiliated,
these figures indicate the vigor of the movement
which shows no sign of abating.[16]

Why are Christian day schools proliferating?
Why are many evangelical Protestants forsaking
their traditional commitment to public schooling
and the "parallel institutions" educational
strategy? There are a number of factors involved.
Some are symbolic of evangelicals' increasing

alienation from the American social order. To them the public school exemplifies trends and practices they deplore in the society at large: widespread uncertainty concerning sources of authority; dissolution of standards; waning of evangelicalism as a culture-shaping force; loosening of custom and constraint; scientism; and government social engineering. Thus when they establish schools which in some measure reflect the civil religion of nineteenth century America and stress the Bible, moral absolutes, basic subject matter mastery, discipline, and varying degrees of separation from state authority and society, they are not only protesting the secular nature of public education, unsatisfactory academic and behavioral standards, and unrest in the schools but also expressing disillusionment with the society that sustains the educational enterprise.

While evangelicals have pointed to discipline problems, declining educational standards, the drug culture, federal meddling, and unresponsive educators as reasons for abandoning the public schools, secularism has disturbed them the most.[17] Although the United States Supreme Court decisions in 1962 and 1963 outlawing mandatory prayer and devotional Bible reading in tax supported schools merely marked the culmination of better than a half-century long process of "de-Protestantization" of public education, many evangelical Protestants translated the removal of these symbols of the evangelical elements of the American civil faith as "yanking" God out of the schools.[18] Rather than making the schools neutral on matters related to religion, they believed that, despite the intent of the majority of the Court, these decisions contributed to the establishment of the religion of secular humanism in the public schools. Such a belief sensitized them to what was being taught in the schools. So while these decisions did not cause directly the rapid growth of Christian day schools, they certainly provoked many evangelicals to scrutinize public education to a greater extent than ever before. The result has often been dissatisfaction with the secular character of the

85

schools which has led them to either attempt to
restore evangelical symbols and perspectives to
public schooling, e.g. voluntary prayer, Ten Commandments plaques, and creationism, or found
Christian educational institutions. As Richard N.
Ostling, a staff writer for the religion section of
Time, has observed: "There is little doubt that
the rulings produced anxiety about the climate in
public schools that is boosting Protestant schools
many years later."[19]

This concern has been evident in recent textbook controversies in, among other places, West
Virginia, New Jersey, California, Indiana, Minnesota, Texas, and Georgia. Here evangelical
Protestants have charged that the exclusion of
Christian values and perspectives from public education and the current orientation of the curriculum has resulted in a de facto establishment of the
religion of secular humanism in the public
schools.[20] They have, for instance, often complained that Man: A Course of Study, the well-
known elementary level social studies curriculum,
embodies the tenets of secular humanism. In this
course they believe moral absolutes are undermined
by an evolutionary framework and situation ethics.
Many evangelicals have also seen evidence of
secular humanism in moral education programs which
are based on the assumption that values are relative, personal, and situational. Summing up this
contention, Charles E. Rice of the University of
Notre Dame Law School has suggested:

> If the objecting parents are
> correct in their claim that the pub-
> lic schools are promoting the tenets
> of a secular religion, it must be on
> the basis that the nonjudgmental
> treatment of moral issues without any
> affirmation of the supernatural is
> itself an implicit assertion that
> contradictory moral positions are
> equally tenable, that there is there-
> fore no objective and binding moral
> order, that the supernatural is not
> a necessary factor in the making of

moral decisions. It is not unreasonable to describe such teaching as an
implicit affirmation of a position
that, in its relativism and secularism,
is authentically religious. The Christian parents' concern is therefore
understandable.[21]
They have likewise been troubled by behavioral
sciences texts which imply that man is a social
animal rather than a unique being created in the
image of God, which belittle belief in an omni-
scient and omnipresent Creator, and which equate
the Bible with myth.[22]

Evangelicals have probably been more concerned
about public school science courses which present
the general theory of evolution as dogma than any
other curriculum issue. In recent years an increasing number of evangelical laymen and scientists have questioned the exclusive presentation of
the evolutionary explanation of human origins and
development. To them such a practice not only
burdens the free exercise rights of students who
affirm divine creation as an article of their faith
but also effectively establishes one of the cardi-
nal tenets of secular humanism, the absolutism of
evolution. Until a more neutral approach which
allows for the examination of evidence of both the
general theory of evolution and the theory of
scientific creationism is widely adopted, this
issue will remain a major source of evangelicals'
discontent with public education.[23]

Reflecting the dissatisfaction of many evangelical Protestants concerning the character of
public schooling, Floyd Robertson of the National
Association of Evangelicals has asserted: "It has
become quite obvious to many that this religion of
secularism has indeed pervaded our public school
system and created an anti-Christian attitude in
all too many cases."[24] Although a majority of
evangelicals still enroll their children in the
public system and continue to wrestle with its
secular nature, a growing number are opting for
Christian day schools. Like nineteenth century

Catholics who established parochial schools to preserve their religion and culture, a significant number of them are founding and supporting schools to counter the secular influence of society and its institutions on their children.

Awakening and profession as well as alienation and protest are involved in the growth of these schools. The Christian school movement is more than just a "counter-cultural" phenomenon. A recrudescent evangelical consciousness, one manifestation of the spiritual ferment of the past twenty years which historian William G. McLoughlin has termed the "Fourth Great Awakening," has prompted many evangelicals to promote Christian education beyond the home and the marginally effective efforts of the Sunday school.[25] Realizing that all education is value oriented and Christian nurture is a full-time endeavor, they have supported schools which embody the biblical beliefs of the church and home. As one parent stated on a Christian school application form: "We believe that our children are gifts of the Lord. We are responsible to train them according to His word not only at home and in church, but in school as well."[26] By embracing Christian day schools which complement the worldview of the home and the church, an increasing number of evangelical Protestants believe they have fashioned an educational configuration in which all components are engaged in their conception of the scriptural command to "train up a child in the way he should go ...."[27]

Zeal for these schools is not universal. Some critics have argued that they represent an abdication of Christian social responsibility rather than a manifestation of a reawakened evangelical sense of commitment and witness. To them the public school is a mission field to be cultivated not abandoned. William H. Willimon of Duke University Divinity School enunciated this position in a provocative article which raised the perennially controverted question of how to be in the world but not of it. He wrote:

In too many communities, parents
who are talented, educated, committed
Christians have withdrawn their children
(along with their time, talent, and
prayers) from the public schools without a thought for their responsibility
as their brother's keeper. Without
children in the public schools, they
have little interest in the needs of
public education .... Certainly there
is much wrong in today's public
schools — mostly the same things that
are wrong with our society as a whole.
Christian parents have good reason to
feel alarmed over many recent developments in public education. But who
will improve it? What kind of society
will we have if all Christians abandon
the public schools?[28]

Others have charged that many Christian
schools were established primarily to maintain
racial segregation. A recent study by David Nevin
and Robert E. Bills suggests, regrettably, that
racism was an important factor in the founding of
some purportedly Christian schools in the South.[29]
Another investigation indicates, however, that
these institutions are not merely segregation
academies. Based on an analysis of Christian day
schools in two states, William Lloyd Turner concluded that religious and academic factors rather
than racial ones motivated parents to remove their
children from the public schools. He explained:

Many authors have charged that
these "Christian" schools are only a
new type of segregation academy, similar
to those that sprang up in the South
after passage of the 1964 Civil Rights
Act. These "new segregation academies"
are said to be adopting a religious
guise in order to claim First Amendment guarantees of religious protection and thus escape federal desegre-
gation regulations. But research
conducted in early 1979 on fundamentalist

89

schools in Kentucky and Wisconsin disputes this claim and suggests that the factors producing this new wave of fundamentalist schools are more complex than previously supposed ....

While both parents and administrators of "Christian" schools in both states insisted that they were not opposed to integrated education, it was found that more than 95% of the students enrolled in fundamentalist schools in these states are white; fewer than 2% are black. No black teachers were employed by fundamentalist schools in either state ....

The motivation for founding and maintaining nonpublic schools appears to be more than racial prejudice. In recent decades religious influences in American public education have eroded rapidly. Many evangelical Protestants have come to believe that the public schools now espouse a philosophy that is completely secular, perhaps even antireligious. Hence many conservative Protestants have withdrawn their children from public schools and have established sectarian schools with quite different standards and curricula.[30]

Although racism has, unfortunately, been a factor in the founding and maintenance of some Christian day schools, the vast majority do not discriminate on the basis of race. Most Christian school associations and spokesmen for the movement condemn racially motivated schooling. In the words of D. Bruce Lockerbie, a respected Christian educator: "The racist stronghold claiming also to be a 'Christian school' is, by definition, an imposter, a fraud. Its reason for being is indefensible by standards of Scripture, the Constitution, ... or common decency."[31] Besides professing nondiscrimination, it appears that an increasing number of these institutions are enrolling minority students, though their proportion of the total student population remains small.[32]

Proponents as well as opponents of Christian day schools have also raised questions concerning the nature and quality of the education provided at these institutions. Several observers have lamented the poor academic standards evident in some schools. Other critics have rightly deplored the "super-patriotism" which characterizes a number of Christian schools. Commentators have also suggested that these schools may shelter students and thus fail to prepare them for life in the "real world."[33]

Regardless of these criticisms, the Christian day school movement continues to flourish. While these recently established schools have yet to attain the stature of the major alternative to public schooling, the Roman Catholic educational enterprise, they are becoming increasingly visible on the educational landscape. Whether or not they ever achieve that status will depend to some extent not only on the resolution of the aforementioned problems but also on responses to a number of more critical questions.

Perhaps the most important question facing Christian day schools concerns their present and future relation to state and federal regulatory agencies. Courts in New Hampshire, Vermont, Ohio, Kentucky, and North Carolina have recently decided cases in which Christian schools claimed that state-mandated minimum educational standards and licensing practices violated their free exercise of religion rights. In all but the last instance state supreme courts ruled that detailed and extensive accreditation standards and teacher certification requirements as applied to Christian schools went beyond the bounds of reasonable regulation and thus unduly burdened free exercise rights. In North Carolina a lower court sustained state accreditation and teacher qualification standards for Christian schools. That decision was, however, overturned by legislative action repealing all state regulation of religious schools except for health, safety, and attendance reporting requirements.[34]

Even if efforts are made to reconcile free exercise rights with state interest in regulating education, more litigation of a serious nature seems likely. As one commentator has noted:

> ... Although nearly all proponents of the Christian school movement agree that the state has a legitimate interest in expecting all children to achieve competency in basic reading, writing, and mathematics skills and requiring safe school facilities, an increasing number of them ... are questioning the authority of the state to license or charter Christian schools under any circumstances. As far as they are concerned, such a procedure is tantamount to imposing the state's philosophy and control on an arm of the church. They raise what may become in the near future one of the most profound and litigated questions in the church-state realm: "What right does the state have to license a ministry of the church?"[35]

Besides the fundamental church-state issue, there are other pressing questions. To what extent, for example, will the public school system attempt to accommodate disgruntled evangelicals? Will proponents of Christian day schools accept the discredited assumption that schooling is a panacea for all problems? How will graduates of these schools fare in society? To what extent will evangelical Protestants "systematize" their schools? What direction will the apparent evangelical "awakening" take in the next decade?

Regardless of its future status, the Christian day school is currently a viable alternative to the public school and its rapid growth indicates that a significant number of evangelical Protestants are reconsidering educational strategy. The Christian day school also symbolizes alienation and awakening among evangelicals, represents a reassertion of parental educational rights, and, most importantly, suggests a crisis in American civil religion in one of the major vehicles of its transmission, the public school.

NOTES

1. Robert N. Bellah, The Broken Covenant: American Civil
   Religion in Time of Trial (New York: Seabury Press,
   1975); Daniel E. Griffiths, "The Collapse of Consensus,"
   New York University Education Quarterly 7 (Fall 1975):
   2-3; Christopher Lasch, The Culture of Narcissism:
   American Life in an Age of Diminishing Expectations
   (New York: Norton, 1978); William G. McLoughlin,
   Revivals, Awakenings, and Reform: An Essay on Religion
   and Social Change in America, 1607-1977 (Chicago: The
   University of Chicago Press, 1978); and William L.
   O'Neill, Coming Apart: An Informal History of America
   in the 1960's (New York: Quadrangle Books, 1971).

2. "In Quest of Leadership," Time, 15 July 1974, p. 23.

3. See, for example, Carl Bereiter, Must We Educate?
   (Englewood Cliffs, N.J.: Prentice-Hall, 1973); Harry S.
   Broudy, The Real World of the Public Schools (New York:
   Harcourt Brace Jovanovich, 1972); R. Freeman Butts,
   "Assaults on a Great Idea," The Nation, 30 April 1973,
   pp. 553-60; Ronald and Beatrice Gross, eds., Radical
   School Reform (New York: Simon and Schuster, 1969);
   Robert M. Hutchins, "The Schools Must Stay," The Center
   Magazine, January/February 1973, pp. 12-23; Allan C.
   Ornstein, "Critics and Criticism of Education," Educa-
   tional Forum 42 (November 1977): 21-30; Joel Spring,
   "Dare Educators Build a New School System?," paper pre-
   sented at the 21st annual meeting of the American
   Educational Studies Association, Colorado Springs, 8
   November 1980; Elmer L. Towns, Have the Public Schools
   "Had It"? (Nashville: Thomas Nelson, 1974); and Peter
   Witonski, What Went Wrong with American Education and
   How to Make It Right (New Rochelle, N.Y.: Arlington
   House, 1973).

4. Seymour W. Itzkoff, A New Public Education (New York:
   David McKay, 1976); and John Martin Rich, Innovations in
   Education: Reformers and Their Critics, 3rd ed. (Boston:
   Allyn and Bacon, 1980).

5. Lawrence A. Cremin, "The Free School Movement: A Per-
   spective," Notes on Education 2 (October 1973): 1-11;
   Mario Fantini, ed., Alternative Education (Garden City,
   N.J.: Anchor Books, 1976); Allen Graubard, "The Free
   School Movement," Harvard Educational Review 42 (August

1972): 351-73; and David Thornton Moore, "Social Order in an Alternative School," Teachers College Record 79 (February 1978): 437-60.

6. Evangelical Protestantism is composed of several ideological subgroups. Richard Quebedeaux has identified four. Ranging from the most conservative to the least conservative on theological and social issues, they are "Separatist Fundamentalism," "Open Fundamentalism," "Establishment Evangelicalism," and "The New Evangelicalism." Although no research has been done on the matter, one would speculate that enthusiasm for Christian schools is greater in the "fundamentalist wing" than in the "evangelical wing." Richard Quebedeaux, The Young Evangelicals (New York: Harper & Row, 1974). See also Augustus Cerillo, Jr., "A Survey of Recent Evangelical Social Thought," Christian Scholar's Review 5 (1976): 272-80.

7. Francis X. Curran, The Churches and the Schools: American Protestantism and Popular Elementary Education (Chicago: Loyola University Press, 1954); Otto F. Kraushaar, American Nonpublic Schools: Patterns of Diversity (Baltimore: The Johns Hopkins University Press, 1972); and Edwin H. Rian, Christianity and American Education (San Antonio, Tx.: Naylor, 1949).

8. Robert T. Handy, A Christian America: Protestant Hopes and Historical Realities (New York: Oxford University Press, 1971), p. 102. See also James C. Carper, "A Common Faith for the Common School? Religion and Education in Kansas, 1861-1900," Mid-America 60 (October 1978): 147-61; Timothy L. Smith, "Protestant Schooling and American Nationality," Journal of American History 53 (March 1967): 679-95; and David Tyack, "The Kingdom of God and the Common School," Harvard Educational Review 36 (Fall 1966): 447-69.

9. William B. Kennedy, The Shaping of Protestant Education (New York: Association Press, 1966), p. 27. See also Robert W. Lynn, Protestant Strategies in Education (New York: Association Press, 1964); and Robert W. Lynn and Elliot Wright, The Big Little School: Two Hundred Years of the Sunday School (New York: Harper & Row, 1971).

10. American civil religion comes primarily from a fre-
    quently tension-producing fusion of elements of the
    Enlightenment ("secular humanism") and Puritan thought
    (evangelical Christianity). See Robert D. Linder,
    "Civil Religion in Historical Perspective: The Reality
    That Underlies the Concept," Journal of Church and State
    17 (Autumn 1975): 412-18.

11. Christian day schools existed prior to the early 1960s.
    The rapid expansion of the number of such institutions,
    however, has occurred since that time.

12. B. Drummond Ayers, "Private Schools Provoking Church-
    State Conflict," New York Times, 8 April 1978, sec. A,
    pp. A1, A23; William J. Lanouette, "The Fourth R Is
    Religion," National Observer, 15 January 1977, pp. 1,
    18; Roy W. Lowrie, Jr., "Christian School Growing
    Pains," Eternity, January 1971, pp. 19-21; Richard
    Ostling, "Why Protestant Schools Are Booming," Christian
    Herald, July-August 1977, pp. 44-47; Ken Ringle, "D. C.
    Suburban School Systems Are Swept by Changes —
    'Christian Schools,'" Washington Post, 31 December 1973,
    sec. B, p. 31; and Elmer Towns, "Have the Public Schools
    Had It?," Christian Life, September 1974, pp. 18-19,
    50-51.

13. Paul A. Kienel, "The Forces Behind the Christian School
    Movement," Christian School Comment, 1977, p. 1. See
    also Joseph Bayly, "Why I'm for Christian Schools,"
    Christianity Today, 25 January 1980, pp. 24-27; Anthony
    Ramirez, "No-Nonsense Schools with Christian Ties Tilt
    with Bureaucrats," Wall Street Journal, 7 December 1978,
    sec. 1, pp. 1, 34; Dorothy W. Rose, "Success Story of
    Christian Schools," Good News Broadcaster, September
    1979, pp. 48-50; and George Sweeting, "When the Bible
    Goes to School," Moody Monthly, September 1979, pp. 64-
    66.

14. Several proponents of Christian day schools have claimed,
    perhaps with some exaggeration, that such institutions
    are being established at the rate of nearly two per day.
    See Thomas W. Klewin, "Make Way for the Christian
    School," Liberty, September-October 1975, p. 18; and
    Lanouette, "The Fourth R Is Religion," p. 1.

15. Ayres, "Private Schools Provoking Church-State Conflict,"
    p. A23; Donald A. Erickson, Richard L. Nault, and

Bruce S. Cooper, Recent Enrollment Trends in U.S. Non-public Schools (Washington, D.C.: National Institute of Education, U.S. Department of Health, Education and Welfare, 1977); Lanouette, "The Fourth R Is Religion," p. 1; Dave Raney, "Public School vs. Christian School," Moody Monthly, September 1978, p. 42; and Towns, "Have the Public Schools Had It?," pp. 18-19.

16. These figures are based on information provided by Gerald Carlson of the American Association of Christian Schools, Washington, D.C., and Lee Ranson of the Association of Christian Schools International, La Habra, California. See also Paul A. Kienel, "Status of American Christian Schools," paper presented at the National Institute of Christian School Administration, Winona Lake, In., 25-30 July 1976.

17. John F. Blanchard, Jr., "Can We Live With Public Education?," Moody Monthly, October 1971, pp. 33, 88-89; Klewin, "Make Way for the Christian School," pp. 18-19; and Lanouette, "The Fourth R Is Religion," p. 1; Raney, "Public School vs. Christian School," pp. 44-45.

18. Engle v. Vitale 370 U.S. 421 (1962); Abington School District v. Schempp 374 U.S. 203 (1963); and Murray v. Curlette 374 U.S. 203 (1963).

19. Ostling, "Why Protestant Schools Are Booming," p. 45.

20. Based on a review of the literature on secular humanism, pronouncements of humanists, such as Paul Kurtz, editor of The Humanist, Paul Blanshard, and G. Richard Bozarth, and an analysis of the Humanist Manifesto I (1933) and the Humanist Manifesto II (1973), Whitehead and Conlan assert that secular humanism is a nontheistic religion that: "denies the relevance of Deity or supernatural agency"; affirms the "supremacy of human reason"; emphasizes the "self-sufficiency and centrality of Man"; assumes the inevitability of progress by either natural or state-aided means, particularly public education; exalts "science as the guide to human progress and the ultimate provider of an alternative to both religion and morals"; and emphasizes the "absolutism of evolution" in all realms. John W. Whitehead and John Conlan, "The Establishment of the Religion of Secular Humanism and Its First Amendment Implications," Texas Tech Law Review 10 (Winter 1978): 17-65 passim. For additional commentary on secular humanism and its role in public

education see Wendell R. Bird, "Freedom from Establishment and Unneutrality in Public School Instruction and Religious School Regulation," Harvard Journal of Law and Public Policy 2 (June 1979): 125-27, 174-85; Harvey Cox, The Secular City: Secularization and Urbanization in Theological Perspective (New York: Macmillan, 1965), p. 18; Alan N. Grover, Ohio's Trojan Horse (Greenville, S.C.: Bob Jones University Press, 1977), pp. 28-89 passim; and Robert L. Toms and John W. Whitehead, "The Religious Student in Public Education: Resolving a Constitutional Dilemma," Emory Law Journal 27 (Winter 1978): 3-40 passim.

21. Charles E. Rice, "Conscientious Objection to Public Education: The Grievance and the Remedies," Brigham Young University Law Review (1978): 860. See also Alan L. Lockwood, "A Critical View of Values Clarification," Teachers College Record 77 (September 1975): 35-50 passim; and Joel S. Moskowitz, "The Making of the Moral Child: Legal Implications of Values Education, Pepperdine Law Review 6 (Fall 1978): 114-26.

22. James C. Hefley, Textbooks on Trial (Wheaton, Ill.: Victor Books, 1976); George Hillocks, Jr., "Books and Bombs: Ideological Conflict and the Schools — A Case Study of the Kanawha County Book Protest," School Review 86 (August 1978): 632-54; Ostling, "Why Protestant Schools Are Booming," p. 45; and Gerald J. Stiles and Louis R. Rittweger, "The Dichotomy Between Pluralistic Rhetoric and Bias Practices," paper presented at the 18th annual meeting of the American Educational Studies Association, Philadelphia, 3 November 1977.

23. Legislation requiring instruction in creationism as well as evolution has been recently introduced in at least a dozen states including Illinois, Georgia, Iowa, Tennessee, South Carolina, and Florida. According to Bird, "School districts in six states currently require or encourage balanced treatment of the theory of scientific creationism and the general theory of evolution, and state-approved textbook lists for five states currently include texts presenting scientific creationism along with evolution." Bird, "Freedom from Establishment and Unneutrality in Public School Instruction and Religious School Regulation," p. 165; and "Evolution, Creationism Backers Tangle over Teaching of

Origins," Christianity Today, 18 April 1980, pp. 50-51.
For an excellent analysis of the creation-evolution
issue and its legal and religious implications see
Wendell R. Bird, "Freedom of Religion and Science In-
struction in Public Schools," Yale Law Journal 87
(January 1978): 515-70. See also Dorothy Nelkin,
Science Textbook Controversies and the Politics of Equal
Time (Cambridge: MIT Press, 1977); and recent issues of
Acts & Facts, a monthly publication of the Institute for
Creation Research, San Diego, California.

24. Floyd Robertson, "The Declining Support for Public
Schools," Christian Teacher, November-December 1976,
p. 19.

25. Adjustments in institutional arrangements, including
schooling, are frequently linked to religious awakenings.
For an informative discussion of the different facets of
the current ferment and possible outcomes see McLoughlin,
Revivals, Awakenings, and Reform: An Essay on Religion
and Social Change in America, 1607-1977, pp. 179-216.

26. Paul A. Kienel, "Ten Reasons Why You Should Send Your
Child to a Christian School," Christian School Comment,
1976, p. 1.

27. Proverbs 22:6.

28. William H. Willimon, "Should Churches Buy into the
Education Business?," Christianity Today, 5 May 1978,
p. 22. See also Ethel L. Herr, "Who's Salting the
Schools?," Eternity, February 1976, pp. 16, 18, 58-59.

29. David Nevin and Robert E. Bills, The Schools That Fear
Built (Washington, D.C.: Acropolis Books, 1976).

30. Virginia Davis Nordin and William Lloyd Turner, "More
Than Segregation Academies: The Growing Protestant
Fundamentalist Schools," Phi Delta Kappan, February
1980, pp. 391-92. Busing has been a factor in the
establishment of some Christian schools in all regions
of the country. It is unclear, however, as to whether
the reaction to busing has been due to racism, resent-
ment of federal coercion, fear of unrest, or a combination of all three. See Russell Chandler, "Popularity of
Religious Schools Rising," Los Angeles Times, 18 June
1978, p. 14; and Towns, "Have the Public Schools Had
It?," pp. 19, 50.

31. D. Bruce Lockerbie, "The Way We Should Go," Christian Teacher, September-October 1976, p. 7. See also "Creed and Color in the School Crisis," Christianity Today, 27 March 1970, pp. 32-33; Lowrie, "Christian School Growing Pains," p. 20; and Ostling, "Why Protestant Schools Are Booming," pp. 45-46.

32. According to G. William Davidson of the Association of Christian Schools International, La Habra, California, most of the 700-plus Christian schools in California are integrated. See also Chandler, "Popularity of Religious School Rising," pp. 1, 14; and Ostling," pp. 45-56.

33. Herr, "Who's Salting the Schools?," pp. 16, 18, 58-59; Lockerbie, "The Way We Should Go," pp. 6-7, 29; Lowrie, "Christian School Growing Pains," pp. 19-21; and Willimon, "Should Churches Buy into the Education Business?," pp. 20-22.

34. State v. LaBarge 134 Vt. 276 (1976); City of Concord v. New Testament Baptist Church 382 A.2d 377 (N.H. 1978); State v. Whisner 47 Ohio St. 2d 181 (1976); Kentucky State Board of Elementary and Secondary Education v. Rudasill No. 78-Sc-642-TG (1979); and North Carolina v. Columbus Christian Academy No. 78-CVS-1678 (N.C. Super. Ct. September 5, 1978). For detailed discussions of these cases see Bird, "Freedom from Establishment and Unneutrality in Public School Instruction and Religious School Regulation," pp. 185-95; James C. Carper, "The Whisner Decision: A Magna Carta for Christian Day Schools?," a paper presented at the 21st annual meeting of the American Educational Studies Association, Colorado Springs, 6 November 1980; and Grover, Ohio's Trojan Horse, pp. 8-89 passim. Recent attempts by the Internal Revenue Service to regulate private religious schools are discussed in current issues of Inform, published by the Center for Independent Education, San Francisco, California, and Outlook, published by the Council for American Private Education, Washington, D.C.

35. Carper, "The Whisner Decision: A Magna Carta for Christian Day Schools?," pp. 28-29.

The Jewish Day School:
An Update and Appreciation

Shimon Frost

The Jewish day school is a unique phenomenon among the various types of non-public schools, religious and non-sectarian, in the United States. Its beginnings go back to the earliest days of Jewish settlement in this country (1654), yet its phenomenal growth is largely a post-World War II development; it is religion oriented, yet non-parochial and lay governed; far from being a monolith, it represents a wide spectrum in religious world outlook and educational philosophy; it was an expression of ethnic pride well before the current vogue for ethnicity; and it favored cultural pluralism when the melting pot theory of Americanization reigned supreme.

History

Schiff notes that "although there were Jewish schools in the U.S. in the 18th and 19th centuries, the present Jewish day school is not an offshoot of any earlier type of Jewish all-day school in this country."[1] The early schools, whether under congregational or private auspices, served the Jewish immigrants as a counterpart to the church-related or private academy permeated with Christian teachings. The Hebraic/Judaic program in these early Jewish day schools was meager and, more often than not, was limited to Hebrew reading skills in the Siddur (the Jewish prayer book), and some Jewish history.

With the advent and growth of the public school as a neutral non-religious schooling instrumentality, the then existing Jewish day schools discontinued operations or converted into supplementary schools for religious education. Jews predominantly opted for the public school concept and have, over the years, been among its staunchest supporters.

103

The mass migration of East European Jews to
the U.S. in the 1880's brought with it the establishment of several yeshivot[2] modeled largely
after the East European pattern, but offering also
a full program of general studies as mandated by
the State educational authorities. The founding of
these schools marks the beginning of the American
Jewish day school as we presently know it. Thus,
the New York based Yeshivat Etz Chaim and Yeshivat
Rabbi Yitzhak Elchanan were founded in 1896 and
1897 respectively. Out of their eventual merger
came the launching of Yeshiva University with its
various schools and institutions of higher learning.

Though Jewish day schools grew and consoli-
dated during the inter-war period, the economic
depression notwithstanding, it was not until 1940
that the flourishing of the Jewish day school
throughout this vast continent really began. It is
estimated that 90% of the Jewish day schools
presently in existence were founded after 1940.
The most recent Jewish school census conducted by
the American Association for Jewish Education[3]
speaks of some 91,000 children enrolled in Jewish
day schools, constituting 26.3% of all Jewish children who attend any type of Jewish school. In
fact, the Jewish day school alone among all types
of Jewish school settings (weekday afternoon supplementary schools for religious instruction, one-
day-a-week schools, etc.), has maintained, and
even slightly increased its enrollment level during
the period from 1962 to 1980, when the total number
of Jewish children attending any kind of Jewish
school declined from 600,000 to 344,000.

Rationale

The motivating factors accounting for the
rapid and dramatic growth of Jewish day schools,
despite the strong opposition of many segments in
the Jewish community, including some of its out-
standing leaders, are manifold. The horrors of the
Holocaust, coupled with Christendom's indifference,
strengthened the striving for Jewish positive

affirmation, while the restoration of a free Israel in the ancient Jewish homeland, along with the revival of the Hebrew language, awakened long dormant sentiments of ethnic pride.

Furthermore, along with Americans of other faiths and ethnic backgrounds, Jews, in ever-increasing number, responded to the mood and temper of our times of return to religion and rediscovery of ethnic roots. Cultural pluralism, championed by the advocates of bilingual education, found its supporters among many Jews to whom the preservation of their ethnic cultural heritage has always been a cherished ideal.

Undoubtedly, the decline in the scholastic caliber of many public school systems on this continent had its share in the increased interest in the Jewish day school on the part of many parents. Added to the last factor was also a considerable feeling of disenchantment with the meager results of supplementary Jewish schooling. On the whole, however, even among non-Orthodox Jews, as pointed out in a recent study, the "motivations for enrolling a child in a day school do not differ markedly from the stated goals of the schools. While the 'secular' motive prevailed, the specifically Jewish component in the total education of the children was also important."[4]

Basic Facts

Of the 91,000 students currently attending Jewish day schools, 72% are enrolled in Orthodox institutions, 11% in Conservative-sponsored day schools, 2% in schools favoring the Reform religious ideology, and 15% in schools defining themselves as "communal or independent." In terms of curricular offerings and general educational policies, however, the latter category of schools, in their overwhelming majority, lean heavily towards a Traditionalist (i.e. Orthodox) orientation. The bulk of Jewish day school enrollment is in the primary and elementary grades (N-8), accounting for

78.5% of the student body. The day high school, however, is gradually gaining in acceptance and enrollment.

In terms of geographic distribution, the American Association for Jewish Education's census, quoted earlier, notes "the steadily rising proportion of students outside New York and its environs. Whereas, in the past census series New York used to be the main center of day school education, according to present figures the schools outside Metropolitan New York now enroll 39.6% of the total."[5]

Governance and Ideological Orientation

Jewish day schools are independent, autonomous institutions, incorporated as voluntary tax-exempt entities and governed by a lay board of directors. The board of directors conducts its business and affairs through a variety of standing committees, foremost among which is the Board of Education, responsible for setting policy subject to the approval of the board of directors.

Many day schools, in fact, most of them, affiliate with national networks of schools along lines of religious and ideological preferences. The largest of these networks, Torah Umesorah, the National Society for Hebrew Day Schools, is Orthodox in orientation and now claims 467 affiliated schools. Torah Umesorah was founded in 1944, at a time when the destruction of the European Jewish community brought to this country a group of renowned rabbis, sages, and scholars who gave the impetus to a system of intensive Jewish education. The Solomon Schechter Day School Association, the network of Conservative day schools, lists 59 affiliates in its most recent directory.

The national networks offer a variety of supportive services in their affiliated schools in areas of curriculum, teacher in-service training, seminars for principals, publications, as well as

106

guidance in management and institutional development.

National ideological affiliation notwithstanding, the Jewish day school is an autonomous institution with the full power of governance vested in a lay board of directors responsible only to the parents and supporters of the school. The influence of the national headquarters of a particular network on the individual affiliate is on the level of advisement and suasion. In Orthodox institutions, particularly of the rightist variety, the views of Orthodox Rabbinic and scholarly authorities will carry much weight on the decision-making by the board of directors of the school.

Communal Support

The attitude of various segments of Jewish society vis-a-vis the day school is reflective of the ideological and religious differences within the Jewish community. This attitude is by no means static. Rather, it is evolving as changing realities in societal developments require novel and diverse responses on the part of those concerned with creative Jewish survival.

Among the religious movements, Orthodoxy - in all its nuances and shadings - is committed to day school education as a sine qua non. In fact, many, if not most, Orthodox congregations have discontinued offering formal religious instruction in a supplementary school setting as part of their synagogue program, since nearly all children of the congregants attend some type of Jewish day school.

Conservative Judaism is on record, through its lay and rabbinic national bodies, as favoring day school education. A position paper, "The Solomon Schechter Day School in the Conservative Movement," published by the Solomon Schechter Day School Association, lists seven such pronouncements and resolutions, spanning from 1957 to 1976. Withal, the Conservative day school is a fairly recent arrival

107

on the Jewish day school scene, and the Solomon
Schechter Day School Association was officially
launched only in 1965. Conservative synagogues
thus maintain a vast network of supplementary
schools for religious instruction, and only a
minority of children from Conservative homes attend the fifty-some Solomon Schechter Day Schools.

Through the 1950's, the majority view among
Reform Jews opposed Jewish day schools in principle.
In 1950, during the symposium on day schools held
at the annual convention of the Central Conference
of American Rabbis (the national organization of
Reform Rabbis), one speaker proclaimed that "the
Jewish all-day school, like Jonah's gourd, has come
up in the night of despair. It will wither in the
broad daylight of renewed faith in freedom and
democratic process."[6] By 1969, however, the Commission on Jewish Education of the Reform Movement,
passed a strong pro day school resolution. As
Syme puts it, "The text reflects an emerging consensus that day school and public school were not
an either/or choice."[7] In the words of the Commission: "The Commission maintains its commitment
to the public school and to part-time Jewish education, perceiving the day school as an attractive
option for those who wished to avail themselves of
it."[8] There are, to date, eight day schools under
Reform Jewish auspices.

Secular Jews have been, by and large, stead-
fast in their avoidance of day school education.
There are, however, a handful of secular bicultural
Jewish day schools, some with a strong Yiddish cultural component in their program offerings. Most
of these schools are in Canada, rather than the
United States.

Curricular Organizations and Content

Jewish day schools, as noted earlier, cover a
wide gamut of points of view in religion, culture
and world outlook. Ranging from the Hasidic day
school through traditional Talmudic academies,

modern Hebraic yeshivot, the Solomon Schechter Day
School, to day schools under Reform Jewish auspices - they present an accurate replica of Jewish
communal pluralism.

This pluralism is reflected in the wide variation in policy and practice, in curriculum organization and content, and in the overall educational
goals and expectations. Reform day schools,
Solomon Schechter Day Schools, communal and independent day schools, and some of the modern Hebraic
yeshivot are coeducational institutions. Some of
the middle-of-the-road day schools, in terms of
religious outlook, will maintain co-ed classes at
least on the elementary level. The Talmudical
academies, the Hasidic yeshivot and other right
wing institutions operate separate schools for boys
and girls. The Hasidic yeshivot and some of the
Talmudic academies instruct Talmud by translating
the Aramaic text into Yiddish; modern Hebraic
yeshivot and Solomon Schechter Day Schools insist
on Hebrew as the language of instruction in the
Hebraic/Judaic program.

The flow of the school day, its length and
number of hours devoted to Hebraic/Judaic instruction, will also vary depending on the type of
school. Some more modern and religiously liberal
schools opt for an integrated school day in which
general studies and Hebraic/Judaic subjects rotate
in the course of the day. Other schools follow a
dichotomized day in terms of programming (Hebraic/
Judaic subjects in the morning, general studies in
the afternoon).

By and large, 15 hours weekly of Hebraic/
Judaic instruction is the norm in most middle-of-
the-road institutions. The Solomon Schechter Day
School Association mandates a minimum of 12 hours
of Hebraic/Judaic subject matter weekly. Some
schools may, because of local circumstances, offer
only 10 hours of weekly instruction in Hebraic/
Judaic subject matter; in rightist and Hasidic
yeshivot a 20-hour learning load in Hebraic/Judaic
course work is not uncommon.

109

The same variations obtain on matters of ultimate educational goals and curricular content. Schiff[9] lists three broad categories of aims and objectives of Jewish day schools. These are: (1) Preparation for Jewish Living; (2) Personality Building; (3) Preparation for American Living. These categories are broad enough to permit a particular school (or network of schools) to give substance and direction to each of the strands listed. Such objectives as "To train Jewish youth to believe in and help insure Jewish survival," or "To develop religiously observing Jews," or "To provide Jewish youth with rich and varied opportunities for pleasurable experience in Jewish living" carry varied connotations to diverse types of Jewish day school educators.

Rabbi Arthur Hertzberg, speaking at a Curriculum Colloquium of the Solomon Schechter Day Schools Association in 1978, listed, among others, the following characteristics of day schools under Conservative auspices:
1) A full commitment to the validity of general culture;
2) A view of Judaism as part of Western civilization and as a world outlook that must be consistent with contemporary categories of thought;
3) The acceptance of pluralism in Jewish life; especially in matters of ritual;
4) The striving for a non-compartmentalized learning experience in our schools in which Judaic and general components co-exist in harmony.[10]

In terms of curricular content in the Hebraic/ Judaic program, schools will vary mainly on the following issues:
1) The grade placement of text studies - (When is the study of the Pentateuch to begin? Is it to be studied from the original text at the very inception? When should the study of rabbinic commentaries to the Pentateuch, notably the Rashi Commentary, be initiated? How much time should be allotted to this subject?)
2) The place of Rabbinics in the day school

curriculum - (Should the Talmud be taught in the
elementary grades? Should it be limited to
Mishnah[11] or should it include Gemara[12]? Should
Codes [Shulhan Arukh][13] be taught on the elementary level? How much time should be allotted to
the study of Rabbinics?)
3) The place of the Hebrew language in the curriculum - (Is the Hebrew language only a medium for
unlocking sacred texts, or should it also be
taught for full literary and communication mastery?)
4) The place of modern Hebrew literature in the
curriculum - (Does modern Hebrew literature - a
largely secular corpus of literary creativity -
belong in schools whose thrust is essentially
religious?)
5) The place of Jewish history and the Zionism/
Israel dimension in the curriculum - (How much
of this material belongs in the day school program? Are these subject matter areas frills or
legitimate disciplines consonant with the
schools' goals and objectives?)

Integrating the Judaic with the General Curriculum

The modern Hebraic yeshivot and the Liberal-
Conservative day schools have been attempting, with
varying degrees of sophistication and success, to
integrate general and Judaic components in the
curriculum. While the general studies program will,
in most instances, follow the prescribed state syl-
labus for elementary and secondary schools, there
are numerous opportunities for "integrating" the
Hebraic/Judaic subjects with general subject matter
areas. Thus, there have been attempts "to create
programs of studies for day schools which would
constitute unitary learning experiences both in
terms of content and approach; unitary, too, in
the sense that they represent a meaningful (not
forced) blending of a Judaic world outlook, the insights of the Jewish humanities, and general
culture."[14]

111

A considerable body of theoretical writings and practical programs has emerged in recent years dealing with this subject.[15] Proponents of the integrative approach in the Jewish day school program have, however, become increasingly aware of the fact that "the subject matter is integrated only in relation to the philosophy of the integrator."[16] In sum, "two or more objectively identifiable phenomena are therefore not integrated with one another. They are integrated only insofar as they are both related to an integrated human personality."[17]

Funding

It is estimated that over $150,000,000 is spent on Jewish day schools, with funds coming from private and Jewish communal and charitable sources. The major source of Jewish communal-charitable grants to Jewish day schools is the local Federation - a voluntary amalgam of Jewish charities through which the community supports health, education and social service agencies, as well as funds for overseas relief via the United Jewish Appeal. Federation support of day schools was a slow process, reflecting the general ambivalence felt by influential segments in Jewish society vis-a-vis the day school concept. This ambivalence has been, by and large, overcome. According to a recent study "day schools are the beneficiaries of the lion's share of all education allocations by Federations."[18]

In 1977/78, day schools received 15.5% of all total Federation allocations. The rationale for Federation assistance to Jewish day schools lies in the high level religious-cultural service rendered by these schools in terms of educating cadres of Hebraically literate leaders in the Jewish community. Since the per pupil cost for educating a child in a day school (with a dual program to boot) is very high (in 1977/78 this figure was $1,065 per child), the Jewish community, through Federation funding, is assisting with subsidies. In 1977/78

112

the income pattern of Jewish day schools was as
follows:

Income from tuition	52.3%
Federation allocations	19.2%
Contributions and fund-raising by schools	28.5%

The American Association for Jewish Education,
the coordinating and service agency for Jewish education on the North American continent, recommends
an income structure for day schools in which income
from tuition would be between 50%-55%, Federation
allocations from between 25% to 30%, and fund-
raising by the school from 20% to 25%.

Despite the high cost of day school education,
most families desirous of this type of schooling
can obtain it as a result of a wide and generous
scholarship policy maintained by Jewish day
schools, either from their own funds or special individual and foundation grants.

Staffing

Staffing of a day school presents a variety of
problems, particularly on the administrative-super-
visory level. "The head of a Jewish day school
(known under a variety of titles as headmaster,
principal, dean, educational director) is essentially an educational factotum whose professional
strength lies in his ability to function compe-
tently on many planes of educational leadership.
This person is, using descriptive titles common in
general education, a 'building principal' (with
responsibilities ranging from supervision of instruction to monitoring halls and scheduling fire
alarm drills), who functions as 'superintendent of
schools' (dealing, as head of the system, with long
range planning and institutional development including some involvement in the ubiquitous fund
raising efforts), acting also as 'director of instruction' (leading the school in programming,
curriculum development and in-service teacher
training). Tangentially, the school head also

113

functions as guidance counselor, advisor to a multitude of lay boards and committees, and not in the least, a religious leader. Individuals who can and are willing to shoulder these multi-faceted responsibilities are hard to come by and hence the 'buyers market' prevalent at this moment in general education does not apply to principalships of Jewish day schools."[19]

As far as the instructional staff is concerned "with the possible exception of the fields of mathematics and science on the high school level, the staffing of day schools in the general studies, especially on the elementary level, presents few difficulties in most communities at this moment given the realities of supply and demand of teachers. The overwhelming majority of general studies personnel in Jewish day schools are Jewish. Here and there Christian teachers are employed. Experience with Christian teachers instructing in Jewish day schools has been generally very good. Christian teachers who accept employment in Jewish day schools take the Jewish religious outlook of the school very seriously and adhere to the school's policies unswervingly."[20]

The staffing for the Hebrew studies presents certain specific problems. Schools committed to an ivrit b'ivrit[21] program find that American trained teachers fully fluent in Hebrew are not easy to come by, particularly for the instructing of middle and upper grades. Not infrequently, therefore, the Hebrew Department is staffed with teachers from Israel.

Though salaries in Jewish day schools are considerably lower than in public schools, it is good to note that in recent years, and certainly in the better established schools, salaries and fringe benefits have risen at least to a respectable level of being competitive with prevailing salaries in the general independent schools.[22]

114

The Impact of Day School Education

Much hope has been placed in the Jewish day school. Not surprisingly, therefore, considerable efforts have been invested, through individual and institutional research, to study the impact of Jewish day school education on the lifestyle of the graduates of the Jewish day school.[23] The findings of these diverse studies seem to converge in the recognition of the lasting and decisive impact the Jewish day school has on its alumni. Thus, Pinsky concludes, among others, that "the alumni (of the Rabbi Jacob Joseph School -SF) have generally preserved their Orthodox identification after graduation" and "the strongest identification with Jewish values are to be found among those responding alumni which have had the most intensive Jewish education."[24] Similarly, the Pollak study found that "They (the day school graduates -SF) were active in communal life, and gave leadership to the organizations with which they were associated. They have retained reading habits, but were not subscribers of Jewish periodicals and did not maintain extensive Jewish libraries. They were charitable in accordance with a scheme learned through their schooling and were more generous in their contributions towards the causes which the Jewish community supports. By and large, they were tolerant of heterodox Jewish life-styles, but tolerance did not extend to intermarriage."[25]

The decisive role of the Jewish day school in forging of Jewish loyalties and lifestyle is also underscored in the Ribner study which sought to compare graduates of three "intensive" schools with those who had had a less intensive Jewish education (23% of the "intensive" group were day school graduates).

A Glimpse Into the Future

Social vogues and preferences fluctuate rapidly in our fast-moving American civilization. Any attempt at prognostication is an exercise in looking into a crystal ball. It is very doubtful whether day school education will ever become the dominant schooling instrumentality for Jewish children. Ideological uncertainty and fear of self-ghettoization, even more than fiscal restraints, added to the traditional commitment of Jews to the public school concept, will probably keep many Jewish families away from the day school idea. Yet the Jewish day school has become a permanent institution in American Jewish life. It will continue to grow, and will make further gains in social acceptance. Even those Jews who have personal doubts and would not consider enrolling their offspring in a Jewish day school, have come to realize that the day school is the most effective arm of Jewish educational endeavor. As long as the American Jewish community has a collective will to maintain a creative existence on these shores, the Jewish day school is here to stay. In fact, it will flourish and add a special hue and bouquet to the wide array of non-public schooling options in American society.

NOTES

1. Schiff, Alvin I. The Jewish Day School in America, p. 20. JEC Press, New York. 1966.

2. Yeshivah (plural - Yeshivot). A school for Jewish studies.

3. Jewish School Census: 1978/79. Information Bulletin No. 44; American Association for Jewish Education. New York. August, 1979.

4. Kelman, Stuart L. "Parent Motivations for Enrolling a Child in a Non-Orthodox Jewish Day School." Jewish Education, Vol. 47. Spring, 1979.

5. Jewish School Census. op. cit., p. 16.

6. Syme, Daniel B. "The Reform Day School: Its History and Future Prospects." The Pedagogic Reporter, Vol. XXIX, p. 14. Fall, 1977.

7. Ibid., p. 15.   8. Ibid., p. 15.

9. Schiff. op. cit., p. 106 and ff.

10. Quoted in Frost, Shimon. "The Needs of the Solomon Schechter Day Schools: A Practitioner's View." Conservative Judaism, Vol. 33, p. 74. Spring, 1980.

11. Mishnah. A collection of Jewish Law and Ethics compiled and edited by R. Yehuda Ha-Nassi at the beginning of the 3rd Century. Written in Hebrew, it provides an expansion and elucidation to Biblical law and is the basis of further elaboration in the Gemara. Mishnah and Germara, jointly, form the Talmud.

12. Gemara. Body of discussions and amplifications on the Mishnah. Written largely in Aramaic, it has two versions, the Babylonian Gemara and the Jerusalem or Palestinian Gemara. The former is more complete and is the one that is commonly studied. The Gemara was completed and edited at the beginning of the 6th Century by R. Ashi.

13. Shulhan Arukh. Literally, "Prepared Table." A concise summary of Jewish law and religious practices arranged as a guide for Jewish living. Written in relatively easy Hebrew, and accessible to any Hebraically literate layman, it was authored by R. Joseph Karo, 1488-1575.

117

14. Frost, Shimon. "Integrating the Judaic and General Studies Curriculum." The Synagogue School, Vol. 24, No. 3, p. 29. 1966.

15. cf. "Integration in Day School Programs." Special Issue of Jewish Education. Winter, 1978.

    Integrative Jewish Learning: The Search for Unity in Jewish School Programs. Edited by Max Nadel. American Association for Jewish Education. New York. 1980.

    Freidenreich, Fradle & Gittelson, Abraham J. Interdisciplinary Integration in the Jewish Day School: A Model of Process. American Association for Jewish Education and Miami Central Agency for Jewish Education. 1979.

16. Greenberg, Simon. "Limitations of Integration." Jewish Education, Vol. 46, p. 21. Winter, 1978.

17. Ibid., p. 21.

18. Budgeting and Financing in Jewish Day Schools. Information Bulletin #41, p. 24. American Association for Jewish Education. New York. March, 1979.

19. Frost, Shimon. "Staffing a Day School." Pedagogic Reporter, Vol. 29, pp. 37-38. January, 1977.

20. Ibid.

21. Ivrit b'ivrit. Literally, "Hebrew in Hebrew." A method of language instruction stressing the communication and speaking aspect of the language taught and predicated on complete avoidance of translation into the vernacular.

22. Salaries of Teachers in Day Schools. Information Bulletin #46. American Association for Jewish Education. New York. September, 1980.

23. Pinsky, Irving I. A Follow-up Study of the Graduates of One of the Oldest Existing American Jewish Day Schools: The Rabbi Jacob Joseph School. Unpublished Doctoral Dissertation. School of Education, Yeshiva University. New York. 1961.

    Pollak, George. The Graduates of the Jewish Day School, A Follow-up Study. Unpublished Doctoral Dissertation. Western Reserve University. Cleveland. 1961.

    Himmelfarb, Harold. The Impact of Religious Schooling: The Effects of Jewish Education Upon Adult Religious Involvement. Unpublished Doctoral Dissertation. The

118

University of Chicago, Department of Education. Chicago, Ill. 1974.

Ribner, Sol. A Study of the Effects of Intensive Jewish Secondary Education on Adult Jewish Lifestyles. Unpublished study. American Association for Jewish Education. New York. 1977.

Heimowitz, Joseph. "Jewish Education Makes a Date: A Study of the Graduates of a Yeshivah High School." Jewish Education, Vol. 47. Summer, 1979.

24. Quoted in Pollak, George. "The Day School in Light of Research." Pedagogic Reporter, Vol. 29, p. 25. Fall, 1977.

25. Ibid., p. 25.

SECTION THREE

RELIGION, MORALITY AND PUBLIC EDUCATION

Manner as Medium for Morals

Gary D Fenstermacher

What follows is a dialogue among members of a family. Its purpose is to show how education, or perhaps better, one view of education, requires consideration of moral matters. Too often the debate over moral education is cast as a question of whether there should or should not be such a thing as moral education occurring in the schools. That seems to me a wrongheaded question. A better way to phrase the question is whether education can take place without dealing with moral matters. It is this latter question that is raised and discussed in the dialogue.

The dialogue format is a risky one for scholars — especially those who purport to be philosophers. One's efforts are instantly compared to Plato's dialogues, with the usual result being renewed praise for Plato's skill at this literary form. In this case, the risk seemed worth taking. I place so much emphasis on the notion of manner that the manner of presenting my ideas became almost as important as the ideas themselves. I thought the dialogue form the best literary manner for exploring the concept of manner in education.

Bibliographic citations appear ridiculous in a dialogue, yet I am indebted to the work of others for many of the ideas that are spoken by the several characters. A short bibliographic essay at the end of the dialogue acknowledges this debt.

Archie: Moral education should be a required part of every school curriculum. The young people of today need help in sorting right from wrong, and in doing the right things. Moral education would teach them to do what is right.

Bert: Do you mean that you want teachers to tell

	their pupils what it is right for them to believe and do?
Archie:	Yes, I do. Of course there will also be good books and materials to help the teacher in this work.
Bert:	How do the teachers learn what it is right to believe and do, so that they can teach this to others?
Archie:	Teachers should be trained so that they can provide effective moral instructions. They should also be picked with regard for their moral character.
Bert:	So, in addition to making teachers responsible for the moral character of their pupils, you would make teacher educators responsible for the moral character of teachers. And where the teacher educators slipped in their work, you expect those who hire teachers to screen out the ones who do not measure up.
Archie:	Your questions indicate you disagree with me. Is that so?
Bert:	Yes, I think I do. You have a view of moral education that seems too simple.
Cathy:	And now the academic mind of Uncle Bertrand will begin to complicate the topic.
Bert:	Sorry, Cathy, but I don't know any other way of handling it. It seems to me that the notion of moral education could mean several different things.
Archie:	It seems clear enough to me.
Derek:	Why not give Uncle Bert a chance to tell us what he thinks the different interpretations are?
Bert:	Thank you. One way of understanding moral education is that offered by your father; that is, telling people what it is right for them to do or believe. I think this is what we are doing when we insist on

124

commitment to and repetition of such things as the Ten Commandments, the Pledge of Allegiance, the Scout Oath, the Golden Rule, and other, similar guides to conduct.

Cathy: If that's what dad means by moral education, I disagree with him. There are lots of people who invoke oaths, pledges, and rules only when it is convenient for them, while ignoring these guides in much of their own behavior.

Derek: What's your alternative?

Cathy: I'm not sure. But I don't like the idea of teaching morality by telling someone else what it is right for them to do.

Archie: Naturally; what child still under the guidance of parents does? You, especially, show a penchant for ignoring advice and finding out on your own.

Bert: There, Archie, you have just hit on another way of moral education.

Archie: How's that?

Bert: By learning yourself what it means to be moral; by trying out ways of doing things, to see what they lead to and how they might be justified.

Derek: You mean that old touchy-feely stuff about, "If it feels good, do it"? A lot of the people I know who talk like that seem selfish, or at least self-centered.

Cathy: No, it's not a matter of doing it because it feels good. But there is something to be said for trying things — for learning on your own.

Bert: I think you have something, Cathy. Let's explore it.

Cathy: I'm not sure I want you to pull the old Socrates routine on me, Uncle Bert. Asking me questions that lead to places which may eventually trap me into a position I don't want to take is not my idea of a good discussion.

Bert: Dear me, where did you develop this dis-
taste for academic discourse?

Cathy: The same place you developed your taste
for it.

Bert: Touché. But give me a try, anyway. Plato
I'm not, so I doubt you will fail to
recognize any traps in my questions. Besides, I am sympathetic to your point of
view.

Derek: Give Uncle Bert a chance. He might just
find himself trapped in his own questions.

Bert: I'm overwhelmed by the filial affection in
evidence here. Such odds only impel me to
try harder, so you might want to be more
gentle. Now, Cathy, what is it for a person to be moral?

Cathy: A moral person is someone who does what it
is right to do.

Derek: Now there's genuine progress.

Cathy: That judgmental outburst is premature,
little brother. Would you care to re-
phrase or apologize?

Bert: What did you find offensive about Derek's
comment?

Cathy: It was rude; it showed a lack of respect
for my thinking; it indicated a lack of
humility on his part.

Bert: In other words, from your brother you seek
consideration, not rudeness; respect, not
dismissal; humility, not pride.

Cathy: Isn't that what I just said?

Bert: Forgive me; you're right. I was setting
up the next question. What would you call
things like showing consideration, respect,
and humility?

Cathy: Traits of character, perhaps.

Derek: Rudeness, disrespect, and pride are also

126

traits of character.

Bert: I agree with both of you. But there are certain traits of character that we generally value in people. These traits we call virtues. The nobler among the virtues are goodness, courage, respect for persons, regard for truth, a sense of justice, and so on. When people act in accord with these nobler virtues, are they not doing what many of us believe it is right for them to do?

Derek: It seems so.

Bert: Then your cynical retort to Cathy's answer was unjustified, for that is precisely what Cathy said: For a person to be moral is for a person to do the right thing. Acting in accord with the several virtues is to do the right thing.

Derek: It appears that I am the one trapped. Sorry, Cathy.

Cathy: Accepted. I'm wondering what virtue has to do with my view of moral education.

Bert: I was coming to that. If the imparting of virtue is the point of moral education, then we can raise the same question Socrates did in his discourse with Protagoras: Can virtue be taught?

Archie: Of course it can. I've been saying that all along.

Cathy: But you want to teach it by telling, and by having people memorize and recite oaths and pledges. That doesn't work, because people can be told what it is right to do and still not do the right thing. They can recite all the rules of good conduct while doing things that are wrong. It's because people can say one thing while doing another that I argued that people have to try to do the right thing.

Archie: And how will they know what to try unless they are told?

127

Derek: You could show them.

Bert: Bravo! I don't think you can make someone
         courageous by telling him to have courage.
         Rather, you have to show courage, and then
         free the person to try to be like you.

Cathy: Now I owe you an apology, Uncle Bert, for
         you just worked out my position for me.
         Moral education is showing others the ac-
         tions that flow from virtue, and providing
         them with the opportunity to practice
         these actions for themselves.

Archie: Why take the long way around? Why not
         just tell a person what to do?

Bert: Telling may have a place in the scheme of
         things. In telling, you indicate to
         others what you regard as important, what
         you value. It could be that while telling
         another the right thing to do does not
         lead the person to do the right thing, it
         does indicate to the person that you place
         a value on doing things in this way.
         Telling people to be fair is a way of
         letting them know that fairness is valued,
         but it seems an ineffective, perhaps even
         wrong, way to get them to be fair.

Derek: I can see, for the reasons Cathy men-
         tioned, how telling is ineffective. But
         how could it be wrong?

Bert: May I postpone trying to answer that ques-
         tion until we finish the discussion with
         Cathy?

Cathy: I thought we concluded that.

Bert: Not quite. We've left your father with
         the impression that he is odd man out —
         in spite of assuring him that telling may
         have a place in moral education. He
         started this discussion by holding that
         teachers should themselves be exemplars of
         moral action. Given the ground we have
         covered, is he very far off the mark?

128

Archie: Maybe there is hope for détente between businessmen and academics!

Cathy: I don't see the connection.

Derek: I think I do. We've agreed that moral education occurs when persons are shown virtuous action, and allowed to try such action for themselves. If moral education is to take place in the schools, then it must be teachers who will demonstrate virtues for their students. Thus, teachers will have to be virtuous themselves.

Bert: So long as we don't confuse virtue with some of the simpler notions of purity and piety, I think you've got it. Teachers serve as models for their pupils, and perhaps even encourage their pupils to attend carefully to what teachers do, while also providing opportunities for pupils to try different forms of moral action for themselves.

Cathy: Hold it. Cannot teachers fake their behavior just as they might tell pupils to do things that are right while themselves doing just the opposite?

Bert: Yes, of course they can. But if they did, would they not be acting inappropriately, perhaps even immorally? Would not pupils recognize the falseness or insincerity of teachers who tried to act righteously solely in order to set an example, without being righteous in their everyday dealings with pupils?

Cathy: Yes, I think so.

Bert: Then, if teachers did so, would they not be modeling for pupils precisely the wrong kind of behavior; that is, the pupils would have as models persons who were false, insincere, perhaps dishonest?

Cathy: Now I see your point.

Bert: Okay. Now I would like to add just one more thing before getting to Derek's

129

question — the one I put aside a moment
ago. I fear some of my colleagues in
psychology will misinterpret the connection between traits of character and virtue, so I want to call traits that pick
out moral or immoral patterns of behavior
"manner". We often say of someone that
he has a kind manner, or adjudicates disputes in an impartial manner, so this word
"manner" is not very far from our everyday
understanding. I just hope you won't confuse the plural form, manners, with standards of etiquette; like table manners or
what is meant when we say of a person that
he shows poor manners. Manner refers to
certain reasonably stable characteristics
of a person, characteristics which pertain
to the person's tendency to do the right
or wrong thing under a given set of circumstances.

Derek: Using the notion of manner in the context
of moral education, is it correct to say
that teachers exhibit manner, and that
pupils will pick up on this manner? They
may emulate the teacher's manner, such
that the teacher is serving as a model for
the pupil.

Bert: You're a quick study, Derek.

Cathy: Either that or he started this conversation with no ideas of his own, and has
found it convenient to embrace yours,
Uncle Bert.

Derek: Aha! Could that remark indicate envy or
jealousy? Is it evidence of an incon-
siderate or disrespectful manner? To whom
ought the apology be directed this time?

Bert: To you. Though this little fit of pique
offers a good occasion to remind you that
indiscretions can occur, and that impru-
dence may be very temporary. If you regard your sister as one who frequently
evidences manner indicative of tolerance,

respect, and fair play, you might reasonably choose to ignore such minor lapses in character.

Derek: Very well, I shall save my vituperative talents for her major lapses in character.

Cathy: In which case they will atrophy from desuetude.

Bert: May we have a truce, and return to Derek's question? He asked how telling might not only be ineffective as a form of moral education, but also wrong. Do you recall?

Derek: Yes. Are you saying that if a method of teaching is ineffective, it is wrong to use that method?

Bert: No, not quite. It may be procedurally wrong to continue to employ teaching methods you realize are ineffective, but certain conditions would have to be in effect before a procedural wrong becomes a moral wrong.

Derek: What might those conditions be?

Archie: I believe that is just the question your uncle was looking for.

Bert: And so it was. Unfortunately I don't know quite how to answer the question without getting complex.

Cathy: It's been my experience that teachers say that when they really don't understand their topic.

Bert: For that I am going to ask you to persevere. Let's go back to manner. Do you see a difference between what is taught, and how it is taught?

Derek: Sure. What is taught is the content or subject matter. How it is taught is the method.

Bert: Agreed. Now we need to make a distinction between manner and method, and this distinction is a subtle one. Take the notion

131

of reinforcement; I'll call it praise for purposes of this discussion. It isn't hard, is it, to picture a teacher who is fair in his dealings with pupils, but does not praise them often — even when they do well.

Derek: I think I had a teacher like that.

Bert: So you agree that a teacher can be fair, yet not an astute user of the methods of praise. Do you also agree that a teacher can be a good user of the technique of praising performance, yet not be fair in her dealings with pupils?

Derek: Yes.

Bert: So there may be teachers who are astute practitioners of pedagogical methods, though lacking in manners which mark a person of high moral character; and there can be teachers of high moral character who may be poor in the use of instructional methods.

Derek: Yes.

Cathy: You agree too quickly. We have agreed that sincerity is a manner that marks a person of moral character. Yet a teacher's praise can be insincere. This shows there is a connection between method and manner.

Bert: There's a connection, all right. What I wanted to make clear is that the two are different from each other. Your example of insincere praise helps to make my point. The instructional methods we pick up from experience in teaching, and learn from psychologists who study education are a different kind of thing from the notion of manner we have been discussing. I warned you the point was subtle.

Cathy: It certainly is. Is it also important?

Bert: It is. Take the unfair teacher teaching

	pupils history. She could make excellent use of such instructional techniques as pacing, appropriate prescription, reinforcement, and opportunity to learn, yet still be unfair in her dealings with pupils. Correct?
Derek:	Correct.
Bert:	Would you say that the unfair teacher is doing wrong?
Derek:	I think so. Let me see the rest of the argument before I commit myself too strongly.
Bert:	There's not much more to it. A teacher whose instructional methods are in accord with what is known about the psychology of learning might be thought an effective teacher, yet she could still be acting wrongly with respect to the manner she employs. Thus a teacher may be effective, though exhibiting a manner that is something less that morally defensible. A teacher may also be ineffective, yet exhibit a morally defensible manner.
Derek:	So there are really three elements in a teaching-learning interaction, manner, method, and content?
Bert:	There may be more, but you have the three of interest to us at the moment.
Cathy:	I don't think you've established the importance of the distinction.
Bert:	Go back to Archie's opening remark that moral education ought to be part of the curriculum in every school. If you were a teacher, given the discussion so far, what would you consider the critical ingredient in moral education?
Cathy:	Manner, I suppose.
Bert:	Would you simply call attention to your manner, saying something like, "Hey, watch me carefully, and do what I do?"

Cathy: If I did do that, it would not be much different from telling pupils what it is right for them to believe or to do.

Bert: You're no less quick than your brother. What would you do?

Cathy: I'd look for a way to display appropriate manners, without insisting that students attend to or copy them.

Bert: How would you do that?

Cathy: I don't know, but I think you do. Tell me, and let me judge the worth of the idea.

Bert: I would search out content areas or subject fields that allowed me to demonstrate what I believed it was worthy for my pupils to model.

Derek: What do you know — I think I'm beginning to see it. You're contending that morals cannot be taught in a vacuum, by themselves — for that would be just like trying to tell a person what it is right to do. Instead, you select different subjects, using them as an opportunity to display different manners. Pedagogical methods are useful here because they help you do the task effectively or efficiently, but they are not the same as manner. Have I got it?

Bert: You do. Can you think of some examples to clarify the point?

Derek: I remember a constitutional law professor I had last year. No matter how carefully we prepared to discuss the cases, she always found a way to scrutinize them that had not occurred to us. She kept saying, "If the rule of law is clear to you, you do not understand it yet." By mid-term, most of us were wishing we had dropped the course. But near the end, we began to understand her point. She was trying to get us to think of new applications for the rule of law, applications that seemed proper but made the rule less clear than we thought it was. Her manner was very analytical. Was she trying to get us to adopt the same manner? Of course! That's exactly what she was trying to do. She used constitutional law as a kind of medium for the manner she was trying to get us to adopt.

Cathy: I wouldn't call that moral education. There's virtue there, but it seems more an intellectual virtue than a moral virtue.

Bert: I wish you had not said that. It opens a vast area of ambiguity, and I am not sure I know how to handle it.

Cathy: False modesty?

Bert: Honest appraisal. There is a relation between the ability to reason well, and acting morally. In order for someone to do what he believes it is right to do, he has to have good reasons for doing it. Being able to think critically and creatively has a bearing on whether we can generate the reasons to act as we think we should.

Derek: Could we complete the other topic before we get off on to this one?

Bert: I would be relieved if we left this topic for a time. Okay, Cathy?

Cathy: All right, but I think a lot of the thesis you have been developing depends on the kinds of connections you can make between being rational and being moral If we can get back to these, I don't mind delaying a bit.

Derek: I wanted to get back to the topic because it occurred to me a moment ago that if you are correct, Bert, then all education is moral education. In so far as a teacher is teaching, that teacher will be exhibiting manner of one kind or another. Pupils who grasp the manner may choose to

135

try to copy it, to use the teacher as a model.

Bert: I've thought the same thing, but I'm not sure it's right. There is a sense, a somewhat less powerful sense than the one you just noted, in which all formal instruction is moral instruction. This less powerful sense is found in the fact that formal teaching involves human relationships among persons. As such, one person always seems in a position to grant or deny rights and privileges, to impose, accept, or refuse duties and obligations, and to advance or inhibit freedom and liberty. In other words, two or more people working together must deal with one another; hence there are many occasions when moral considerations will arise. In this sense, all education has a moral property about it. But to say that all education has moral elements is not the same as saying that all education is moral education. I think that in order for education to be moral, it must specifically aim at getting matters of morality across to pupils. It cannot be incidentally moral, as in the case of two or more persons simply engaged in a common task.

Derek: I follow your point, though I do not yet see how it bears on my idea that all education is moral because teachers are always displaying manner of one kind or another.

Bert: It isn't enough that a teacher is displaying manner; in order for education to be moral in some specific and important sense, the teacher must intend to display manner, and have this intention covered, so to speak, by some purpose having to do with moral education.

Cathy: That's pretty abstract. Can you restate it more clearly?

136

Bert: I'll try. In the late 1970s, many educators latched on to the idea of basic skills education. The purpose of this approach was to make sure that pupils learned to read, write, calculate, and have a minimal understanding of social and economic life. The teachers who were caught up in this movement spent much of their time on presenting information to pupils, on drills and exercises, and on testing for mastery of basic skills. These teachers, by and large, had no intention to impart morality to their students, nor did they suppose that it was their purpose to do so. They did not see themselves as instructors in moral matters, nor did they often try to impart moral insight. If anything, their intention was to be amoral.

Derek: Yet they could not be amoral, because something of a moral nature was always present, just as you said earlier.

Bert: Yes, but remember that I called that form of moral instruction incidental. I want to distinguish it from intentional moral education.

Derek: Is your notion of manner critical to your idea of intentional moral education?

Bert: Absolutely. Intentional moral education is generally what we were discussing a little while back. It is the selection of a subject matter which sustains manners believed critical to the amelioration of life. It is the way we enter into our heritage, and prepare our future. Your word "medium", Derek, may be the best choice of terms. Too often we have viewed the teacher as the medium for content, wherein the teacher serves as a kind of transfer device for getting knowledge and understanding from texts and materials to the heads of pupils. Intentional moral education, of the kind I am putting forth, places the teacher in a far more pivotal

137

position. Here content and manner are tightly related to one another, as the teacher uses content to open the way for the display of manner, and the student's understanding of the content opens the way for him to recognize the teacher's manner, and to choose to model it.

Cathy: It's still all very abstract.

Bert: Let's say you were interested in helping another to gain respect for life. Your intention is to bring those you teach to the point of valuing living things, and avoiding, where possible, creating the conditions leading to death. How would you do this? You said some time ago you would not just tell people to respect life. Do you still hold to that position?

Cathy: Yes, I do. I would try to find other ways to create a respect for life.

Bert: What ways?

Cathy: Would having animals around, and showing others how to care for them be an example?

Bert: On my view it would. Would you also care for them yourself? Would you treat them tenderly, feed them regularly, seek veterinary assistance when they are ill, and attempt to stop those who would do harm to your animals?

Cathy: Of course.

Bert: And in doing so, would you not be displaying a manner, that manner characteristic of respect for life.

Cathy: Yes.

Bert: My contention is that in displaying this manner, you are showing others how to have respect for life. You might also show them the skills needed for feeding the animals, for cleaning their habitats, and for nursing their illnesses. It is in how you do these things that your manner becomes apparent. If you have great respect for life, you will do these things differently from the way you would do them had you only a passing interest in the life and welfare of animals.

Cathy: I see your point, at the elementary level of pet care. How do you get from there to the academic subjects taught in schools and colleges?

Bert: Are there not great works of literature that deal profoundly with respect for life, and with the welfare of fellow human beings? Could not human ecology be studied from the perspective of respect for life? What of biology, and astronautics?

Derek: How did astronautics get in there?

Bert: Do you recall that when the first astronauts returned from the moon, they were quarantined? Their isolation was done from fear of the possibility that they might have picked up some form of bacteria that would be harmful to life on earth. Respect for life was the reason for the quarantine.

Cathy: It's all still somewhat vague.

Bert: Earlier I called some virtues noble virtues. The list included goodness, courage, respect for persons, regard for truth, and a sense of justice. If teachers intend to encourage these virtues in their pupils, how would they do it?

Derek: They would have to find a way to display the manner that is characteristic of such virtues.

Bert: And how might they do that?

Derek: By dealing with content that provides them the opportunity to display these virtues.

Bert: And what kind of content might this be?

Derek: Well, I guess that if you wanted to deal in depth with these virtues, you would have to find content that dealt with them in depth. Such as literature, history, philosophy; perhaps drama, and maybe even opera.

Cathy: I think I'm having some trouble with this because I don't see how a teacher can, in the usual classroom setting, display a manner that rises to the level you are describing.

Bert: Suppose you are right, Cathy, and suppose, too, that I am right about the central importance of manner in moral education. Can you see how your concern might be handled?

Cathy: I have the feeling you're leading me again. What is the point you would like me to make?

Bert: In many cases, content extends the reach of the teacher for displaying manners characteristic of the nobler virtues. You cannot always create situations in the classroom that elicit the more profound aspects of virtue, so you turn to works of literature, music, art, poetry, science, and logic to help you. You confront the student with Dostoyevsky or his literary characters, with Beethoven or his music, with Matisse or his works. Their manner is open to the student to imitate as is the manner of the teacher. Where the teacher cannot plumb deeply enough in the classroom setting, books, records, museums, galleries, and theatres abound to extend the lesson.

Cathy: So one does not read great works, or listen to or look at them just to learn more about them. Part of the reason for studying great people and their work is to engage the manner exhibited by them or the characters, events, or things they create.

Archie: I've been very quiet for some time now, and would like to re-enter this discussion. Bert, the view you're developing seems to permit just the kind of discussion I've been saying ought to occur in schools. Moses, Solomon, and Jesus were great persons. They exhibited a manner that seems to me to evidence a great deal of moral depth. What you've said indicates to me that religious instruction should take place in the schools. My original point about telling persons what they should do still sounds good to me, even after all the conversation among you, Cathy, and Derek.

Bert: I'm sure it seems that way to you, Archie, but there are difficulties with your position.

Archie: I was sure you would find some.

Bert: I'm not as unsympathetic as you might think. A teacher who intended to engage in moral education might reasonably turn to scriptures and religious figures to extend his reach beyond the limiting circumstances of the classroom. However, it turns out that it is very difficult for most of us to deal with religious persons and events dispassionately. It can be done, but it isn't easy. For too many of us, our passions run high in this area, and we are unable to maintain our commitment to other critical virtues while pursuing those that religious studies so abundantly and fruitfully portray.

Cathy: Would I be correct in saying that we are getting back to my question about the relation between the intellectual virtues and the moral virtues?

Bert: You would be. Among the so-called intellectual virtues are the ability to think clearly, critically, and creatively, showing a regard for evidence, respecting truth, remaining open to alternative

141

explanations, and maintaining a modicum of detachment from our inquiries. As we encounter religious figures, the intellectual virtues are easily compromised. Our temptation is no longer to encourage others to choose and try, but to believe what we believe in the way we believe it. In short, many of us too readily lapse into indoctrination. Because we consider indoctrination a less than satisfactory way to educate, we err on the conservative side by proscribing, at least in the public schools, religious studies — unless we can show beyond doubt that intellectual freedoms are uncompromised by these studies. I am not saying that this is the reason why the founding fathers built a wall between church and state; I am saying that this is one reason why it makes sense to have such a wall.

Cathy: You gave me a clue to the connection between the intellectual and the moral virtues. If moral education is designed to encourage pupils to choose certain persons, or the manner of certain persons, and try this manner for themselves, then the pupils must have a way of deciding whether they made a good choice. They must be able to assess the effects of their trials, to make judgments about what they are doing. To do so, they need to be able to think clearly and critically, to take account of available evidence, and the other things you mentioned. If I am right, the choose-and-try approach to moral education is incomplete without the intellectual virtues; it would be like handing a person a loaded gun without also providing the means to learn from its use.

Bert: The metaphor is not only vivid, it is apt. The choose-and-try approach, as you call it, is a bit like a loaded gun. That is why we attempt to reduce the risk by providing young people with the best possible

142

	models we can find. In the hopes that when they choose, they will choose what is best, and when they try, they will try to do what the best models we have provided them do.
Archie:	Well, at least my views have not been completely destroyed by this august group. I did say at the outset we ought to seek the best teachers, and train them well for their work.
Cathy:	But you also said that those teachers ought to tell their pupils what to believe and how to act. You never mentioned manner, nor did you seem at all willing to permit choice and trial. Have you changed your mind about this?
Archie:	No, I don't think so. Perhaps I'm a little less confident of my view than I was when we started. But I still prefer it over the position you and your uncle have taken.
Derek:	Your manner is both gracious and stubborn, dad.
Archie:	If you consider that a fault, son, I look to your generation to rectify it.
Bert:	At the risk of having the last word ...
Cathy:	How could it possibly be otherwise.
Bert:	We've covered much ground, and I wonder whether the main point is still with us. If we look to education to liberate the minds of pupils, then education is indeed a moral matter. Who among us would say that a person is educated if he or she seldom knew the right thing to do, or seldom did the right thing. Yet the mind is not liberated when it is crammed full with rules, for these serve mostly to constrain. Freeing the mind is providing for choice, and for trial, and preparing the chooser to learn from these trials, to evaluate them, revise them if necessary, or even

143

discard the ideas that produced them. To
preserve the feature of choice, we must
depend less on compulsion and more on
freedom and opportunity. The idea of manner indicates how moral education may take
place under conditions of opportunity and
freedom, as it is in adopting the manner
of one we choose to model that we make a
choice and try a course of action. How
far our models can take us, and how far we
can travel from our models depends on the
depth and breadth of our knowledge and
understanding. If we are familiar with
only a few things, and these only
modestly, it means we have had few models,
and we cannot venture very far without
them. If we have insight into many things,
and command much of human life and history,
we have been fortunate to have had many
models, and are able to venture far from
them. Teachers who would liberate the
minds of their pupils are inescapably involved in their moral education. As such,
their charge is to exemplify the manner of
the persons they wish their pupils to become. To this end, all the resources of
the human race are at their disposal.
Putting them to use is a matter of first
attending to one's own manners, as this is
the primary means of attending to the
moral education of those we would teach.

Archie: Bert, do you think if I could state my
position the same way you stated yours,
you would be persuaded to mine rather than
yours?

Bert: Maybe. Let's discuss it. Do you think
that if you were to state your position in
the same way I stated mine, you would still
believe what you believe?

Cathy: Dad, you should have let him have the last
word.

Many of the ideas presented in the dialogue are based on the work of contemporary philosophers of education, particularly the modern British school of philosophy of education. Among the leaders of this school are R.F. Dearden, P.H. Hirst, John Passmore, and R.S. Peters. Though their work appears in many different books, the articles from which ideas in this dialogue are drawn are contained in a single text: R.F. Dearden, P.H. Hirst, and R.S. Peters, eds., Education and Reason, Part 3 of Education and the Development of Reason (London: Routledge and Kegan Paul, 1975). In this same text, Gilbert Ryle writes on the question of whether virtue can be taught; his ideas have influenced the treatment of virtue in the dialogue. While I have developed the notion of manner in my own way, it was suggested to me by two of Peters' essays; one, entitled "Education and Human Development," appears in the text mentioned above (pages 111-130); the other appears in, R.S. Peters, ed., The Philosophy of Education (London: Oxford University Press, 1973), see especially pages 24-26.

The work of other philosophers accounts for the ways I approach moral education, providing the background for my interpretation of the British school. The two classics in this field are Plato's Protagoras (the Jowett translation, revised by Martin Ostwald, with an excellent introduction by Gregory Vlastos, is published by Bobbs-Merrill (1956) under the title, Plato's Protagoras), and Aristotle's Nicomachean Ethics (translated by H. Rackham, and published by Harvard University Press, 1962), William K. Frankena's analysis of Aristotle in Three Historical Philosophies of Education (Chicago: Scott, Foresman and Company, 1965) is, in my view, one of the best discussions of the bearing of Aristotle's thought on educational theory and practice. Frankena's Ethics (Englewood Cliffs, J.J.: Prentice-Hall, 2nd ed., 1973) is a lucid introduction to the field, should the reader wish to gain a broader grasp of moral issues often unmentioned in discussions of moral education. For a powerful argument on the nature of morality within social order, and what it means to be moral within the usual conditions all of us face, see Kurt Baier, The Moral Point of View (N.Y.: Random House, 1965).

Two collections of essays provide worthy reading for those who wish to explore the complexities and refinements

145

in moral education: Nancy F. and Theodore R. Sizer, <u>Moral Education: Five Lectures</u> (Cambridge, Mass.: Harvard University Press, 1970); and Barry I. Chazan and Jonas F. Soltis, eds., <u>Moral Education</u> (N.Y.: Teachers College Press, 1973). The bibliographies contained in the Chazan and Soltis anthology, as well as in Frankena's <u>Ethics</u> offer happy hunting for those whose interest in the topic develops beyond that of passing acquaintance.

Why Civic Virtue and Self Interest
Should Provide the Moral Core of
Citizenship Education

Robison B. James

From the 1770's through the 1970's, a remarkable debate was carried on in this country. In the
midst of the struggle for independence and the
founding of the new nation, some of the best minds
ever to engage in public controversy[1] debated this
question: What qualities of character and moral
commitment must American citizens possess, if the
republican form of government they were establishing was to survive?[2] In order to pursue a
similar question here — the question about the
moral core of citizenship education in U.S. public
schools — we could hardly do better than to try,
in the first place, to get clear about what was involved in that unfolding dispute.

The Great Debate

Although the two sides in the debate argued
with extraordinary intellectual skill, the question
was anything but academic. The penalty for accepting the wrong answer to their question, they
fully believed, would be the collapse or fatal
skewing of their costly experiment in liberty and
self-government.

On the one side were men like the cousins
Samuel and John Adams of Massachusetts, and, with
more moderation, Thomas Jefferson of Virginia.
They championed "civic virtue," the frugal, hardy,
sacrificial, disciplined devotion to the common
good, which they also called "republican virtue,"
or "public virtue." No people who lacked such virtue, they urged, could long enjoy the blessings of
liberty. Without it the people would splinter into
greedy, lawless factions and plunge the affairs of
livelihood, commerce and state into such chaos that
only some new tyrant would be sufficient to impose
tranquility once again.

147

So strongly did these men feel that liberty
could not endure without civic virtue that they
wrote a stern warning to this effect into the constitution of Virginia in 1776, and thereafter into
the constitutions of at least three other of the
original states. And it was a lasting thing. No
subsequent constitution for the State of Virginia
has omitted that warning, and such a warning stands
now also in the constitutions of at least six
states besides that of Virginia.[3]

There was indeed a tremendous surge of public-
spirited virtue in the 1770's — enough to establish democratic governments in the several states
and to win a war with Britain. But by the 1780's
there was an ominous increase of such unvirtuous
things as insurrections, cancelled debts, inflated
paper money and the election of demagogues in the
states. For example, a few months after the Shays
rebellion was put down in 1786, Shaysites got themselves elected to the Massachusetts legislature in
enough numbers to gain relief from their debts by
passing a law.[4]

In the light of such events, a great deal of
opinion during the 1780's began shifting to the
view, as it was expressed in a newspaper of the
time, that "virtue, patriotism, or love of country,
never was nor never will be till men's natures are
changed, a fixed, permanent principle and support
of government."[5]

The newer view — and it constituted the other
side of the national debate I am tracing here —
focused on self-interest rather than virtue. It
simply accepted as a fact that human beings will
usually pursue their own self-interest, not least
as citizens and in the affairs of state. But this
view also involved the belief that acquisitive or
ambitious motives of this sort could be harnessed
so as to serve and protect the common good. How
this could be done was shown by those supremely realistic men[6] who labored through a Philadelphia
summer in 1787 to frame the checks and balances of
the U.S. Constitution. Congress must check the

President and vice-versa, the judiciary must be
separate, and Congress must be pitted against itself in House and Senate.

That Constitution is itself the chief monument
of this point of view. Among the finest spokesmen
of this perspective were Alexander Hamilton and
John Jay of New York, and James Madison of Virginia.
Not coincidentally, the three were the authors of
an historical series of 85 newspaper columns, ap-
pearing in 1787-88 and later collected as The
Federalist, which explained the Constitution and
urged that it be ratified.

In the Federalist Number 51, Madison explains
the underlying assumptions: "Ambition must be made
to counteract ambition. The interest of the man
must be connected with the constitutional rights of
the place."[7] Or, as an interpreter who wrote about
the time President Nixon was forced to resign expressed this view, "if officials in one part of the
government should be insufficiently moved by ambition and self-interest, a necessary balancing restraint would be lacking and the danger would increase of concentration of power in the hands of
others."[8] Madison called this a "policy of supplying by opposite and rival interests, the defect
of better motives." He thought it "might be traced
through the whole system of human affairs, private
as well as public."[9] I believe he was right.

So where are we left? In 1774 and 1775 Samuel
Adams' call for America to base itself on republican virtue and be a Christian Sparta[10] might have
seemed to make sense. In those years there was an
almost magical coalescence of a united people in
different places. Giddy with liberty, and yet con-
ducting themselves usually with restraint and de-
corum, they formed committees, councils and con-
gresses which acted on local, state and Continental
scales as actual governments, even before independence was declared. And there was Lexington and
Concord, and Bunker Hill.[11]

But by the 1790's, after the strain of America's

longest war before Viet Nam, and after the confusion and strife which followed, thoughtful
Americans were not sure they could depend, year in
and year out, upon anything more lofty than self-
interest within the breasts of the citizenry. That
wasn't all bad, though. "America would remain
free," Gordon Wood sums it up, "not because of any
quality in its citizens of spartan self-sacrifice
to some nebulous public good, but in the last
analysis because of the concern each individual
would have in his own self-interest and personal
freedom."12

If we leap forward a moment, however, we can
see that we have by no means heard the last of
virtue. To take but one example, it was virtue
which guided Jefferson, elected President in 1800
and 1804, as he dismantled the pretensions, patronage and power which the Federalists had brought
to the federal government during their glittering
decade of the 1790's.13

Both/And

I obviously have a didactic interest here.
But what do we do with such a story as the above?

The easiest thing in the world is to decide
that one side or the other won: That side is right,
the other all wrong. I think that conclusion would
be a mistake, although I confess that I have told
the story in such a way as to tilt it a bit towards
self-interest. I suppose I have suggested, at
least implicitly, that virtue is needed only in
supplemental doses and from time to time — or that
virtue would not be available in larger quantities
than that, so that we had better settle for it as
only a periodic supplement to self-interest.

Actually, although I believe large, supplementary bursts of virtue are needed from time to
time within our national life (in time of war, or
in a disaster, for example), I also believe that
virtue is needed as a constant counterpoint to

self-interest. It is needed, in my judgment, both within the moral makeup of our citizens individually, and in the kinds of moralizing we do at each other in our public discourse. For such reasons, it is only to be expected that I would like to see both values played up in our enterprises of citizenship education.

Are not these values inconsistent, however? To be sure, many people manage to join them together in their operating lifestyles. For example, they compete hard in order to earn more, and also give regularly and even sacrifically to benevolent causes. Even so, virtue and self-interest do a lot of quarreling when they are called upon directly to guide our conduct or shape our character.

Granting that, however, I believe this measure of inconsistency is a recommendation rather than a drawback for the citizenship education I have in view. For one thing, this inconsistency helps mightily to alleviate any uncomfortable implications of a state-prescribed morality. I have drawn my two values out of a swatch of history — out of a definitive phase of Americans' national struggle to fulfill their destiny, as they saw it. One could hardly be an American citizen without coming to terms somehow with the principal moral claims embodied in that story. True enough. But still there may be other parts of our story exuding other values, or I may have burdened one or both of my values with a biased definition. And if it were not I, it would be someone else doing such things. Or other things. Thus, the minute the public school system gives backing to any proposal thus conceived, we are confronted with the question of whether one person's moral preferences are about to be imposed upon others in some authoritarian manner.

Of course, virtually any proposal which attempts to convey the main values of the American way has an inbuilt protection of sorts against authoritarianism. Such an effort simply cannot leave out those rights and values which have to do with freedom of conscience, of expression, of

151

religion, and with the equal dignity and worth of
every human person. If our schools managed to
convey or instill such values, the result should be
to diminish the amount of authoritarianism which we
would otherwise be inflicting upon one another.
This inbuilt protection against authoritarianism is
in no way peculiar to my proposal, however. On
this point, I would hope only to run sufficiently
with the pack not to get off the main road.

What is probably different about my proposal
is that the apparent inconsistency of my two
values, or their "uneasiness of combination," means
that the teacher must be extraordinarily dull not
to leave the imprint of his or her personality on
the subject matter itself — not just on the way it
is put across, but on what that content is. "I
taught exactly the same two values she did," you
might say. Perhaps. But that isn't all you did.
You also conveyed a particular way of relating, or
of balancing the two. Does self-interest come
across as something necessarily to be suffered in
society, but a bit cribbed, mean or venal, at least
by comparison with what a great heart will care
about, namely, virtue? Or does virtue enter the
picture as the stuff of childhood dreams, nice to
think about on Sunday morning, perhaps, but only on
the fringes of the real world where one must provide for one's family?

It is not even required that you decide self-
interest and virtue are inconsistent. You're just
not supposed to leave either one of them completely
out, or fail utterly to appreciate those actors in
the human drama who somehow picked the "wrong"
value, as you see it, to get excited about. I find
this to be far more an incitement to serious
thought and to individuality of approach than any
kind of straitjacket. And yet each teacher will be
grappling with much the same content.

Why is it so important to keep both these
values in the picture in citizenship education?
Part of the reason is that the story of the country
in which we are citizens cannot be savored in

152

anything like its full dimensions, nor can one be
ready to share in the continuation of that story
very well, if one is systematically unresponsive to
one or the other of these values — since each has
been the moving force in so much of what this country has been up to.

But there are reasons more strictly moral or
ethical why it is important to come to terms with
both these values. An aptness only for public-
spirited virtue can get pretty shrill, an aptness
only for self-interest pretty mean. And, beyond
that, at least three key American values, liberty,
equality and justice, turn out to be rather different, depending upon which of our two core values
is given the upper hand. This means that the very
possibility of communicating about these moral
issues is lost, to say nothing of the possibility
of resolving them, if we have firmly shut the door
on one or the other, virtue or self-interest.

Seen under the sun of public virtue, liberty
is fully participating in government, unimpeded, as
well as in other aspects of the corporate life. In
the light of self-interest, by contrast, liberty is
not being bothered in the course of one's actions
(so long as one does not bother others), and it is
also being secure in the possession of one's
property, able to use it as one freely chooses.
From the point of view of republican virtue,
equality is likely to mean equality of results with
everyone in general (at least up to some minimum
satisfaction of dire needs) in the number of goods
one enjoys or has. Alternatively, from the point
of view of self-interest, equality means at most
the equality of opportunity to better one's self;
and it may only mean being equally able with others
to claim what one has earned (and only what one has
earned) and to stand somehow equal "before the
law." And the two diverse notions of justice will
track fairly closely these two diverse notions of
equality, respectively. I have sharpened the contrasts somewhat between the two values in the way I
have stated their different implications. Something like a balance of virtue and self-interest

153

often prevails, however, so that the contrasts are blurred, and a good deal of discussion and thought is provoked concerning the meaning of the "liberty," "equality," and "justice" which we seek.

Some Advantages of Including Self-Interest in Ethics Education

I am interested in the moral education component of preparing the young for citizenship — or, as I prefer to call it, the ethics education component. In such an undertaking, it is not surprising that we should treat the high claims of "civic virtue." For example, the public interest in a livable environment is likely to be noted as a constraint on any reckless pursuit of greater and greater profits. But shall we treat self-interest with appreciation, in ethics education of all places — especially if we begin to think about the possibility of inculcating it somehow as a value?

Actually, a substantial amount of demanding content is generated by self-interest as a moral principle. The late Martin Diamond has pointed this out in a very perceptive contrast of our "modern" view of government — as stated by Madison, especially — with the classical view of Aristotle and others that one purpose of government is to make the citizens good or virtuous. Diamond starts out by distinguishing acquisitiveness from avarice. Avarice is the inordinate desire to have, whereas acquisitiveness is the desire to get. (Often it is the inordinate desire to get, to be sure.) The acquisitive person will be driven to cultivate a panoply of excellence of character. They turn out to be the bourgeois virtues: venturesomeness, hard work, temperance, moderation, the ability to delay gratifications to achieve a goal, and even a sturdy bit of justice. Justice enters because one must acquire justly, or not too unjustly, if the whole scheme of competitive strivings is to continue to allow the competitors to accumulate or produce more and more goods. Honesty, which is the "best policy," comes into the picture at this point. It

154

is part of fair play and justice. So acquisitive self-interest yields quite a bit of morality. I do not agree with Diamond, however, that we can develop all the principles of public morality which are appropriate or needed in our form of government on this basis alone, apart from civic virtue.[14]

Over and above such considerations, I believe it is realistic to expect <u>seven benefits</u> to flow from playing up self-interest, as well as virtue, in the ethics education we give to future citizens.

(1) We could make our ethics education a great deal more honest and realistic. I offer the unsubstantiated guess that some of the ineffectiveness of various programs of character or moral education stems from the fact that the students may have felt what was being presented was "too good to be true."

(2) I believe ethics education of the sort I am suggesting would be a lot more fun and a lot more interesting to everyone. On several occasions, as a member of a state legislature, I have attempted to explain for classes of school children how government works. All the talk of structures and procedures serves mainly to glaze their eyes over. If I can spice up what I am saying with something a bit "naughty," or with some narrative of conflict, conniving, or shrewdness, however, interest seems to pick up at once.

(3) One of the problems with ethics, moral, or character education is the problem of having it mesh <u>with</u>, and come up naturally within, the treatment of the various subjects in the curriculum. Many teachers, I suspect, would see an ethics interlude as something along the lines of stopping the action cold, marching a plaster saint upon the stage of discussion, and having that plastic individual model his halo like an item of women's ready-to-wear in a fashion show. If the treatment of ethics has something more of the earthy about it, it might be more naturally a part of the curriculum.

(4)   Rather than ethics education obscuring or
simply being irrelevant to the way in which our
public and social institutions actually work, such
ethics education as I am proposing could provide
one of the most intense points at which insight and
comprehension could come about.   I can explain to
someone how the Virginia General Assembly works on
paper.   But that person has only a dim idea of what
actually is going on in the real world until I have
been able to show him how some of the power blocs,
the legislative maneuvers, and the like, operate.
Rather than ethics education gliding over all the
likes of this, clucking "that's a no-no" all the
while, ethics education would actually be cracking
open such institutions and showing how they work.

(5)   Another advantage of the kind of ethics
education I am proposing is that it would be unlikely to set the students up for what I might call
"the young activist's two-wave syndrome."   The two
waves I have in mind here are two successive ways
in which a young person may encounter social problems and social opportunities.   In the first wave,
the young person becomes aware and concerned, and
quite possibly also becomes involved.   In social
encounters of this sort, young people in particular
are able to exhibit a prepossessing sensitivity
and moral passion.

But moral passion can rather easily pass over
into moral arrogance.   Some of the young activists
of the 1960's and early 70's have made this all too
clear.   Our society, like any other, has fallen
into some long-standing habits concerning the way
it wishes to go about its business.   For that reason, it does not suffer reforming upstarts gladly,
particularly if they are young, and most particularly if they are absolutist and cocksure to boot.

It would be a pity if ethics education were to
give us too many youths of such a supercilious sort.
But it could happen.   A little ethics, like a
little learning, is a dangerous thing.

But worse than the strident confrontations of

156

the "first wave" is what comes next. The second
wave is disillusionment. It is giving up, dropping
out, growing cynical, any or all of the above. To
the young it all becomes quite clear. A world too
wicked to hear their word is a world not worthy of
them. They tried. Because they tried, because
they once burned brightly with a higher hope, and
because they were given a rude rebuff, they have
earned the right now to be as mean and as little
concerned as they choose to be. They'll get theirs
while the getting is good. That's the second wave.
I would hope our ethics education will give students hopes for better things, to be sure, but also
that it will steel those hopes with more realistic
expectations for what can be done, and more realistic notions of how to go about getting it done.

(6) According to Harold Berlack, the most
basic dilemma of citizenship education (he calls it
"political education"), which is the same as the
dilemma of schooling itself, is the dilemma of
"continuity versus change." It is the fact that
the purpose of schooling is both (a) the purpose of
    passing on to others in the society the
    traditions and inclinations to act that
    will insure a reasonably close resem-
    blance of present social processes and
    forms with future social processes and
    forms,
and also (b) the purpose of
    helping the young become increasingly
    self-conscious and competent in ques-
    tioning the adequacy of existing societal
    solutions (e.g., its present traditions,
    social-economic forms) to the changing
    conditions of social-political life.[15]

I would like modestly to suggest that my proposed approach to ethics education resolves this
dilemma without ever having to try. Instead of imposing upon ethics education from without some kind
of protocol to keep such endeavors from straying
too far to the right or to the left, my proposal
defines the subject matter itself in such a way
that, if the teacher adequately handles both sides

157

of that subject matter — both the "public virtue" and the "self-interest" sides of it — the teacher will thereby give scope to both the continuity and the change aspects of the mission of the schools. This is so because (a) the progressive and reformist proclivities of the American ethos find their heart in the call for "public virtue" while (b) the very soul of America's predilections of a conservative stripe is to be found in the way we bless, unleash and protect our people's self-interested strivings.

(7) Finally, I cannot suppress my opinion that ethics education, somewhat along the lines I have elaborated, would make sure that the student is confronted with a more adequate ethic. As I view the matter, good ethical theory is ethical theory which makes ameliorative sense of the actual situations in which people confront obligations — the obligations which ethics is purportedly discussing, clarifying, and instilling. Another way of putting this last point is to make two moves: first, I should point to the self-interested and acquisitive drives which are so large a part of what makes any human being "tick," and then I should urge that any ethics which does not explicitly provide some appropriate and provisional sanction for such drives is not a very adequate ethic.

We might take Lawrence Kohlberg as an example here. He does a good job with these acquisitive drives in elaborating his Stage Two of "instrumental relativism." But then he goes astray with the Pollyanna assumption that our moral reasoning will simply outgrow or rise above such baser levels. The real job (or one of them, anyhow) is to work out the relationships between Stage Two and the higher levels of normative thinking — without just shoving Stage Two into the basement and branding it temptation or bad or "what ought not to be in any case."[16]

Reflecting now on what is said in this section, I should repeat that, in the ethics education

I am suggesting, all the exacting requirements for
virtue, public-spiritedness and concern for others
remain valid, binding and imperative. The American
ethos walks on two legs, not merely on one leg.

Those two legs, or two values, ought to provide the moral or ethical core of citizenship education, in my judgment. There certainly are other
values which are integral to democratic society.
R. Freeman Butts elaborates ten "civic values," as
he calls them, namely, justice, equality, authority,
participation, personal obligation for the public
good (each of these undergirding the unity of our
democratic society); and also freedom, diversity,
privacy, due process, and international human
rights (the latter five undergirding the pluralism
of our democratic society, he thinks).17

But virtue and self-interest are somehow at
the heart of such values, a key to the rest. These
two are sufficient for that. In fact, they are
well nigh overwhelming.

NOTES

1. As Gordon S. Wood points out, the leaders of the
   founding generation were at one and the same time the
   ranking intellectuals of the time and the practicing
   politicians of their day. See his "The Democratization
   of Mind in the American Revolution," The Moral Foundations of the American Republic, edited by Robert H.
   Horwitz (Charlottesville: University of Virginia Press,
   1977), pp. 102-128. Precisely because they were so successful and virtuous as republican statesmen — in
   "opening up the system," as we would say — they ensured
   that their generation would be the only one of such
   "philosopher kings." As one divine wrote in 1803, much
   of the intellectual leadership of America had fallen by
   1800 into "the hands of persons destitute at once of the
   urbanity of gentlemen, the information of scholars, and
   the principles of virtue." See Wood op. cit. (within
   this note, note 1), p. 122.

2. This debate is a major theme running through the 653
   pages of Gordon S. Wood's The Creation of the American
   Republic, 1776-1787 (Chapel Hill: University of North
   Carolina Press, 1969). Wood makes use of an astonishing
   number of quotations from the newspapers, letters,
   pamphlets and books of the period, all at an impressive
   level of eloquence.

3. A. E. Dick Howard, Commentaries on the Constitution of
   Virginia, Vol. I (Charlottesville: University of
   Virginia Press, 1974), pp. 281-282, 282n. See Ibid.,
   Art. I, Sec. 15 of the current Virginia Constitution, as
   follows. "Qualities necessary to preservation of free
   government. That no government, nor the blessings of
   liberty, can be preserved to any people, but by a firm
   adherence to justice, moderation, temperance, frugality,
   and virtue ...." Other states with similar warnings are
   New Hampshire, South Dakota, Vermont, West Virginia,
   Wisconsin and Massachusetts.

   One virtue only, that of "frugality," was removed from
   the 1870 Virginia constitution. It reclaimed its place
   in the next constitution, that of 1902, however, thus
   restoring George Mason's phrase to its original integrity.

4. Gordon S. Wood, in Bernard Bailyn, et al., The Great
   Republic (Lexington, Mass: D. C. Heath & Co., 1977),
   p. 329.

5. _Providence Gazette_, December 29, 1787, as quoted in Wood, _Creation of the American Republic_, _op. cit._ (note 2 above), p. 610.

6. Richard Hofstadter, "The Founding Fathers: An Age of Realism," in Hofstadter, _The American Political Tradition and The Men Who Made It_ (New York: Alfred A. Knopf, 1948), pp. 3-17.

7. _The Federalist_, edited by Jacob E. Cooke (Middletown, Conn.: Wesleyan University Press, 1961), p. 349 (emphasis added).

8. Robert A. Goldwin, "Of Men and Angels: A Search for Morality in the Constitution," _The Moral Foundations of the American Republic_ (note 1 above), p. 10, emphasis added.

9. _Federalist_, _loc. cit._ (note 7 above).

10. Wood, _Creation of the American Republic_, _op. cit._, (note 2 above), pp. 118, 421.

11. _The Great Republic_ (note 4 above), pp. 258-260.

12. _Ibid._, p. 612.

13. _The Great Republic_ (note 4 above), "Government Without Power," pp. 360-368. Compare "The Hamiltonian Program," pp. 341-350.

14. Martin Diamond, "Ethics and Politics: The American Way," _The Moral Foundations of the American Republic_ (note 1 above), pp. 39-72, especially pp. 62-68.

15. Harold Berlak, "Human Consciousness, Social Criticism, and Civic Education," in _Building Rationales for Citizenship Education_, edited by James P. Shaver (Arlington: Va.: National Council for the Social Studies, 1977), p. 35.

16. In 1979 Kohlberg declared the following to be "the best introduction to the cognitive-developmental approach to moral education of Piaget or myself currently available": R. H. Hersh, D. P. Paolitto and J. Reimer, _Promoting Moral Growth_ (New York: Longman, 1979), p. ix. Valuable to me has been Kohlberg, "Moral Stages and Moralization," in _Moral Development and Behavior_, edited by Thomas Lickona (New York: Holt, Rinehart & Winston, 1976), pp. 31-53.

162

17. R. Freeman Butts, <u>The Revival of Civic Learning: A Rationale for Citizenship Education in American Schools</u> (Bloomington, Ind.: Phi Delta Kappa, 1980), pp. 121-163, especially p. 128. See also Butts, "Curriculum for the Educated Citizen," <u>Educational Leadership</u>, 38 (October, 1980), pp. 6-8, as well as several other articles in the same issue.

Religious Pluralism and
Public Education

Seymour W. Itzkoff

Historical Considerations

On the surface, it would appear that the problems of religious pluralism and public education
are discrete and not interconnected in our historical evolution as a nation. True, they are
separate problems with their own subject matter and
traditions. Yet there is an interesting set of historical intersections and even an evolving theoretical dialectic that renders their relationship
relevant for examination in a short paper such as
this.

The problem of religious pluralism enters our
historical consciousness at the earliest stage in
the American experience. The openness of our geography and history, the initial diversity of
Protestant and other Christian as well as Jewish
immigrants to this land, the ostensible search for
religious freedom of the refugees to the Colonies,
paradoxically contained an early hostility to the
ideal of pluralism. In spite of this prima facie
context for religious pluralism, there was early on
a hard fought battle as each group tried to carve
out its own orthodoxy within its own particular
geographical and social turf. Thus began the
travels of Roger Williams to Providence and Thomas
Hooker to Hartford, two among many searching to
find a secure home for their own religious persuasions.

During the early Colonial period, education was
the apparent ward of the state, but usually through
the regnant church of the community and its minis-
terial leader. One cannot speak of a public educational system in a real sense until the beginning
of the nineteenth century. By then the problem of
religious pluralism had long been addressed by
legislatures of enlightenment persuasions, firmly
committed to the view that religious pluralism was

an especially valuable dimension of the new nation's corporate experience.

The relatively heavy-handed symbiosis of church and state in New England, the relatively conservative, if not post-medieval attitude of many sects persuaded the avant garde intellectuals who instigated the revolutionary and constitutional periods, that church and state ought to be separated to evolve in their own respective and individual manner, in consonance with their quite different services to the individual's heart and the public weal. The separation of church and state was explicit in the First Amendment to the Constitution, in 1791, and the commitment to a religious pluralism based on individual choice firmly established by this act of the founding fathers, especially those from the middle Atlantic and southern states.

While the idea of a public education was not yet in the mind's eye of this political and philosophical leadership, the value to the public of an education was certainly so. For, with the gradual concentration of populations in small cities, an increase in the semi-rural eastern population along easy access communications lines, new intellectual winds were readily perceived. After 1750, a real flourishing of independent educational efforts seems to have swept through the colonies. New secondary academies, a proliferation of free lance teachers in the towns, often young ministers, sometimes formerly indentured and without congregations, began to spread a new educational ethos.

The new Enlightenment educational values were definitely non-statist, nor public. The ideal of the diminished state argued for a free, independent, private and indeed pluralistic educational pattern. The new outlook persuaded that unencumbered reason could find the means for intelligence's own honing and perfection. The tutelary guidance of church and state needed to be held in abeyance. And, except for minor demands, a hankering for the older synthetic state-church schooling relationship,

166

education was given back to the individual as his own obligation. Success or failure would now depend on his will, intelligence, and personal predispositions.

As evidence of this privatism in education yielding presumed public "good" we have only to harken to the Constitution which makes no mention of education. In fact one can point to the Tenth Amendment to the Constitution for a real and crucial insight into the situation. For it is in this Tenth Article that the inherent religious pluralism pointed to by the First Article is extended by implication to education: "Article X, The powers not delegated to the United States by the Constitution, nor prohibited by it to the States, are reserved to the States respectively, or to the people."

Nineteenth Century Public Schools: The Problem Begins

In principle, as the nineteenth century began, we were indeed a pluralistic society both in religion and education. In practice, especially as legislation began to establish Common schools, the jockeying for advantageous religious positions moved quickly. And that was the essential problem. In any associated or even remote area of public life, the entrance of governmental involvement inevitably brought with it those eager institutions that sought a preferred piece of the public pie.

One cannot argue, however, that the inception of a public education was by any means a conspiratorial endeavor by government to carve out special privilege. It happened by necessity. Times changed, new needs, movements became evident, and events would have their way.

Mid-nineteenth century forces of modernity had their impact on religious institutions as well as education. The same trends which gave impetus to the Common School seem to have welded a consensus among the various Protestant sects. In the

extremely decentralized setting of the states and
their diverse communities, local religious impact
was clearly evident in the school. Rather than denominational sponsorship, as in the seventeenth and
eighteenth century, a new religious consensus seems
to have enveloped the Common School program and
atmosphere.

What one might call a non-denominational
Protestantism had wafted over the new public education. And for a few decades a vigorous battle took
place over the nature of this quasi-religious influence and by the varying dissenting sects who
were de facto excluded from public tax support for
their own schools. Prominent among these dissenters of the mid-nineteenth century were the
Catholics. The Catholic opposition at first con-
centrated on opposing the use of Protestant hymns,
prayers, and the King James Bible in the public
schools. It had become clear by the 1840's that
local tax support for the various denominational
schools was not to be forthcoming. The Catholic
effort was characterized by a clearly minority appeal for a true multi-religious set of school patterns, a pluralism in religion and education to be
carved out of the evolving Common School pattern.

But this was not to be, as the powerful
Protestant majority literally challenged the poorer
Catholics to establish their own privately-sup-
ported school system. Thus, Bishop Francis
Kenrick's appeal in 1842 to the Board of Comptrol-
lers of the Philadelphia Public Schools to be sensitive to the rights and needs of the Catholic
children in the school system, went largely un-
heeded.

Without great public support, such dissenters
from a new establishment form of religious and
educational cooperation were forced on to their own
resources, establishing schools where possible,
keeping their children home until the advent of the
late nineteenth century compulsory education laws,
or else, especially in the case of Jews, acquiescing
to the majoritarian pattern in order to receive the

educational sustenance of modernity which the schools provided.

There can be no question as to the bitterness of the Catholic minority, who in starting their own parochial system left no stone unturned in their quest for equal tax support. They considered the public schools a truly ancillary state institution purveying the basic values of the Protestant majority. To this very day, the Catholic position has been to argue either for direct support for their own schools, or else financial support to the parents in the form of a voucher which would allow them to compete equally with the public educational establishment.

Secularization and Dominance

The founding fathers were well aware that the preservation of religious pluralism, an important principle to them, depended on the clear disassociation of religion and the state. This was especially underlined by the prescient Jefferson in his "high wall of separation" letter to the Danbury Baptists in 1802.

On the other hand, it was just as clear to the varying and contending sects, ever sensitive to the opportunity to recruit new adherents to their denominational standard, that government could be a powerful ally in their quest for survival if not dominance. The non-denominational compromise of the 1840's engineered by Common School advocates such as Horace Mann, however, acted as a time bomb, eventually resulting in explosive late nineteenth century consequences that the adherents to the compromise could not have predicted.

In the fifty to sixty years remaining of the nineteenth century, a storm of intellectual, social, and scientific change swept over the western world. What had been a benevolent partnership of public school with the great middle of Protestantism turned into a torrent of secularization as the new

169

knowledge demands swept the education hungry masses into the rapidly evolving public school system. The unexpected result was that by early in the twentieth century a solid ensconcing of the new progressive movement in education had taken place with all its largely naturalistic and scientific orientations. In a sense, the old religious establishment had been in a turn, left out in the cold.

This was ironic, for, while the Protestant churches reverted largely to the fulfilling of the private needs of their communicants in family and neighborhood, the Catholics were now building a burgeoning if yet deprived educational system. Church, school, and family here were firmly locked into an alliance which although it excluded Catholic students from the secular knowledge and the wealth and power that flowed from it, at least preserved the Catholic community. In this set of circumstances it did prepare the ground for its later power advances at mid-twentieth century.

The extent to which the liberal secular, pragmatic movement in education led by John Dewey dominated education in those early twentieth century decades is seen in the Supreme Court's 1925 Oregon decision (Pierce v. Society of Sisters). The decision which came down in favor of the Society of Sisters and allowed them to maintain their schools showed how close the United States came to a state-controlled and run educational system dominated by the seemingly regnant scientific materialism of this era. The attempt to close down private education failed in this case. But as tax support for the public schools began its geometric progression toward mid-century, it became clear that the value system both implicit and explicit embedded in public education was enacting both an intellectual as well as an economic squeeze on the diverse religious contenders for influence and their communicants in the private sector.

With the exception of the Everson decision of the Supreme Court in 1947 which allowed for bus transportation to the child in private schools and,

170

implicitly, other aid under the child welfare
statutes, the courts did not give an inch to religious educators. In spite of a wild and desperate
flurry of court cases well into the 1960's the tradition of the high wall of separation held strong.
Eventually, even the powerful Catholic school system lost its hold. The economic strains on both
Church and family were too great.*

    If the religious pluralism of our nation was
secured in the face of contentious attempts to obtain public funds for such denominational support,
churches were seemingly pressed into the intimate
and communitarian role which the founding fathers
had recommended, and with which, with the exception
of the liberal Jewish community, few sects would
long be satisfied. The entire dialectic of religious pluralism and public education can be summed
up in a nutshell: the domination of a secular
naturalistic value system in the public school inevitably aided religious pluralism but diminished
the social role of religion. To the extent to
which religious denominations became involved in
public education or other state infatuations it reduced the dimension of religious pluralism. Here
they could have become dangerously associated in
either a singular or a multiple state religion, inevitably reducing the range and scope of religious
pluralism.

    This situation with its almost enigmatic con-
sequences for the future, leads us directly into a
discussion of the contemporary American situation
and the possible ramifications for both institutions, public education and religion, in our national life.

The Present Situation

    We have noted the intensely litigious character

----

*From 6.5 million students in 1965 to about 3.8
million students in 1979.

of Catholic and public school relations in the
post-World War II period. There can be no doubt
that as the schools were affected now by the enormous American growth in wealth and corporate power,
the absorption of the schools into governmental
and professional power plays, decreasingly responsible to their local communites, they likewise
moved farther away from the moral and social controls usually exercised through church and family.

But even while the hostility between Catholic
and other orthodox and fundamentalist religious
groups and the schools was exacerbated in the
1950's and 60's, the church also partook of the in-
stitutionalizing power and the allure that emanated
from government. It is no accident that Will
Herberg's Protestant, Catholic, and Jew reflected
on the significant depolarization, even deplurali-
zation, among the major faiths, the "big three."

Herberg's argument was simple. Big religion
had become an intimate part of the American social
scheme, accepted, wooed by the political institutions, a necessary moral symbol for American social
life, to tell ourselves that indeed we had not in
our intercourse with Mammon completely lost our
spiritual virginity. In the process the three religions looked more and more alike. By partaking
of the same waters of social power and national
respectability they had lost their sharp edges and,
unfortunately, a great deal of their uniqueness.

Of course, the easily visible consequence of
all of this entering into the mainstream of contemporary history could be seen in the activities
of the 1960's. Men and women of the cloth were now
involved in psychological therapy, Viet Nam demonstrations, social crusades against segregation, ad
infinitum.

Also, as the crush of students sifted out of
the public schools into the colleges, new Con-
gressional bills supporting not only secular colleges and universities but also the nontheological
segment of denominational institutions gave these

172

schools a tremendous shot in the arm. Again, the trade off for governmental aid was that non-Catholic students and professors now appeared in Catholic institutions as well as other nominally denominational institutions of higher learning.

The impact on the religions was clear. In the realms of morality, relationships between the sexes, birth control, divorce, political attitudes, the heretofore conservative Catholics were hardly to the right of the reformed Jews or the Presbyterians. Up to our own time, the only real deviation of the church from the secular center lies in the area of abortion. The so-called right to life movement while supported by the Church and many Catholics has become a rallying point behind which all religious conservatives can join. In a sense, the old pluralism has dissolved to now become a dualism between conservatives of all faiths against liberals of all faiths with regard to a mere handful of moral issues: abortion, homosexuality, perhaps even poor old Darwin and evolutionary theory.

As we enter the 1980's, our situation is truly perplexing. Doubtless, the major religions have come together in terms of sanctioning the similar overt behaviors and attitudes that their respective communicants display from day to day. The modern Catholic is today a person of this world and not the next. The orthodox Jew still masters the skills of trade, business, craftsmanship that the modern world demands. Yet, on the other hand, as the great mass of American graduates of the public as well as the independent educational sector share behaviors and attitudes, there is a growing dissident movement in religion as well as in education.

The so-called Christian Day Schools are symptomatic of this trend. But so is minister Jim Jones of the terrible massacre in Guyana. The very structure of traditional religion now shows cracks not necessarily in its accommodations with the secular world, but in the worrisome streak of irrationality and fundamentalism reflected in the

173

dissidents from the established and coopted "big three."

There is an explanation for this phenomenon which will lead us toward our conclusion. The new schismatics in both religion and education, in the fact of their extremism and indeed hatred of established social and moral life are not the products of a blind fate. In the absorption by government of all facets of our independent pluralistic social and religious life, in the enormous growth of power which is now embedded in the public schools and stifles any independent educational movement, we have created an institutional miasma against which pluralities have become isolated and thus irrelevant. The only alternative for dissenting associations seem to be the extremes, now creating breaks in the basic discourse of intellectual and social communication.

Extreme situations breed extreme solutions. The growth and non-responsiveness of the public schools can only produce those who would now sacrifice all reason, power, and civility in their attempt to avoid the universal snare of our corporate image. To the extent that the orthodox religions have wallowed in respectability and amiability, to the extent that public education has become totally politicized, religious minorities must go elsewhere. This means they must travel far, toward the extreme situation.

Conclusion

The future of religious pluralism in the United States is inextricably intertwined with the evolving nature of public schooling. The vastness of the public educational enterprise contrasts sharply with the paucity of real pluralistic divergence and creativity in the religious domain. By contrast one notes that in the eighteenth century the various religious sects carved out important roles in the active social life of their time. They were at the forefront of activity and not in

174

the jungles of South America, or chanting on street corners.

The lack of a real center for the private domains of life — family, community, schooling, religious fellowship, ethnic identity — argues for the continued desiccation of the religious realm. The piling up of power by government and its quasi-governmental satellite institutions means the continued disappearance of pluralistic alternatives in our culture. This trend will continue not because it is necessary. In our late twentieth century postindustrial society, big government has become an albatross on the free, educated middle classes. One cannot predict what the breaking point will be and when the centralization tide will ebb and retreat.

The mere return of options of choice in those deeply felt personal areas of religious, communal, and educational life could have an exhilarating impact on the creative thrust of our culture. A public education responsive to its diverse publics could be a beneficiary. On the other hand, schools freely sponsored by religious associations could add a rich leaven to our cultural loaf. We might experience progressive religious movements who would not fear the curriculum of modernity, and would not automatically hearken back to the sixteenth century.

A continuation of the present trend is fraught with danger. Lurking behind the religious irrationalists and schismatics is a cloud that can only be described as an ominous political portent. Irrationalism knows no limit. Power breeds counterpower. Such a trend would mark the end of freedom of thought and expression and of course lead to the demise of any forms of religious pluralism or enlightened public education toward which our society could aspire.

BIBLIOGRAPHY

Bailyn, Bernard. Education in the Forming of American Society. New York: Norton, 1972.

Butts, R. Freeman. The American Tradition in Religion and Education. Boston: Beacon Press, 1950.

Edwards, Newton and Richey, Herman. The School in the American Social Order. Boston: Houghton Mifflin, 1963.

Fellman, David (ed.). The Supreme Court and Education. New York: Teachers College Press, 1960.

Herberg, Will. Protestant, Catholic, Jew. New York: Doubleday, 1955.

Itzkoff, Seymour W. A New Public Education. New York: McKay-Longman, 1976.

Kliebard, Herbert (ed.). Religion and Education in America: A Documentary History. New York: Intext-Crowell, 1969.

Sheehan, Lourdes. "Catholic Schools in 1979: A Unique Tradition and Challenging Future." Review Journal of Philosophy and Social Science. Vol. IV, No. 2, pp. 132-141.

Tiedt, Sidney. The Role of the Federal Government in Education. New York: Oxford University Press, 1960.

177

Civil Religion and the
American Public Schools

June Edwards

> ... there actually exists alongside of
> and rather clearly differentiated from
> the churches an elaborate and well-
> institutionalized civil religion in
> America, [which] has its own seriousness
> and integrity and requires the same
> care in understanding that any other
> religion does.
>
> Robert N. Bellah

Denominational religion has always had a close
association with American schools. In the colonies,
education was viewed by most as a function of the
churches rather than the government. For the
Puritans, literacy was necessary in order to read
the Bible and learn the precepts needed for gaining
salvation. With the idea of the common school,
begun in Massachusetts, educational institutions
became state run, but were still largely dominated
by Protestant interests. Henry Barnard, for instance, first U.S. Commissioner of Education, urged
the reading of the (Protestant) Bible in public
schools in order to develop a Christian morality.[1]

The ongoing pressure of Catholics to wrest
money from the state to support their own schools,
the recent court cases on prayer and Bible-reading
brought by non-Christians, and the attempts by
fundamentalists to remove "obscene" and "blas-
phemous" books from classrooms and libraries attest
to the continuous entwinement of organized religion
and public education. Not so obvious, however, is
the involvement of the government with another kind
of religion, one that permeates our society and
cuts across class and sectarian lines. This "civil
religion" undergirds the everyday actions of
American citizens and is the basis for the organi-
zational structure and moral values that mold our
public schools.

179

What is Civil Religion?

The term was first used, as far as we know, by the French philosopher Rousseau in his book, The Social Contract, published in 1762.[2] There he set down what he perceived to be the roles of the state and its citizens in an ideal society. The American founding fathers were influenced by Rousseau's writings and those of other Enlightenment thinkers and incorporated some of their ideas into the political foundations of this country.

In more recent years, scholars have written about the effect of such political beliefs upon the development of a uniquely American cultural "religion." Philosopher John Dewey spoke of the "common faith" that molds and regulates our society. Theologians J. Paul Williams and Sydney Mead wrote respectively of the "societal religion" and "the religion of the Republic." Political columnist Walter Lippmann talked about the "public philosophy." Sociologists Robin Williams and Will Herberg labeled it the "common religion" and "The American Way of Life," while church historians Martin Marty and Catherine Albanese preferred "religion-in-general" and the "real religion" of the American people.

Though these terms do not necessarily mean the same thing, the general thrust has been that there is a "religion," or set of values and normative behaviors, held in common by the majority of Americans that gives a sense of unity and purpose and provides meaning for lives. This civil religion need not conflict, though it sometimes does, with whatever church affiliations people hold. Often, in fact, it is actively supported by denominational institutions, particularly by those of conservative Christian traditions.

"... the separation of church and state has not denied the political realm a religious dimension," said Bellah in his original article on civil religion:

> ... there are ... certain common elements
> of a religious orientation that the great
> majority of Americans share .... This
> public religious dimension is expressed
> in a set of beliefs, symbols, and rituals
> that I am calling the American civil
> religion.[3]

The most basic belief that lies deep in this
tradition is that Americans are God's chosen people
who have a divine mission to carry out God's will
on earth. America is a promised land, led by God
to establish a new social order that will be a
light unto all nations. Like Moses, General
Washington led his people out of tyranny and into
the land flowing with milk and honey. This God,
actively involved in history and with a special
concern for America, is a rather austere being,
noted Bellah further, "much more related to order,
law, and right than to salvation and love."[4]

Besides this messianic belief in their country's mission, Americans share a set of symbols and
rituals that serve as important elements for
molding national solidarity. Among the saints of
the civil religion, for example, are Washington,
Jefferson and Lincoln, who symbolize all that is
honorable and good in political leadership. The
scriptures are the Declaration of Independence, the
Constitution, and the Bill of Rights. Sacred
shrines, such as Bunker Hill, Gettysburg, and Arlington Cemetery are visited by thousands each year
with solemn reverence, while the national holidays
of Thanksgiving and Fourth of July are honored by
joyous celebrations. Through such rituals as
saluting the flag and singing the national anthem,
Americans lose their sectarian differences and become united in a common societal faith. (Some say
that football games and other spectator sports
serve the same function.[5])

Since Bellah's discussion, scholars from many
different disciplines have put forth their own interpretations of "civil religion," and have argued
about its legitimate use. Naturally, they do not

agree. In the winter, 1980, edition of the <u>Journal of Church and State</u>, Ellis M. West analyzed some of these conflicting definitions and proposed what he calls a "neutral definition of civil religion," in which he attempted to incorporate what is meant by "civil" and what is meant by "religion" into a workable, objective definition:

> "civil religion is a set of beliefs and attitudes that explains the meaning and purpose of any given political society in terms of its relationship to a transcendent, spiritual reality, that are held by the people generally of that society, and that are expressed in public rituals, myths, and symbols.[6]

West's article is fruitful in that it points out the difficulty of using a term that is now commonly expressed but interpreted in many different ways. After analyzing thirteen years of discourse on the meaning of civil religion, however, his "neutral" definition sounds very much like Bellah's original version. What I want to discuss here are the worst manifestations of civil religion in our society and schools and propose what ought to be the best. For this purpose, Bellah's earlier concepts, briefly described above, will function quite well.

The point Bellah made, and I concur, is that civil religion is with us and will always be. As another sociologist, Robin Williams, stated:

> Every functioning society has, to an important degree, a common religion. The possession of a common set of ideas, [ideals], rituals and symbols can supply an overarching sense of unity even in a society otherwise riddled with conflict.[7]

The question, thus, is not whether civil religion does or does not exist in our society, but what form we should permit it to take. Educators, who have been given the awesome responsibility of influencing children's values, attitudes, and behaviors, have a crucial role to play in this determination.

Civil Religion at Its Worst

One form that civil religion can take is that of nationalism, in which the state itself becomes a center of worship. This happens when groups or individuals attempt to make the nation, in effect, a god — a supernatural, transcendent force that demands unmitigated loyalty and unquestioning obedience. Nazi Germany, of course, comes to mind. In the 1950's, Senator Joseph McCarthy and his followers had a similar goal in their pursuance of "communist sympathizers." Every country or cultural group cherishes a common set of historic events and traditions that help bind them together as a people. But when these rituals, symbols, traditions and events become of paramount importance and take on a marked degree of emotional intensity, nationalism becomes a religion.

As we saw earlier, an important aspect of civil religion is the celebration of national holidays. Particularly important in nationalism are those days related to American war victories. In an interesting article first published in 1953, anthropologist Lloyd Warner analyzed small town Memorial Day services and interpreted them as ritualistic "cult of the dead" ceremonies. Said Warner, "Memorial Day is a cult of the dead which organizes and integrates the various faiths and national class groups into a sacred unity."[8] In small towns, especially, Protestants, Catholics, and Jews and people of other faiths gather together in harmony to pay tribute to their common dead.

Warner further discussed the effect war has had on communities and demonstrated how it draws people closer together. "It is in time of war that the average American living in small cities and towns gets his deepest satisfactions as a member of his society."[9] The hate of a common enemy serves to unify a community, while the belief that everyone must sacrifice strengthens their sense of

183

importance. (This was, of course, before the tragic divisiveness of Viet Nam.)

In his book, Nationalism: A Religion, Carlton J. H. Hayes stated that the god of nationalism is a jealous god, primarily one of battles. He demands, above all, the loyalty of his subjects. Intolerant of dissenters, this national god considers traitorous behavior the worst sin of all. In return for the ultimate sacrifice — the death of a son in battle — the family is assured of eternal salvation and glory.[10] Thus, families who have given at least one relative to appease the all-powerful, national god — in small towns this would include almost everyone — share in cultic ceremony both the pain and the pride that accompanies such sacrificial slaughter.

Though nationalism in most countries is also tolerant of other religions, in America it is curiously allied with Christian churches, especially those who call themselves fundamentalists. Hanging side by side in many churches are the Christian and American flags as symbols of equal importance and reverence. Displayed on the walls are the lists of members who died in wars — but not those who died for any other reason no matter how valiant. Wearing red, white and blue uniforms, children in private evangelical schools follow their morning prayers and Bible reading with the singing of the Star Spangled Banner.

This fusing of God and country, said Bellah, is frequently used by such groups as the American Legion as a religious excuse for attacking non-conformist or non-conservative ideas or groups and for gaining support for their own special interests and beliefs.[11] A more recent example of this is the Moral Majority, a right-wing religious/political group founded by Jerry Falwell in Lynchburg, Virginia, credited with influencing the 1980 conservative presidential landslide. One of the greatest threats to America today, claimed fundamentalist preacher Tim LeHaye, is secular humanism. The worst part is that humanists have a one-world view:

184

They want to take from the haves
and give to the have-nots. They want
to bring everyone down to a minimal
standard. These are the attitudes of
the leaders of our day, the reason we
are in the moral mess we are in
today .... They make decisions based
not on what is good for America, but
what is good for the world, and anyone who holds this view is not fit to
hold office in the United States.[12]

Thus, anyone who disagrees with the jingoistic beliefs of the Moral Majority leaders is branded as
irreligious, immoral, and unfit to hold political
office in our country.

Besides demanding a god-like worship of the
nation, desiring to suppress dissension of any kind,
and treating tragic wars as though they were
glorious enterprises, civil religion at its worst
is an exultation of male WASP culture. It extols
the heritage of white European immigrants, particularly those of Puritan descent, and ignores the
contributions of all others. The mighty deeds that
are told with reverence are those of white male
conquerors. The idea of America as a New Eden, as
a place of religious, social, political and economic freedom, relates only to those of European
background.

Certainly Indians, Blacks, Orientals and
Chicanos do not share this perception of America.
As Ralph Ellison illustrated in his book The
Invisible Man, the culture of blacks in our country
was rendered invisible.[13] This was also true for
other minorities and women. What was not invisible
in historical accounts and societal attitudes was
derogatory. Although an attempt has been made in
recent years to rectify this problem, much more
must be done to counteract years of neglect and
prejudice. Stated black historian Charles H. Long:

It is no longer possible for us to
add the "invisible ones" as addenda to
European dominated historical method,
for such a procedure fails to take into

185

account the relationship of the omitted
ones to the Europeans .... Nor is it
possible ... to begin the project of
writing history in which the ideological values of blacks and Amerindians
dominate ... for it could not make
sense of that problem of invisibility
which allowed us to raise the issue of
our discussion.[14]

Besides the omission of cultural contributions
was the commission of insidious deeds. Bellah
cited the slaughtering of the Indians, lynching of
blacks, atom-bombing of Japanese, and napalming of
Vietnamese as particularly vicious manifestations
of nationalistic civil religious behavior.[15] When
one believes that God has chosen the white man in
America to rule the world, it follows that the
destruction of others is simply doing the will of
Divine Providence. According to this view, any
means is morally right if the world is thus "made
safe for democracy." Such righteous and bloody
beliefs have often found their strongest supporters
within American public schools.

Schools and the Worst in
Civil Religion

In his book, the Noise of Solemn Assemblies,
sociologist Peter Berger wrote, "... a good case
could be made for seeing public schools as the
principal agency in our society representing our
politically established cultural religion in almost
pure form."[16] What Berger obviously had in mind
was that schools generally reflect civil religion
at its worst rather than civil religion at its
possible best.

In the past, and still in most places today,
public schools have served as the enforcer of the
status quo, as a mirror of the general community.
The values espoused have been those of the dominant
white Anglo-Saxon, largely Protestant, middle-class
who are, as J. Paul Williams put it, united in the

conviction that the continuous bettering of the
standard of living is an all important goal. "The
values most generally shared in American culture,"
he said, "reflect a low rather than a high understanding of our faith in democracy."[17]

What specifically are these values? According
to the sociologists mentioned earlier in this
essay, the values can be lumped generally under
the heading, "The American Way of Life." Three of
the most prominent are:

1. Success is achieved through competition —
a value underscored in every aspect of educational
life, from the electing of school board members and
the hiring of the staff, to tests and report cards,
football contests and cheerleading tryouts.

2. The good life is the active, practical
life. The "doers" of the world, the achievers, are
admired. The philosophers, the dreamers, the poets
are looked upon with distrust if not disapproval.

3. The good person is the socially well-
adjusted — the kind who gets along well in bureau-
cratic, institutional settings where radical
criticism is suppressed and conformity blessed.
Where conflict is dreaded and status quo affirmed.
Where punctuality and neatness are more important
than creativity.

Though these values are not in themselves
either good or bad, they are not shared by all cultures within our society but are taught to all
children who enter public schools. Thus, students
from ethnic groups, social classes, or ideological
persuasions that value cooperative living or individuality, for instance, are penalized overtly or
subtly for their families' values.

Besides enforcing white, middle-class values,
public schools reflect society in other ways. The
situation that the Moral Majority wants, the separation of the haves from the have-nots, has certainly
been prevalent in schools. As recent revisionists

187

clearly documented, many of the practices in public
schools have deliberately been aimed at steering
the upper and middle classes towards college and
professional careers while pushing minorities and
lower class children into low ability groups, vo-
cational programs and menial occupations.[18]
Nothing is intrinsically wrong, of course, with
non-professional careers. The objection is that
students have been slotted for their "place in
society" early in life on the basis of the stereo-
typical judgments of educators and cultural biases
of "scientific" testing.

Another way schools reflect the civil religion
of society at its worst is in the hierarchical organization itself. The administration mimics the
white-male domination found in society at large,
and especially in traditional religious institutions. Few school administrators are female and
few come from any minority groups. In general, the
lower the pay and status, the more likely a school
position will be filled by a woman or ethnic minority. Schools, then, reflect by their very organization the belief that only white males have
the intelligence and decision-making abilities
needed for educational leadership. (The first is
particularly ironic when one considers that a large
proportion of principals and superintendents were
chosen for their supposed ability to handle teenage
boys via coaching rather than for their intellectual achievements.)

The ritualistic, cultic behavior demanded of
its students by public schools is another aspect of
societal religion. Such behavior has frequently
served to camouflage or retract the democratic
values found in the very documents revered by educators and society as a whole, especially the First
Amendment of the Bill of Rights. For instance, the
demand that all students say the Pledge of Allegiance and salute the flag infringed upon the religious freedom of Jehovah's Witnesses.[19] Compulsory
attendance beyond the eighth grade affronted the
beliefs of the Amish.[20] The reading of the New
Testament, the saying of prayers, and the observance

in classrooms and assemblies of Christmas and
Easter offended the faith of Jewish and other non-
Christian students.[21]

Finally, public schools have been examples of
the worst in civil religion by the choice of textbooks, which serve as value inculcators as well as
subject matter instructors. Throughout social
studies texts and elementary readers, particularly,
can be found the dogma that America is God's New
Israel and WASP males are made in God's image.[22]
As Frances Fitzgerald wrote in America Revised, her
study of the history books, past and present, used
in public schools:

> Ideologically speaking, the his-
> tories of the fifties were implacable,
> seamless. Inside their covers, America
> was perfect: the greatest nation in
> the world, and the embodiment of democ-
> racy, freedom, and technological progress.
> For them, the country never changed in
> any important way: its values and its
> political institutions remained constant
> from the time of the American Revolution.[23]

Hayes pointed out that the civil religion of
society demanded that schools be held strictly ac-
countable for any lapse from the official "theology," no matter how misleading or insidious.
Teachers or authors who proposed an explanation for
a historical event or depicted a revered figure in
ways not in keeping with the nationalistic doctrine
could lose their jobs or have their books banned or
burned.[24]

Though such texts have now been altered to
include more data on blacks, Indians and other cultures and show women in something other than an
apron, the need to sell books to the largest possible audience still limits publishers' commitment
to scholarship of integrity. "Truth," added
Fitzgerald ruefully, "is a market commodity determined by what will sell."[25] For the kind of civil
religion thus far described, neither freedom nor
truth are necessary components of what the believers call "democracy."

Hope for the Future

We have talked thus far about the negative aspects of civil religion in American society and schools, the elements that breed prejudice, dishonesty and national chauvinism. But civil religion need not take this form. Like all religions, said Bellah, the civil one has its "demonic distortions." What critics often do is compare the worst of civil religion with the best of other traditions.[26] But civil religion also has its best. The point of this essay is to compare the worst of civil religion with what it could and ought to be, and to show how this could be manifested in public schools.

First of all, American civil religion should not be the worship of the nation, claimed Bellah, "but an understanding of the American experience in the light of ultimate and universal reality."[27] It should be, rather, the conscience of society, the highest standard by which our nation is judged. "At its best civil religion would be realized in a situation where politics operates within a set of moral norms, and both politics and morality are open to transcendent judgment."[28] Said Sydney Mead, civil religion regarded as democratic faith is essentially prophetic; its ideals and aspirations stand in constant judgment over people as a reminder of standards by which a nation is to be judged and found wanting.[29]

What are these "religious" standards by which a nation is to be judged? The founding fathers wrote in the Declaration of Independence, Constitution, and Bill of Rights certain principles to ensure the survival of the new republic and to give unprecedented freedoms to its citizens. Unfortunately, limited by the prejudices of the times, these freedoms mainly applied to white males, particularly those who owned property, and excluded women as well as Indians, blacks and other minorities. Nevertheless the Bill of Rights was worded in such a way that far broader interpretations can be applied today than was, perhaps, originally intended.

In the 1930's a surge of interest into the
real purpose and meaning of democracy and how it
could be incorporated into schools appeared in the
writings of John Dewey and his followers. Here can
still be found some of the most astute and persua-
sive elucidations of the ways in which our democratic faith ought to be practiced in concrete
situations, particularly in public schools. A
succinct description, representative of the thought
pattern of these thinkers, resides in Boyd Bode's
Democracy as a Way of Life, published in 1937.[30]

According to Bode, democracy is not a name for
an authoritarian or compartmental political belief.
Rather, it is a point of view, an attitude, a value
system that cuts across the whole mass of our traditional beliefs and habits. It does not set pre-
determined boundaries for beliefs, but provides a
basis for which beliefs and values are to be judged.
In other words, democracy is hostile to the setting
up of "democracy" as an absolute as it is to any
other kind of tyranny.

In a similar vein, John Childs later suggested
in Education and Morals that democracy is still an
experiment.[31] It is the best social system yet
devised for preserving the most freedoms for the
most people, although there are, of course, many
problems in the actualization of democratic principles. It is quite possible that some time in the
future something better may evolve. However, in
the meantime we should be loyal to democracy and
actively teach our young its precepts and practice
its principles in all aspects of American life —
and especially in our educational institutions.
This cannot be achieved in a separate course
labeled "citizenship" or "government." Democracy
has to be lived to be understood. "Teaching democracy in the abstract," said Bode, "is on a par
with teaching swimming by correspondence."[32]

Though the deliberate teaching of democratic
ways is criticized by some as being another form of

191

indoctrination, proponents deny this claim. In the first place, as both Bode and Childs pointed out, an essential element of democracy is the freedom to investigate other alternatives and to question the democratic one. Democracy should not become a god to be worshiped, nor should it be forced upon anyone. But believers in the democratic creed, especially teachers, should not be humble about teaching or practicing its principles.

Schools can never be value-free or value-neutral. Educators must select carefully how they wish to influence their students. The whole purpose of education is to foster some types of growth and hinder others. As Childs stated:

> In order to encourage, we must also discourage; in order to foster, we must hinder; in order to emphasize the significant, we must identify the non-significant; and, finally, in order to select and focus attention on certain subject-matters of life, we have to reject and ignore other subject-matters. Were our values different, our selections and rejections would also be different.[33]

The question is, then, in what ways should schools attempt to alter the beliefs, behaviors and attitudes of students? What are the moral standards that should act as the conscience of the educational establishment? If civil religion at its best is ever to reign in our society, the models on which all parts of public schooling should be based are the democratic principles on which our country was founded.

The first and foremost value is respect for each individual person. Democracy proclaims the worth and dignity of every human being. Thus, schools should oppose all forms of discrimination — whether based on religion, sex, race, color, class, national origin, or sexual preference. Teachers, administrators, and staff personnel must consciously seek to unlearn their own prejudicial attitudes and behaviors and teach democratic ones

to students. School rules, regulations and practices must be continuously and stringently examined
to see that they meet this demand. All books
selected for classroom use should either be free of
discrimination, or the teachers should take classroom time to discuss with students where prejudices
exist and why they are detrimental to a democratic
society.

Furthermore, any administrative policy that is
designed, consciously or unconsciously, to keep individuals or groups "in their place," is anti-
thetical to democracy. As mentioned before,
testing programs that have the effect of limiting
minorities and lower class students to subordinate
positions and the bias against females and non-
whites in places of leadership should be scrutinized and challenged.

A second principle is dedication to historical
truth. A democratic teacher will not tolerate
racial, ethnic, or sexual slurs in the classroom or
school at large, nor will she or he choose textbooks that contain them, because such speech and
writings are based on falsehoods. Social studies
books that dwell on the exploits of white male conquerors teach students that "might makes right" and
denies validity to the experiences of all other
peoples. A dedication to truth prohibits one from
teaching that Indians are savage, Chicanos are lazy,
blacks are intellectually or morally inferior, and
women are helpless — connotations which have been
frequently found in American school books, at least
until recent years.[34] In testimony given before
the Senate Committee on Indian Education, a spokes-
person said emotionally:

There is not one Indian in this
country who does not cringe in anguish
and frustration because of these textbooks. There is not one Indian child
who has not come home in shame and tears
after one of these sessions in which he
is taught that his people were dirty,
animal-like, something less than human
beings. We Indians are not just one

193

more complaining minority. We are the
proud and only true Native of this
land.[35]

Stereotypes of any kind have no place in the classroom, except perhaps as negative role models for
what ought to be learned and practiced.

Nor should textbooks that attempt to be
"neutral" or "objective" with regard to history be
chosen. In a lengthy article examining freedom and
racial equality in high school history textbooks,
University of Chicago Professor Mark Krug proclaimed:

> There is no such thing as a
> factual, objective history .... If, as
> it usually does, the textbook evades
> the basic evil of slavery and bondage
> of men and its violation of the spirit
> and fundamentals of a free democratic
> society ... it shows a clear bias
> against the equality of all men and
> deserves the condemnation it has re-
> ceived from black scholars.[36]

By their absence of opinion, textbook writers con-
done the practices that make a mockery of democracy.
A dedication to the democratic faith demands the
courage to speak out on values and interpret historical events in light of the "scriptures" on
which our society is based.

Another principle extremely important to
democratic educational institutions is freedom of
inquiry and a critical examination of any belief.
Students and teachers must have the right to study,
discuss, analyze, and criticize any doctrine, belief or body of knowledge that captures their interest. This is crucial to the preservation of
freedom of thought and speech. Schools must not
deliberately withhold any information or forbid
access to any. Protestors like the Mel Gablers of
Texas who wish to keep students from reading any
material that conflicts with their belief system
must be forcefully resisted. Though democratic
teachers do not select textbooks that contain
sexist or racist interpretations, such books might

be read in the classroom as source material for an in-depth study of sexism or racism. Students would not be forbidden to read the books, but such materials would not be chosen as models for good scholarship.

Only by reading widely and questioning can students make responsible decisions about the worth of ideas, including the idea of democracy. As the court said in a 1978 censorship case in Massachusetts, "The most effective antidote to the poison of mindless orthodoxy is ready access to a broad swing of ideas and philosophies. There is no danger in such exposure. The danger is in mind control."[37]

The above, of course, does not exhaust the values contained in democratic theory, but merely touches upon some of the most basic. Though the values themselves are critical, what is equally so is the willingness of citizens to proclaim their virtues and work for their actualization. Far more is needed than ritual and rhetoric. An important vehicle for promoting civil religion in its best form, as it was in its worst, is the American public school. In this sense, the state is intimately involved in a special kind of religion and always will be. The concern should not be over the state's entanglement, but over the religion's doctrine and methodology.

Conclusions

We have in our American society a potently active civil religion that exists alongside traditional Christianity and other religions. It has, as Bellah stated, its own belief system, scriptures, rituals and creed that, most of the time, do not conflict with denominational institutions. The kind of civil religion that has permeated our society in much of the past, however, has had its "demonic distortions" that conflict with the principles of democracy. In its purest form, American religion should be the moral standard by which our

195

country judges its actions and rectifies its mistakes. If public schools are to be true to the faith on which they were supposedly founded, they must forthrightly fight all attempts to suppress discussion and dissension, limit freedoms, promote discriminations, or bar access to knowledge.

Democracy, however, should not itself become an object of worship. It is as wrong to make an absolute of this system of thought and mode of behavior as any other. What is needed is the development of attitudes and thinking processes whereby persons use democratic principles and judge situations for themselves. Uniformity of thought is not the aim. American citizens should dedicate themselves with a religious intensity to promoting the good life of liberty, justice, and the right to pursue happiness, but should not force its acceptance on all or prohibit the exploration of other ways of living. As Childs said, it is possible that something better may yet evolve. Until that time, however, we should prize individual freedom and welcome cultural diversity, but also be loyal to the underlying principles that allow these virtues to flourish.

Educators, most importantly, should seek to instill in students, by daily actions as well as teachings, a dedication to the democratic way of life in its truest sense. They should state these values openly and make judgments about their own conduct as well as that of others, particularly those in charge of governmental institutions. For schools, said Mark Krug, "there is no place for neutrality, obfuscation or equivocation on the basic values in the American tradition or the American dream. On these values, including the worth of the individual, the rule of the majority, freedom of speech, and the equal rights and opportunities of all citizens, we have the right to demand an a priori and an outspoken commitment from teachers and textbook writers."[38]

American civil religion is a basic part of our culture and will continue to be. But as citizens

we have the right and the responsibility to mold
this religion in constructive ways. In our public
schools, civil religion has often exhibited itself
in ways not in keeping with the democratic principles our society values. Though we cannot undo
the past, we can restructure the present and the
future. The Pledge of Allegiance we take should
be more than to the flag and the republic. It
should be to the democratic creed that undergirds
our nation. Schools cannot singlehandedly solve
society's problems, but they can help breed in the
young an eagerness to investigate, a dedication to
truth, and a commitment to liberty and justice for
all. Such a civil religion should be the heart of
American public schools.

NOTES

1. R. Freeman Butts, Public Education in the United States (New York: Holt, Rinehart and Winston, 1978), p. 85.

2. Jean Jacques Rousseau, The Social Contract (New York: E. P. Dutton, 1952).

3. Robert N. Bellah, "Civil Religion in America," American Civil Religion, ed. Russell E. Richey and Donald G. Jones (New York: Harper & Row, 1974), p. 24.

4. Bellah, p. 28.

5. See Michael Novak, The Joy of Sports (New York: Basic Books, 1976).

6. Ellis M. West, "A Proposed Neutral Definition of Civil Religion," The Journal of Church and State, Winter, 1980, p. 40.

7. Robin Williams, American Society: A Sociological Interpretation (New York: Alfred A. Knopf, 1952), p. 312.

8. W. Lloyd Warner, "An American Sacred Ceremony," Richey & Jones, p. 91.

9. Warner, p. 105.

10. Carlton J. H. Hayes, Nationalism: A Religion (New York: The MacMillan Co., 1960), p. 164.

11. Bellah, p. 36.

12. Quoted in Richard Kenyon, "Moral Majority Sure of Right," The Milwaukee Journal, Sept. 20, 1980, p. 5.

13. Ralph Ellison, The Invisible Man (New York: Random House, 1952).

14. Charles H. Long, "Civil Rights-Civil Religion: Visible People and Invisible Religion," Richey & Jones, p. 213.

15. Bellah, "American Civil Religion in the 1970's," Richey & Jones, p. 269.

16. Peter L. Berger, The Noise of Solemn Assemblies (Garden City, N.J.: Doubleday, 1961).

17. J. Paul Williams, What Americans Believe and How They Worship, 3rd ed. (New York: Harper & Row, 1969), p. 367.

18. See Joel Spring, The Sorting Machine (New York: D. McKay & Co., 1976).

19. <u>West Virginia</u> v. <u>Barnett</u> 319 U.S. 624 (1943).

20. <u>Wisconsin</u> v. <u>Yoder</u> 406 U.S. 213 (1972).

21. <u>Abington School District</u> v. <u>Schempp</u> 374 U.S. 203 (1963).

22. See <u>Dick and Jane as Victims: Sex Stereotyping in Children's Readers</u> (Princeton, N.J.: Women on Words and Images, 1972); Richard C. Turner and John A. Dewar, "Black History in Selected American History Textbooks," <u>Educational Leadership</u>, Feb., 1973, pp. 441-444.

23. Frances Fitzgerald, <u>America Revisited: History School-books in the Twentieth Century</u> (Boston: Little, Brown & Co., 1979), p. 10.

24. Hayes, p. 271.

25. Fitzgerald, p. 31.

26. Bellah, "Civil Religion in America," p. 33.

27. <u>Ibid.</u>, p. 40.

28. Bellah, "Civil Religion in the 70's," p. 271.

29. Sydney Mead, "The 'Nation with the Soul of a Church'," Richey & Jones, p. 60.

30. Boyd Bode, <u>Democracy as a Way of Life</u> (New York: Mac-Millan Co., 1937).

31. John Childs, <u>Education and Morals</u> (New York: John Wiley & Sons, 1950), p. 195.

32. Bode, p. 75.

33. Childs, pp. 19-20.

34. See Jeanette Henry, <u>Textbooks and the American Indian</u> (Indian Historian Press, 1970).

35. Quoted in Henry, p. 9.

36. Mark M. Krug, "Freedom and Racial Equality: A Study of 'Revised' High School History Texts," <u>School Review</u>, May, 1970, p. 300.

37. <u>Right to Read</u> v. <u>Chelsea</u> 454 Supp. 703 (1978).

38. Krug, p. 350.

The Impact of Schooling on Children's Acquisition of Values

Marilyn M. Maxson

The passage of Senator Jesse Helms' bill to return voluntary prayer to the public school in the United States Senate in 1979 reflects a growing concern by some segments of the population with the place of moral/ethical issues in public education. While the bill is currently languishing in a House subcommittee the concern has yet to ease. Public interest groups such as Jerry Falwell's "Moral Majority" which support the return of prayer to the school have become pressingly vocal in recent years. In one sense these groups are pushing for more control of the public school and its curriculum. At a more basic level, however, they are saying in effect that, "we believe public schools influence children's beliefs and values. Since they are publicly financed and open to all regardless of creed we want to mandate what ideas, and even textbooks, our children come in contact with."

As educators we have spent little time examining the question of whether or not public schools in fact do have any impact on children's acquisition of values. The question may be moot as far as the public is concerned since schools are perceived as having an effect. The fact, however, that we as educators implicitly and explicitly have agreed with that assumption without being able to say precisely what that effect is has left us open to repeated attacks on what and how we teach. Wouldn't it seem prudent before attempting to introduce into the curriculum such values as respect for the rights and beliefs of others to examine whether or not schooling can have an impact on that value?

Since their inception one of the primary purposes of American public schooling has been the transmission of values. From Horace Mann and Henry Barnard through William T. Harris and John Dewey up to the present day public schools have

201

been asked to accomplish such diverse tasks as promoting good citizenship behaviors, passing on the
cultural heritage, instilling ideals of ethical behavior, and developing national common values. As
long as these ideals have matched local beliefs
about what is good, and right, and proper there has
been little public interest or concern over what
schools have taught. But as control of public
schools and their curriculum has moved away from
local homogeneous communities, and schools have become more responsive to city, state and national
interests, more and more public outcries of indig-
nation and alarm have arisen.

Not too long ago an English teacher critiqued
the traditional role of women utilizing such books
as The Stepford Wives and Growing Up Female In
America. She so angered a small Indiana community
that not only was she without a job at the end of
the year, but the community held a public burning
of objectionable textbooks.[1] Nor is that an isolated case. Other communities have banned student
dictionaries for defining obscene words flatly
stating that some words students don't need to
know.[2] While the courts have stepped in to settle
a few of the disputes, as in cases of what constitutes obscenity, they have done little more than
set wide, if somewhat confusing parameters of what
is legally acceptable.[3]

The public's continued objections to what is
taught, how it is taught and what is used in
schools leaves educators attempting to sort through
a tangled web of divergent, frequently conflicting
beliefs about what children need and ought to know.
While the public and educators alike may be in
general agreement on the abstract goals of education, such as developing codes of ethical behavior
and sound practices of good citizenship, no one
seems to be able to agree on how specifically these
goals will be reached. Witness the growing concern
over the teaching of morals in the public school.
Even though widespread agreement exists that they
need and should be taught, as evidenced by recent
Gallup Poll responses,[4] how they should be taught

has come under fire repeatedly. One has only to
pick up the paper to find that yet another community has banned and burned the Values Clarification handbook.

A Theory on Value Change

The continued censorship of textbooks and
teachers over the years indicates that the public
feels schools have a great deal of influence on
children's values. Even the Supreme Court appears
to be in agreement if one examines the verdicts in
such cases as Wisconsin v. Yoder where Amish
parents successfully argued that their children
left the Amish way of life after contact with the
public high school.[5] While most educators admit
that schools do serve as one socializing agent in
children's acquisition of values,[6] in fact, few
studies have been done below the college level to
determine what, if any, impact schools have on
values.

One theory by Florence Kluckhohn and Fred
Strodtbeck argues that values change only over an
extended period of time.[7] Unless a person's value
system is unstable little if any change will occur
in any given period. As they put it:
> there is a limited number of common
> human problems for which all peoples at
> all times must find solutions ... while
> there is variability in solutions of
> all the problems, it is neither limit-
> less nor random but is definitely vari-
> able within a range of possible solu-
> tions ... all alternatives of all
> solutions are present in all societies
> at all times but are differentially
> preferred. Every society has, in ad-
> dition to its dominant profile of
> value orientation, numerous variant or
> substitute profiles. Moreover ... in
> both the dominant and the variant pro-
> files there is almost always a rank
> ordering of the preferences of the

203

value-orientation alternatives. In
societies which are undergoing change
the ordering of preferences will not
be clear-cut for some or even all the
value orientations.[8]

According to the Kluckhohn and Strodtbeck
theory the potential for a change in values occurs
in the ordering of the variant profiles. Since the
variant profiles are closely aligned with the
dominant one, a person might alter his value
preferences, but he would not change his values except over a considerable period of time. One implication of this theory is that schools may have
some impact on a child's value preference but they
cannot change the values themselves. For example,
where the school consciously attempted over a
period of time to sway a child's attitudes and beliefs toward respecting all people despite their
race and creed it might make an impact on those
children who already possessed that as one of their
dominant or variant values. The schools would be
expected to be only minimally successful, however,
with those children whose culture and family life
do not contain that value.

On the other hand, Kluckhohn has found that
basic value changes can occur in people who do not
have a well integrated belief system. Given "a
fairly sustained impact of one or more external
forces upon the system" persons will begin to examine their values and possibly change them.[9] This
could mean that if children come to school without
well integrated belief systems then schools over a
period of ten or twelve years may have a great deal
of influence on their values.

The Development of Children's
Values

Determining when the stabilization of children's values occurs is difficult. Psychological
studies indicate that children's behavior patterns
may be established as early as age four or five.[10]

While behavior alone cannot be used as the sole means of determining one's values, frequently it is used by researchers as an indicator of what a person actually believes.[11] In the case of children, however, their actions may not be tied to a value per se.

Milton Rokeach defines a value as "an enduring belief that a specific mode of conduct or end-state of existence is personally or socially preferable to an opposite or converse mode of conduct or end-state of existence."[12] The definition implies the ability to think abstractly and make reasoned choices among possible alternatives. Research by Piaget indicates that children are unable to think abstractly until about the age of twelve. Before that age actions are based on previous experience and their concrete reality — which may be quite different from that of an adult's.

When I was about seven or eight years of age my parents took my brother and me along with my grandmother on a trip across the western United States. Since my father was unwilling to make frequent stops my mother carried water and Kool-Aid along for us to drink. To minimize the spills, whatever we didn't drink went out the window. Generally being seated in the back, after a week or so I was getting tired of looking through a wet window. One day I stopped my mother just as she was about to dispose of the contents of a glass and rolled down the back window. Unfortunately, my brother and grandmother were sitting next to it. After the initial horror my mother asked why I had done it. Being just as surprised as she was by the results I answered truthfully, "But I didn't want to get the window wet!"

Whether because of developmental constrictions as Piaget has contended or lack of experience as others have noted,[13] the incident illustrates perfectly how children are unable to reason their actions through to all the possible ramifications. In most cases they will try something out, and often are just as surprised as I was to find where their actions have led them.

While Piaget's research provides insights into the child's cognitive development, Lawrence Kohlberg has researched the stages people go through in their moral development. Utilizing Piaget's developmental sequence Kohlberg has described six separate stages (later reduced to five) people appear to utilize in making moral decisions. According to Kohlberg, although a person may stop anywhere along the line, he or she must go through each stage in the proscribed order before proceeding on to the next stage. To some extent these stages are bound by age. Until persons have reached the level of abstract reasoning they are unable to grasp the idea that we obey the law not because we will be punished if we don't (Stage 1), or significant others will dislike us (Stage 3), but because society has made rules so that all may live together in accord (Stage 4).[14]

Although Kohlberg's work has been criticized for a number of shortcomings,[15] it is helpful in understanding why a young child finds it difficult to explain another child's behavior. A common scenario in schools is the teacher asking, "Johnny, why do you think Mary took Mike's truck and put it in her desk?" Johnny often answers, "I don't know." And, after a moment's thought he might respond, "Maybe she wanted it." The teacher generally persists with something like, "What do you think about stealing?" Immediately, Johnny answers, "Stealing is wrong and Mary should be punished."

Johnny's answer is typical of a Stage 1 response. He is probably five or six years old and has yet to see that Mary might have taken Mike's truck because Mike did something mean to her (Stage 2). Given enough time Johnny should progress, through interactions with others, to the next stage, and by the time he is an adult be able to understand the full implications of his and other's actions and attach some higher-order meaning to them.

If Piaget and Kohlberg are correct, children's reasoning ability, both cognitively and morally, is restricted by maturation, if not experience, and subject to continual change. While their works are useful as descriptive measures of children's developmental changes they tell us little about where children derive their values, how values can be changed, or what influences if any school has on the development of values.

Research on Value Change

In his book The Nature of Human Values Rokeach posits that children initially learn values "in isolation from other values in an absolute, all-or-none manner."[16] That is, we teach children a value like honesty outside the context of other values which interact with it. But, as adults, when we use our values in any given situation we do so with regard to the relative importance of our other values.

Most of us have had the experience of meeting friends on the street and being asked how we like their new hairstyle. When it's attractive we answer truthfully. But, if we happen to be with a five year old and we tell them it's attractive when the opposite is true, we spend a great deal of time explaining to the child why we weren't entirely honest. We have learned as adults to automatically weigh such values as friendship, honesty, and consideration of others in making our decision on how to respond. But the child has not had the experience or maturation necessary "to integrate the isolated, absolute values" he or she has learned "into a hierarchically organized system, wherein each value is ordered in priority or importance relative to other values."[17]

While Rokeach's work does not deal with the development of values in children he has done some interesting work with changing adult values. Believing that the ultimate purpose of one's values "is to maintain and enhance" the self concept,

Rokeach postulates that a value will undergo a change only if it is endangering the concept of self.[18] By supplying a person with information about contradictions in his or her belief system the person will attempt to change values to more accurately reflect his or her own conception of the self, thus bringing about related behavioral and attitudinal changes.

In a study of 366 Michigan State University students Rokeach attempted to change student values of freedom and equality. Dividing students between experimental and control groups, he provided the experimental groups with information about contradictions they had between the selected values and their conceptions of themselves. Rokeach found that not only was it possible to change student values in a single experimental session, but that these changes were still evident 15-17 months later. He concluded that "genuine and lasting changes in values, attitudes and behavior" were possible through self-confrontation techniques,[19] and that perhaps "merely telling a person about his own values and giving him a free hand to compare them with those of significant others ... [might] be a sufficient condition for initiating value change."[20]

Rokeach acknowledges that changes in a person's values could be brought about by merely reading a book or attending a lecture. But, he qualifies his remark by noting that change will occur only if a person is aware of the contradictions in his/her belief system. Since much of what goes on in a person's life conceals these existing contradictions few people are aware of the inconsistencies in their values, or the need for change.

Although Rokeach's work does not deal directly with the impact of schooling on students' values, it does imply that teachers have within their means the power to change a student's values. In order to bring about these changes, however, two conditions must be met. First, contradictions must exist in the student's belief system. Second, the teacher must provide the means to disclose these contradictions to the student through self awareness.

The Impact of Schooling on Values

A recent study by Herbert Hyman and Charles Wright concluded that "education produces large and lasting good effects" on values.[21] By analyzing data from national surveys done over a twenty-five year period Hyman and Wright found that respondents, in general, differed significantly by age and educational level on questions dealing with, among other things, civil liberties and equality of opportunity. Not only did the study show clear differences between the college-educated and those with a high school or elementary school education, but generally it displayed differences between those with a high school education and those with an education to grade eight.

Two other points from the study are worth noting. First, although education appears to make a difference, its effects are somewhat dispelled by low social class position. In other words, a well-educated blue collar worker tends to reflect values more closely aligned with the people with whom he works and lives. On the other hand, those with less education but a high social position apparently do not change their values to match their better educated peers. Results from other studies by Rokeach seemingly confirm these findings.[22]

Second, aging apparently has some effect on values. Hyman and Wright noted that values tended to decline, particularly among the better educated, with the onset of old age (61-72 years). Since differences persisted among the educational levels, they concluded that values derived from education endure even into old age.[23] Although Rokeach has recorded similar findings he has interpreted them to mean that values continuously change as one advances from adolescence to old age.[24] This in fact may be the case if one examines Hyman and Wright's data on hierarchy of values.[25]   While differences exist among educational levels, broad fluctuations are evident across age ranges within the same educational levels.

The major research by Hyman and Wright with some support by Rokeach indicates that schools do have some impact on children's values.   However, as Rokeach has indirectly noted, and Alan Peshkin has more forcefully pointed out, the teacher's and school's best interests generally lie with those of the local supporting community.[26]   To attempt to shape values that might be considered as falling under the domain of other socializing institutions like the church and family is to invite severe criticism.   For that reason alone many teachers and school districts have preferred to give overt teaching of values a wide berth.

Schooling and Values: The Unanswered Questions

How effective schools are in shaping students' values is still a debatable point.   Many questions remain unanswered.   We do not know for instance how children develop their values.   Indicators are that the early years, prior to the formal schooling experience, are the most formative with parents and significant others being the most influential.   But, if parents and schools disagree on basic values, then do ten or twelve years of formal schooling carry the necessary weight to change children's values along the lines that schools might prefer?

Neither do we know what about the schooling experience influences, or possibly changes, a child's values.   Is it the curricular materials used in schools?   Is it the teacher?   Or, is it the interactions with classmates?   Could it be a combination of all three?   Possibly the effects of formal schooling can only be seen in relation to other experiences outside the realm of the school which impinge on the child's life.

The data by Hyman and Wright do little to support or refute the theory of Kluckhohn and Strodtbeck. Basically, we do not know what values children bring to school with them, nor what values they have when they leave. If we grant that schools do have some influence on children's values, then which values? Surely, not all of them, because as educators we cannot even pinpoint all it is that children learn at school. We do know that much of what children learn at school is incidental to the formal educational experience. Do they also learn values in an incidental way?

Michael Apple has argued that as educators we have spent a great deal of time researching the wrong questions.[27] There is a lot of research (with a lot of non-significant results) on such things as specific teaching methods. But, we have very little research on any of the questions underlying our basic assumptions about education and schooling. Since we have not asked the right questions we do not have some very critical answers. If we ever hope to effectively combat such things as censorship of textbooks we need more definitive answers to questions about our influence on children. And, if as educators we really believe that we make an impact on students' lives then shouldn't we know in what ways we might expect that we are doing so?

NOTES

1. A. Arons, Book burning in the heartland, _Saturday Review_, Oct. 21, 1979, 24-29.

2. D. C. Massie, Censorship in the schools: something old and something new, _Today's Education_, 69(4), 1980, 30-34.

3. In the most recent cases on obscenity the courts appear to be side-stepping the issues of academic freedom and obscenity, and saying that local school boards have the right to serve as the evaluators of community standards in selecting textbooks. See, _Pico_ v. _Island Tree_, 474 F. Supp. 387 (1979), and _Bicknell_ v. _Vergennes_, 475 F. Supp. 615 (1979).

4. See the following issues of _Phi Delta Kappan_ for complete poll results: Sept. 1974, Dec. 1975, Oct. 1976, Sept. 1977, Sept. 1978, Sept. 1979.

5. _Wisconsin_ v. _Yoder_ 406 U.S. 205 (1972).

6. Most college textbooks refer to the public school as a socializing agent of society. This is particularly true of social studies methods texts. See, for example, J. Jarolimek, _Social Studies in Elementary Education_, 5th ed. (New York: Macmillan, 1971), p. 4.

7. F. R. Kluckhohn & F. L. Strodtbeck, _Variations in Value Orientations_ (Westport, Conn.: Greenwood, 1961).

8. Kluckhohn & Strodtbeck, p. 10. (emphasis deleted)

9. Kluckhohn & Strodtbeck, p. 366.

10. See, A. L. Butler (ed.), _Current Research in Early Childhood Education_ (Washington, D.C.: American Association of Elementary-Kindergarten-Nursery Educators, 1970), and F. Redl & D. Wineman, _Children Who Hate_ (New York: Free Press, 1951).

11. See, M. Rokeach, _The Nature of Human Values_ (New York: Free Press, 1973), particularly, Part 4, Long- and short-term change in values, attitudes and behavior, pp. 215-319.

12. Rokeach, p. 5.

13. D. C. Phillips & M. E. Kelly, Hierarchical theories of development in education and psychology, in _Stage Theories of Cognitive and Moral Development: Criticism_

213

and Applications, Reprint No. 13, Harvard Educational Review (Cambridge, Mass.).

14. T. Lickona, How to encourage moral development, Learning, 5(7), March 1977.

15. See, for example, R. S. Peters, Why doesn't Lawrence Kohlberg do his homework?, in Moral Education ... It Comes with the Territory, D. Purpel & K. Ryan (eds.) (Berkeley, Ca.: McCutchan, 1976), 288-290.

16. Rokeach, P. 6. (See note 11).

17. Rokeach, p. 6.

18. Rokeach, p. 216.

19. Rokeach, p. 319.

20. Rokeach, p. 332.

21. H. Hyman & C. Wright, Education's Lasting Influence on Values (Chicago: Univ. of Chicago, 1979), p. 60.

22. Rokeach, p. 73.

23. Hyman & Wright, p. 37.

24. Rokeach, p. 73.

25. See, Hyman & Wright, Table C.1, pp. 85-86.

26. A. Peshkin, Growing Up American: Schooling and the Survival of Community (Chicago: Univ. of Chicago, 1978).

27. M. W. Apple, Ideology and Curriculum (London: Routledge & Kegan Paul, 1979).

Moral Education:
A Comparative Perspective

Samuel M. Craver

As John Wilson once observed, "Moral education is a name for nothing clear. Yet morality and education are two things ... about which most people hold strong views of their own."[1] While this dichotomy makes moral education difficult to write about, the importance of the topic makes it imperative that educators come to grips with some of its essential elements and characteristics. Due largely to the general cultural confusion brought about by unprecedented changes in modern life, morality is a crucial issue today. Major institutions are undergoing bewildering change. Traditional values seem to be losing their once familiar places. Numerous theories and approaches to moral education have been put forward to deal with the issue of morality, but as one recent volume on the topic indicates, "... no one educational model, of those available at present, is sufficient."[2]

For present purposes, three views on moral education will be examined — those of John Dewey, Lawrence Kohlberg, and John Wilson. These three are chosen because they illustrate some of the major focal points in moral education theory: each seeks to sort out the moral confusions in society, each attempts to devise a methodological approach, and each is illustrative of some of the major problems confronting the serious-minded moral educator. The intent is to highlight some essential elements in moral education and to assess the major recommendations of these three theorists.

John Dewey

John Dewey's philosophy looms large in the history of American education, and although his influence has waned over the years, there is much in his philosophy that is pertinent to the contemporary concern with moral education. Indeed, many

215

contemporary theorists, including Lawrence Kohlberg, claim connections with Dewey's view.[3]

The problem of cultural confusion which exists today is not a new phenomenon. The splintering effects of rapid change in American society were a concern for Dewey and others early in the twentieth century. Education, Dewey held, is central to any intelligent effort to regain a sense of direction, and morality must be central to this educational effort. As he put it, "A narrow and moralistic view of morals is responsible for the failure to recognize that all the aims and values which are desirable in education are themselves moral."[4]

For Dewey, the overriding aim of education is growth, by which he meant the increased capacity to learn and to participate in life's activities. His technical definition of education contains his concept of growth: "... that reconstruction or re-organization of experience which adds to the meaning of experience, and which increases ability to direct the course of subsequent experience."[5]

The concept of experience is fundamental to Dewey's view of education. He thought that the key to understanding ourselves and the world about us is experience. Thus, experience is a loaded word in Dewey's philosophy. Experience in its primary manifestations is passive; it is something that happens to us and is simply undergone, suffered or enjoyed. In the secondary sense of meaning or significance in conscious life, experience is a re-sult of reflection or thought; consequently, it becomes active and characterized by intent, fore-sight of consequences, and activity. Experience, then, is a "double-barrelled" word, that is, it includes the actual undergoing (primary experience) and reflective thought on the meaning of what was undergone or will be undergone in future situations (secondary experience). In the educational context, this involves <u>thinking</u>, or making a backward and forward connection between what we do to things and what we enjoy or suffer as a consequence. Dewey did not think that experience is primarily a cognitive affair, but he did insist that "... the measure of value of an experience lies in the perception of relationships or continuities to which it leads up."[6] Thinking, or the perception of relationships, is the intentional effort to discover specific connections between our actions and their consequences so that there is continuity between thought and conduct.

For Dewey, thinking is the method of educative experience.[7] The idea of education as growth and the reconstruction of experience necessarily involves thinking, for it is through thinking that one expands capacity to deal with subsequent experience, or in other words, to grow in the educational sense of the word.

Now it is possible to grow in many directions, and not all growth is beneficial or desirable, for one can grow in undesirable capacities as well as more desirable ones. Thus, growth needs a direction; hence, the moral concern becomes paramount. This does not mean that the young should be given a separate kind of moral education where moral conventions and truths are laid down in some didactic fashion; rather, the moral concern should pervade all education. In Dewey's view, experience occurs in a world of language, institutions, customs, ideals, suffering, and any number of other influences. It is largely a social world, the world of human experience, striving and conflict, and it is full of moral significance and moral confusion. It is the world in which education, as the reconstruction of experience and as growth, must necessarily and inevitably occur.

Moral education is too often conceived as didactic instruction in virtues or character traits usually remote from the immediate understanding of the young. For Dewey, this kind of approach is too "goody-goody," for if school is to prepare for life in society, it must bring in or provide examples of life in the wider society for the needed learning. Since it is not possible to bring in everything, nor would it be desirable to do so, selection must

217

be exercised. The guiding principle of this selection, in Dewey's opinion, is human or social well-being and social progress.[8] Thus, Dewey's objective, in terms of growth in moral education, is a social objective. In its simplest terms, this means growth in democratic living rather than mere "getting along." Democracy was a crucial concern for Dewey, and he saw it as larger than just a political device: "A democracy is more than a form of government; it is primarily a mode of associated living, of conjoint communicated experience."[9] In this respect, the curriculum is considered as a means of enabling the young to reconstruct and understand the human or social context of action. In Dewey's view, "There is no fact which throws light upon the constitution of society, there is no power whose training adds to social resourcefulness that is not moral."[10]

But there must be an individual-social balance. What is needed is modulation, a movement from a social center to a more distinctly intellectual center as a means by which human ties and bonds may be ordered and understood. The materials and studies that are brought into the school must be adapted to the needs and capacities of individuals so that ideas become moving ideas or motive forces active in the life of the young. If growth is the end, then the acquiring of knowledge and the development of understanding must be marshalled toward this end. The subject matter of the curriculum, however judiciously selected, is empty of moral significance for the individual until it becomes moving and active in his life.[11]

In fact, Dewey held that the problem of moral education in the school is one of maintaining the vital connection between knowledge and action. This is seen in his definition of education as the reconstruction of experience (learning from and adding to the meaning of experience; in short, gaining knowledge) and increasing ability to direct the course of subsequent experience (using this knowledge in action or conduct). This is what he meant by growth.

Thus, Dewey did not see moral education as a separate endeavor; rather, the moral concern must suffuse all education. It is growth in capacity to live and participate in a democratic social context so that what one receives balances with what one gives. What one receives and gives is not external possessions, but a widening and deepening of conscious life and meaning. As Dewey put it, "Interest in learning from all the contacts of life is the essential moral interest."[12]

During his lifetime, Dewey wrote some forty books and 700 articles. His work has generated a considerable body of critical literature. Several recent criticisms relate primarily to Dewey's tendency toward vague, general descriptions of key concepts, such as growth, democracy, and the social,[13] (all of which lie central to his concept of moral education). Another criticism of his work is that while he showed insight into such problems as the relation of knowledge and action, he never really tells how specifically to bridge the gap between the two.[14] Perhaps the chief, enduring value of Dewey's philosophy for moral education lies in the comprehensive manner in which he related moral education to the needs of democratic society.

Lawrence Kohlberg

The work of Lawrence Kohlberg holds a significant place in the contemporary literature on moral education. Indeed, when the topic of moral education is mentioned, many educators equate it with Kohlberg's name or with his cognitive stage theory of moral development.

Kohlberg maintains that every person is a "moral philosopher," child and adult alike, and this is because there are universal forms of moral thinking which may be described as "cognitive developmental stages."[15]

Briefly, moral development occurs across five

219

stages[16] grouped into three levels:

    I.   Preconventional Level.
        Concern for external consequences to self.
        Stage 1.   The punishment-and-obedience orientation.
        Stage 2.   The instrumental-relativist orientation.
   II.   Conventional Level.
        Concern for meeting external social expectations.
        Stage 3.   The interpersonal "good boy-nice girl" orientation.
        Stage 4.   The "law-and-order" orientation.
  III.   Principled Level.
        Concern for fidelity to self-chosen moral principles.
        Stage 5.   The "conscience" and respect for the "rights, life, and dignity of all persons" orientation.

According to Kohlberg, stage development occurs in an invariant sequence, although the rate of development may vary and some children may become arrested at any stage. Stages are comprised of "structured wholes," total ways of thinking rather than mere attitudes toward particular situations. An individual is not always at a given stage, but may be in transition from a past stage to a future stage. Rarely are the stages developmentally removed from one another. While there are differences in the rate of development, stages are universal across cultures and social conditions.

Two assumptions are central: (1) moral development has a cognitive core, and (2) the origins of morality are interactional. The more mature stage of moral development is the more structurally adequate, an adequacy resting on the cognitive criteria of differentiation (prescription) and integration (universality). The stage sequence is not "wired into the nervous system" nor is it determined by "natural-physical forces" of the environment. Movement from one stage to the next involves cognitive reorganization rather than cultural conditioning or the addition of new information. A cognitive conflict or imbalance "drives" the movement from stage to stage. Basically, each stage is defined by a "... new cognitive-structural mode of role-taking in conflict situations."[17]

Kohlberg has argued that moral development is a result of moral conflict, primarily between competing claims of human beings. Where such conflict is resolved on a principled basis, it is usually on principles of fairness, equality, and reciprocity — in short, justice. "Moral" is defined in terms of judgment, and the formal character of the judgment rather than its content. At the highest or principled level, moral judgments tend to be "universal, inclusive, consistent, and grounded on objective, impersonal, or ideal grounds." Thus, moral is defined without considering specific content, doctrine, or personal standards. The definition is toward a formal philosophical sense in which justice is supreme.

Only principled-level thought has the formal features of moral judgment. Kohlberg bases this view, in part, on R. M. Hare (formal features are prescriptivity and universality characterized by autonomy of choice and obligation) and Immanuel Kant (prescriptivity and universality are characterized by the categorical imperative to "so act as to make the maxim of thy conduct the universal will"). This is not taken in the absolute formal sense (such as Kant, who would not tell a lie even to save a victim from murder because lying would violate the imperative); rather, it is taken in a "softer" sense of formal where moral obligations are towards "concrete other people in concrete situations."[18]

As is inevitable with any theory that gains prominence, Kohlberg's approach has encountered mounting criticism. One area of contention is his argument for the primacy of justice[19] as the highest level, or stage six, of development. This has led, at least in part, to his revision of the stages from six to five and a de-emphasis of justice as the highest principle. Instead, he now argues that moral education must occur in a just environment or "just community" and has de-emphasized the upper, or principled level, as a realistic objective.[20]

In spite of the revisions, Kohlberg still maintains that moral education involves the stimulation of development up through the stages, as opposed to the teaching of fixed truths. Moral education is a matter of aiding the child in a direction he is already heading rather than merely imposing an external pattern upon him. The role of the teacher is to present the child with realistic moral conflict issues; however, where formerly Kohlberg maintained that hypothetical problems depicting moral dilemmas were sufficient for moral development to occur, he has recently come out for the necessity of aiding children to confront value content to the extent that the teacher must become, at least in part, an active socializer and advocate. The major constraint in this process is the explicit recognition on the part of the democratic teacher and students as to the socializing and advocacy role of the teacher. For moral education to be successful, Kohlberg holds that it must be conducted in a just school environment.

Part of Kohlberg's efforts at revision relate to problems associated with moral action flowing from moral knowledge. It is commonplace that knowing what to do does not mean that it will be done. Kohlberg takes the position that children live in a world of much immoral behavior. We cannot afford to wait until children reach the principled level to deal with their behavior. Moral action presupposes a concern about moral content or moral knowledge,[21] (a point reminiscent of Dewey's position on knowledge and action).

Since the stages are still present in Kohlberg's approach, this may also continue to be a point of contention. Of course, Kohlberg did not

222

invent the notion of stages, but expanded on the stage sequence ideas of Jean Piaget. Both Piaget and Kohlberg have maintained that stages have a scientific status, but D. C. Phillips and Marvis E. Kelly have challenged this claim, arguing that the hierarchy may belong more to the conceptual nature of the materials of study in the curriculum, which go from simple to complex, than to the psychological nature of the child.[22]

Phillips and Kelly use as a further example Jean Piaget's view of the conservation of substance at the level of concrete operations. In one of his experiments, several children were given balls of plasticene, and after they had formed the balls into other shapes they were asked if they were now the same amount, weight, and volume of material. At about age eight a child will say the same amount, at a later age the same weight, and still later the same volume. Piaget thought that the appearance of such concepts could not be explained by experience, but rather by the cognitive development of the child. It was in this manner of reasoning that he came to conclude that there are invariant stages of cognitive development. But Phillips and Kelly maintain that it is just as reasonable to suppose that when a child's attention is drawn to such problems he begins to notice things which are relevant to his growth of knowledge. An older child, with more experience, has had more opportunity to refute false hypotheses and to advance nearer the truth than a younger child. In short, rival explanations to stage development are possible, and in this case, experience is a possible explanation.[23]

In view of the criticisms his theory has engendered, Kohlberg has softened many of his earlier stands. He states:
> I realize now that the psychologist's abstractions or moral "cognition" (judgment and reasoning) from moral action, and the abstraction of structure in moral cognition and judgment from content are necessary

223

abstractions from certain psychological research purposes. It is not a
sufficient guide to the moral educator who deals with the moral concrete
in a school world in which value content as well as structure, behavior
as well as reasoning, must be dealt
with.[24]

If his theory has internal difficulties, Kohlberg
has still made a major contribution to moral education. He, probably more than any other single
figure at the present time, has brought the need
for moral education to the public's attention, and
has stimulated the development of materials and
activities in schools across the country.

John Wilson

John Wilson, a British philosopher and educator, is perhaps less well-known to Americans than
either Dewey or Kohlberg, but he has been very influential in moral education developments in
Britain, and to some degree in Canada, and, more
recently, the United States. Basically, his approach to moral education encompasses this
departure point:
Any serious attempt on moral education,
whether theoretical or practical, must
begin by listing the components or attributes which constitute a morally
educated person — the 'pieces of
equipment' which can be seen as logically
necessary.[25]

Thus, Wilson's approach is based neither on a view
of society and experience, as in Dewey's case, nor
upon a psychological stage hierarchy, as in
Kohlberg's case; instead, Wilson looks to the
logically necessary components of what it means to
be a morally educated person.

Wilson attempts to clarify the general distinction of "moral" as a particular kind of human
thought and action involving characteristics of intention, understanding, and knowing what one is

224

doing. For Wilson, to act morally one must know
what he is doing and do it freely rather than by
force. Morality begins when one thinks that he
ought or ought not do to something. The person
acts for a reason and is not coerced by causes.
Moral action must be rational, and to be rational
the reasons must be causally operative and not mere
rationalization. In short, the person must act as
a moral being.[26]

A moral being can be described as a "morally
educated" person, with the emphasis not simply on
overt behavior, but on the nature of motives,
reasons, and intentions. Thus, morality involves
examination of the attitudes, feelings, and dis-
positions one has. The essence of moral education
is not the inculcation of right choices but clarification of feeling and disposition.[27] It is
through internal and external dialogue (the examination) that one gets the opportunity to react to
the facts in a more discriminating way. Morality
is largely a matter of making decisions based on
clarified attitudes or feelings, both our own and
those of other people; in other words, the peculiar
function of morality is to bring one's inner
attitudes into "a right relationship with other
people."[28]

It has long been held that facts and values
are of differing logical orders. While Wilson does
not deny that there may be a difference, he does
maintain that moral values are not necessarily ir-
rational and arbitrary; instead, they have their
own criteria of success, and there are ways of
deciding that one moral belief is better than
another. Words descriptive of these criteria include "reasonable," "rational," "unprejudiced,"
"sensible," "wise," and "sane." These words are
indicative of the ways in which, or the reasons for
which, a person comes to have moral beliefs.
Wilson's approach is toward a principled morality,
but here a clarification is needed of what Wilson
means by the term "principle." In short, he makes
a distinction between what may be called "first
order" principles and "second order" principles.

"First order" principles deal with the content of moral beliefs, that is, <u>what</u> one believes. Wilson's effort is not to answer the question "what are the right moral views?" Rather, he is after "second order" principles entailed in the question "what are the rules of procedure, or the canons of relevance, which we actually use to assess the merits of a moral view?" Thus, "second order" principles are those principles by which we can assess the merits of moral beliefs or describe the morally educated person. General rules of procedure are that we should (1) stick to the laws of logic, (2) use language correctly, and (3) attend to the facts.[29] The specific criteria for describing and assessing moral beliefs of a morally educated person are that the beliefs must:

  (1) be autonomous or freely held;
  (2) be rational;
  (3) be impartial or interpersonal;
  (4) be prescriptive, that is,
      a. suitable for all people on similar occasions, and
      b. such that the believer commits himself to acting thusly; and
  (5) take precedence over the believer's other opinion.[30]

Second order principles do not deny that there is such a thing as moral knowledge. Educating people in the moral sense entails educating them to derive their beliefs from sound bases, not just teaching them to repeat truths correctly. In other words, the approach is intended to serve as the educational foundation for moral beliefs.

Wilson stresses that a rational defense of morality has to relate to human interests. In one sense, a great deal of immorality and irrationality results from ignorance or disregard for the feelings and interests of other people. Part of the solution to this problem lies in being clear on our own feelings or interests, for by failing to be aware of our own feelings, we distort our impressions of others'. In another sense, Wilson contends that we need to submit our moral views to a social test and discussion where rules of procedure tend to be followed more effectively. Alone, we may be tempted to distort rules to our own ends or treat moral questions as if they were only arguments about fact or logic. Part of the solution is to create contexts or follow general principles designed to show how we really see ourselves, other people, and the world in general.

Morality is not defined in the interpersonal sense, for there are legitimate moral questions concerned with what Wilson calls "personal prudence" (personal moral beliefs that may not directly involve interests of other people), and questions of "mental health" (personal inadequacies requiring conscious learning rather than psychiatric or mental treatment). However, it is readily apparent that it is quite difficult to state categorically that a given belief or question is solely "personal," i.e. that no one else's interests are involved, especially when the belief or question involved is considered apart from any concrete circumstances. The prime consideration is the interpersonal one. For Wilson, the awareness of feelings, both personal and social, involves being able to give correct descriptions in a public language, or in rational terms. Since there is no single behavior pattern of moral adequacy for all people, the only general criteria are the criteria of moral rationality.[31]

According to Wilson, "first order" principles or moral content will be present to some degree in practically every educational situation, and this raises the problem of indoctrination. Wilson's effort is to devise criteria for moral education from a neutral or non-partisan basis, but he also recognizes the necessity and inevitability of moral content. While we do not just want children to get the "right answers," we can use "right answers" to help morally educate them. Some rule-governed behavior and conditioned responses are necessary. The proper course is not to confuse these preconditions with moral education.[32]

Preconditions — groundrules, working principles, social mores — serve the purpose of setting the stage for moral education. They provide a framework or springboard for people to choose their moral beliefs and values. For the educator to try to impose values is immoral, but it is just as immoral for the educator to fail to create or utilize frameworks within which choices can be made. A basic question is "What groundrules are necessary to achieve educational ends?" Educators have no moral rights over children, only a mandate to protect and educate them so that they grow up into free adults. The desire to ensure that children have a solid framework, and the desire not to indoctrinate, constitute a dilemma of some proportions. Wilson is of the opinion that these two elements are compatible as long as educators do not think that they have to build their own values into the framework or that the framework alone will morally educate.[33]

Thus, educators need a neutral or non-partisan standard (but not aimless relativism). We have to go to the question, "What would a rational person want?" The criteria of rationality are not the be-all and end-all of moral education, however. Many moral questions are particularly elusive, and practical conditions, such as economic necessity, survival and so forth, may present compelling departures from a non-partisan standard. But if this is the case, we should be clear as to the reason for the departure in each instance.[34]

Wilson's approach to moral education has been criticized for its emphasis on rational procedures to the exclusion of other pertinent considerations. Among these are the role of norms and values of the community which, while they may be of lesser concern than reasoning skills, are nonetheless a crucial factor in moral education. Then, too, there is the view that the school can teach more than the form of moral reasoning, for it can also teach knowledge about values and the mastery of content that must go into a rational program of moral education.[35] Nevertheless, Wilson provides

a fairly clear and concise account of procedures
and criteria for moral education; and he does
recognize norms and values as "preconditions."

Conclusion

This brief survey of three approaches to moral
education indicates some of the difficulties facing
educators in sorting out the various approaches to
moral education. Each of the three has strengths
and weaknesses. Dewey provides a broad treatment
of moral education against a background of the
nature of experience, the democratic society,
growth as the aim of education, and education itself as a moral enterprise. His approach is comprehensive, and it provides a perspective characterized by breadth in which the various parts fit
together in a systematic fashion, a comprehensiveness lacking in Kohlberg and Wilson. Yet, Dewey's
recommendations often lack specificity and some of
his key concepts are vague. Still, his philosophy
provides educators with landmarks they need in
traversing the landscape of moral education. The
relation of knowledge and action is one of these
landmarks. Another is the need to keep the ends of
education in focus, especially in terms of growth
and its social consequences in a democracy.

Both Kohlberg and Wilson provide specificity,
but they do not provide comprehensiveness.
Kohlberg approaches moral education from a narrow
stance of the cognitive structural elements. He
attempts to find an invariant, universal structure
upon which to base moral education. This allows
him to fill in specific details, but it is on this
very structure that his approach has faced increasing criticism. Nevertheless, he does provide
a schema for taking students from the simple to the
more complex, and while his explanations may be
flawed, his direction has much to offer.

Wilson seeks an approach aimed at defining
what constitutes a morally educated person and
identifying the procedures which will produce that

person. He gives a fairly clear-cut approach
lacking in both Dewey and Kohlberg, an approach
free from entangling vagueness or psychological
abstractions. However, this simplicity may ignore
other pertinent issues extending beyond rational
procedures alone. Here both Dewey and Kohlberg
offer some correctives, for they see moral growth
in terms of a democratic society or a just community.

A major point emphasized by all three authors
is that moral education, whatever else it may include, is at the very least concerned with reflective rational thought and its development or
cultivation among young people. The significance
of this should not be lost, for all three, in spite
of the wide range of differences in approach,
theoretical orientation, and style, are in agreement on the centrality of thinking. For them,
thinking and moral development go hand in hand.

Another point which calls for emphasis is the
matter of content in moral education. Dewey is,
perhaps, most explicit of the three on this issue,
for he sees the entire curriculum potentially involved in moral education. In the more specific
sense, however, Dewey believed that cultural norms
and traditions are important ingredients if approached in the reflective, reconstructive sense of
educational growth. Kohlberg, especially in his
revisions, emphasizes the need to consider value
content as well as cognitive development, although
he has not as yet stated his views on this in any
in-depth fashion. Wilson recognizes content as
"groundrules, working principles, or social norms."
These are necessary ingredients for moral education,
but are preconditions rather than moral education
per se. The point is that all three consider content to be important, although their attention is
primarily directed at the ends and process of moral
education. This suggests that educators need to
exercise care and scholarship in the selection of
content in moral education with their focus on the
educational ends to be achieved.

Perhaps a final point to be drawn from this brief survey is that educators need to be familiar with a variety of approaches to moral education. This familiarity should not be based on a mindless eclecticism that randomly picks and chooses; rather, it should involve scholarship and the desire to increase professional competence, for the issues involved in moral education are complex, for which no easy solutions or patch-work panaceas exist.

1. John Wilson, et al. <u>Introduction to Moral Education</u> (Baltimore: Penguin Books, 1967), p. 11.

2. Richard H. Hersh, et al. <u>Models of Moral Education: An Appraisal</u> (New York: Longman, Inc., 1980), p. viii.

3. For a critical appraisal of the Dewey-Kohlberg connection, see Jeanne Pietig, "Lawrence Kohlberg, John Dewey, and Moral Education," <u>Social Education</u>, Vol. 44, No. 3 (March, 1980).

4. John Dewey, <u>Democracy and Education</u> (New York: Macmillan Paperback Edition, 1961), p. 359.

5. <u>Ibid.</u>, p. 76. 6. <u>Ibid.</u>, p. 140. 7. <u>Ibid.</u>, pp. 153-163.

8. John Dewey. <u>Moral Principles in Education</u> (Carbondale, Ill.: Southern Illinois University Press, Arcturus Books Edition, 1975), pp. 13-17.

9. <u>Democracy and Education</u>, p. 87.

10. <u>Moral Principles in Education</u>, p. 43.

11. <u>Ibid.</u>, p. 48.

12. <u>Democracy and Education</u>, p. 360.

13. See, for example, Anthony Flew, "Democracy and Education," and R. S. Peters, "John Dewey's Philosophy of Education," in <u>John Dewey Reconsidered</u>, edited by R. S. Peters, The International Library of the Philosophy of Education (Boston: Routledge and Kegan Paul, 1977), pp. 76-101, 102-123.

14. Sidney Hook, "Preface," in <u>Moral Principles in Education</u>, p. xvi.

15. Lawrence Kohlberg, "Stages of Moral Development as a Basis for Moral Education," in <u>Moral Education: Interdisciplinary Approaches</u>, edited by Clive M. Beck and others (Toronto: University of Toronto Press, 1971), p. 34.

16. As reported by Thomas Lickona, "How to Encourage Moral Development," <u>Learning</u>, Vol. 5, No. 7 (March, 1977), p. 38. Kohlberg formerly claimed six stages. See, for example, Lawrence Kohlberg and Richard H. Hersh, "Moral

Development: A Review of the Theory," Theory Into
Practice, Vol. 16, No. 2 (April, 1977), pp. 54-55.

17. "Stages of Moral Development as a Basis for Moral Education," p. 51.

18. Ibid., p. 61.

19. See, for example, R. S. Peters, "Why Doesn't Lawrence
Kohlberg Do His Homework?" in Moral Education ... It
Comes With the Territory, edited by David Purpel and
Kevin Ryan (Berkeley, Cal.: McCutchan Publishing
Company, 1976), pp. 288-290.

20. As reported by Howard Muson, "Moral Thinking: Can It Be
Taught?", Psychology Today, Vol. 12, No. 9 (February,
1979), p. 57.

21. Lawrence Kohlberg, "Moral Education Reappraised," The
Humanist, Vol. 38, No. 6 (November/December, 1978),
pp. 13-15.

22. D. C. Phillips and Mavis E. Kelly, "Hierarchical
Theories of Development in Education and Psychology," in
Stage Theories of Cognitive and Moral Development:
Criticism and Applications, Reprint No. 13, Harvard
Educational Review (Cambridge: The President and
Fellows of Harvard College, 1978), p. 172.

23. Ibid., p. 190.

24. Kohlberg, "Moral Education Reappraised," p. 14.

25. John Wilson, "First Steps in Education, Morality, and
Religion," Philosophy of Education 1977: Proceedings of
the Thirty-Third Annual Meeting of the Philosophy of
Education Society (Urbana, Ill., Philosophy of Education
Society, 1977), p. 41.

26. John Wilson, et al., Introduction to Moral Education,
p. 60.

27. Ibid., p. 65. Wilson's use of the term "clarification"
should not be confused with "values clarification," a
theory popular in the United States. Wilson's approach
is decidedly rational.

28. Ibid.   29. Ibid., p. 76.   30. Ibid., p. 77.

31. Ibid., p. 89.   32. Ibid., pp. 126-127, 140.

33. Ibid., pp. 142-143.   34. Ibid., p. 163.

35. Harry S. Broudy, "Response to Wilson," _Philosophy of Education 1977: Proceedings_, pp. 52-53.

Resolving the Dilemma of Religious and Humanistic Moral Education in Public School Curriculum

William F. Losito

Some issues continually reemerge in public education though the formulation of the issues may differ according to time and place. Among those issues must be included questions about religious and moral instruction in public school curriculum. Frequently enough, religious and moral education are popularly thought to be coextensive when debate ensues about what should or should not be included in the curriculum. In other quarters, morality is thought to be exclusively a form of humanistic inquiry and knowledge logically autonomous from religious inquiry.[1]

In the context of formulating curriculum policy for public education, these different perspectives prompt different recommendations and arguments. For those who contend that instruction about morality is logically inseparable from religion, they typically argue against the inclusion of moral instruction in public education because it would necessarily be a form of Constitutionally prohibited religious instruction. For those who maintain that moral knowledge and inquiry are logically autonomous, humanistic enterprises, they characteristically advocate the inclusion of moral instruction in public school curriculum. They argue that moral instruction contributes to an important dimension of human development and it does not represent an abridgement of the separation of Church and State.

These incompatible curriculum policy recommendations, which serve as a focal point for contemporary educational debate, presuppose different views about the relationship between religious and humanistic moral inquiry. The purpose of the present essay is to present an alternative policy recommendation concerning moral education in public school curriculum that is rationally justifiable.

Such an alternative policy recommendation must include as part of its justification: 1) some general interpretation of the policy and guidelines for its implementation, 2) a position with accompanying arguments concerning the relationship between religious inquiry about morality and humanistic inquiry about morality, and 3) arguments for/against certain version(s) of moral education in the curriculum.

Any policy recommendation about moral education is dependent upon a satisfactory resolution of the prior issue concerning the relationship between religious and moral inquiry. In addition, arguments for or against a certain form of moral education must be presented, because supporting a policy recommendation involves more than resolving questions about religious/humanistic moral inquiry. The desirability of a curriculum policy depends upon a number of social and political considerations, as well as its consistency with adequately defined purposes of public education.

And thirdly, any alternative view must indicate and justify some general guidelines for the form and manner of inclusion (of the type of inquiry) in the school curriculum. For even if a type of inquiry can be shown to be desirable in general, a specified manner and form still need justification. For example, age, geography, and culture of the potential students dictate some plausible constraints. In the case of religious and humanistic inquiry about morality, the religious pluralism of contemporary society and the Constitutional requisites of separation of Church and State pose legitimate shaping influences on how those forms of inquiry might be included in the public school curriculum.

The alternative view here proposed is that religious and humanistic inquiry about morality are logically autonomous but are conjunctively desirable for inclusion in the public school curriculum in a manner that does not abridge the Constitutional separation of Church and State. According to this view, religious and humanistic inquiry about morality constitute logically distinct forms of inquiry about morality. Their logical distinctness does not entail them being contradictory in their conclusions, however. Ideal standards for human conduct (the sense of 'morality' understood throughout this essay) can be inquired about both from the religious perspective and through the use of human reason alone. Instruction about religious morality and humanistic morality are both desirable in public school curriculum, but only if both are included and in a manner consistent with restrictions arising out of the purposes of good education and the legal context of American society. The policy recommendation advocated goes beyond the "desirability" argument to the claim that instruction about both religious and humanistic moral inquiry <u>should</u> be included in public school education. The remainder of this essay will be an explication of this alternative view and a presentation for some of the "common sense" reasons for accepting the position.

First, we will look at that part of the thesis which contends that religious and humanistic inquiry are logically distinct, although not contradictory in most of their main features.

Autonomy of Humanistic Moral Inquiry

It is not the purpose of this section to argue for a particular system of humanistic morality or set of ethical norms. It is sufficient to point out that humanistic moral inquiry can, in principle, be valid and that its judgments need not contradict religious judgments about the same human conduct.

First, let us examine the primary argument against the possibility of humanistic inquiry and knowledge about morality. A serious challenge to this logical possibility in the Anglo-American tradition has been the doctrine of logical

positivism. The logical positivists, typified by
A. J. Ayer, hold that the only meaningful statements are those which are verified in principle
through sense experience.[2] Now, statements about
the good life and moral norms for human action are
not justified through sense experience according to
the logical positivists; so humanistically derived
moral norms are not knowledge claims about the object world but rather expressions of personal
feelings and emotions by the user.

If the thesis of logical positivism obtains,
it seriously challenges the possibility of a
rational, humanistic morality. Historically,
logical positivism lost credibility on its own
grounds. For the lynchpin proposition of logical
positivism — "only those statements verified in
principle through sense experience are meaningful" — itself is a statement which is not verified
through sense experience, and therefore is not
meaningful according to its own criterion. Attempts have been made to patch up the logical
positivistic thesis and thereby dismiss the legitimacy of humanistic inquiry about morality. The
death knell was sounded for logical positivism,
though, when several academicians persuasively argued that even some of the fundamental notions of
theoretical physics, the paradigm of scientific
knowledge, are themselves non-empirically verifiable.[3] A position like logical positivism which
rules out the possibility of scientific knowledge
certainly cannot be tenable. Dismissing the thesis
of logical positivism does not in itself justify
the possibility of humanistic inquiry about morality, but it does remove one of the traditional conceptual obstacles to such a position.

The importance of the line of argument used to
refute logical positivism is that it provides a
clear direction for affirming the plausibility of
humanistic moral inquiry. The critics of logical
positivism pointed out that some scientific claims
are accepted for criteria other than their disposition to be empirically verified. Such criteria
for acceptability would include logical consistency,

clarity, fruitfulness, and compatibility with our
common sense, consensual judgments. The adoption
of such non-empirical criteria enables us to con-
ceive of human inquiry producing some ideal standards for action that would be rationally acceptable.

It is a fact of our social existence that we
share common moral norms for the conventional
regulation of our public conduct (if not also our
private conduct). William D. Ross has listed and
explicated some of those general moral precepts
which he thinks are socially consented to as prima
facie ethical responsibilities:

1. Not to harm others.
2. To make reparation for harm done by us.
3. To keep our commitments.
4. To repay our benefactors.
5. To treat people at least as well as
   they deserve to be treated.
6. To improve ourselves in some ways.[4]

While these ethical norms are not empirically verifiable, they certainly do represent, as Ross maintains, examples of ethical norms accepted con-
sensually by our society as useful, consistent
rules for guiding public moral conduct. And even
though the application of these norms to concrete
situations is not perfectly clear, a common core of
meaning has emerged through public debate and discussion. Richard Purtill has formulated some of
the clarifying guidelines and qualifications for
these prima facie moral precepts. An example of
these clarifications for the first of the ethical
norms cited above is:

Do not harm persons, or perform actions
which will probably harm persons, except
a. When the action is for the long-term
   good of the person(s) being harmed and
   is done with their consent where
   feasible.
b. When all other possible actions will
   cause greater harm to persons.
c. When the person has by his own free
   choice deserved to be harmed and the
   person doing the harm is the

   appropriate person to inflict this
   harm.

 d. When an important obligation to make
   reparation to other persons or an extremely important commitment makes
   some harm or risk of harm to persons
   unavoidable. Occasionally relatively
   minor harm to persons may be justified by extraordinarily important
   obligations to benefactors or the opportunity to give extraordinary help
   to deserving persons.[5]

So, if one adopts some reasonable criteria for the
acceptability of theoretical generalizations other
than on empirical grounds, humanistic morality is
not just a possibility, but a social reality which
we accept as a basis for social conduct, much of
our statutory/case law, and public policy. To be
sure, humanistic ethical norms are not true with
certitude; they share attributes of openness and
tentativeness with other forms of human knowledge,
such as the natural and social sciences. And the
application of these ethical norms to complex contemporary situations, like the issues of genetic
engineering and abortion, does not lead to easy
solutions and frequently leads to divided, controversial social judgments. But the tentativeness of
its generalization and the difficulty of application does not negate the existence of humanistic
morality.

  Another reason for accepting the possibility
of humanistic morality is that it is acknowledged
and even included in several religious traditions.
As Paul Hirst[6] has pointed out, the Christian
Scriptures enunciate the position that morality can
be known outside of faith and revelation:

   For instance, pagans who never heard of
   the Law but are led by reasons to do what
   the Law commands, may not actually 'possess' the Law, but they can be said to
   'be' the Law. They can point to the substance of the Law engraved on their
   hearts — they can call a witness, that
   is, their own conscience — they have

accusation and defence, that is, their
own inner mental dialogue. (Paul's
Letter to the Romans, 2:14-16)
Under any standard exegesis of the passage, Paul is
claiming that the good life can be known and interpreted without the aid of revelation. An addi-
tional implication of Paul's discourse is that
there is no essential prescriptive difference between the norms dictated by the "Law commands"
(religion) and what "reason" concludes from "inner
mental dialogue" (humanistic moral inquiry).

Humanistic morality is autonomous in the sense
that acceptable moral norms for social conduct can
be formulated and justified. This autonomy does
not, however, necessarily imply exclusivity or con-
tradiction between humanistic morality and religious morality. It is logically consistent that
similar/identical ethical norms can be produced by
two or more independent procedures of inquiry.

Autonomy of Religious Moral Inquiry

Most religions and religious traditions espouse a set of norms for moral conduct. The norms
are derived from a "holy book" (or an interpretation thereof), direct revelation/inspiration from a
transcendent being, or some other communication
from the transcendent being through an intermedi-
ator (or intermediators). The source of moral
norms in religious inquiry is essentially different, then, from humanistic moral inquiry, where
the source is exclusively rational reflection on
human experience. There have been three lines of
arguments advanced against the autonomy of religious moral inquiry: 1) a denial of the existence
of a transcendent reality and/or deity; 2) reduction of religious moral inquiry to humanistic moral
inquiry; and 3) the claim that religious morality
is superfluous, because it does not add any legitimate prescriptions not already found in humanistic
morality.

The attempt to negate religious moral inquiry by denying the existence of transcendent reality is not a fruitful line of criticism. While there are reasonable arguments against the existence of transcendent reality, they can be countered with arguments from the viewpoint of religious believers. The arguments of religious believers, as well as the long religious tradition in civilization, do not with public certitude prove the existence of transcendent reality, but they do establish the religious mode of consciousness, understanding, and inquiry as legitimate human endeavors. Pointing to the pluralism of religious and religious moralities likewise does not negate the legitimacy/autonomy of religious moral inquiry. Within the tradition of humanistic moral inquiry, there also is a pluralism of positions, such as utilitarianism, contractarianism, existentialism, etc.

The more substantial challenge to religious moral inquiry comes from the claim that religious moral inquiry can be translated/reduced to humanistic moral inquiry. Such a position is advanced by C. M. Hamm, who holds "that there is no way in which knowledge of the good and right can be based on religion."[7] Hamm attempts to substantiate this conclusion by distinguishing two types of religion, R_1 and R_2. R_1 religion is the traditional form which includes dogma, priesthood, ceremonies, sacred books, and public assembly. R_2 religion is a life orientation that usually includes a sense of human dignity and commitment to something. Hamm dismisses R_2 religion as a source of religious morality because it encompasses everyone and everything as religious. This would make R_2 religious morality indistinguishable from humanistic morality because religious moral inquiry could be defined as moral norms derived exclusively from rational reflection on human experience. This would entail religious and humanistic moral inquiry being coextensive.

Hamm turns to R_1 religion as a possible conception for autonomous religious moral inquiry.

The essential characteristic of R_1 religion according to Hamm is the central role of a religious leader. The source of religious morality is the conduct and expressed thought of this religious leader. Hamm argues that it is not logically consistent to maintain that the religious leader has knowledge of morality independent of human experience and reflection.[8] Religious moral inquiry under R_1 religion would be just another form of humanistic moral inquiry; its only distinguishing feature would be that moral knowledge and inquiry would be attributed to the thinking of a religious leader rather than a social produce/process attributable to non-religious leaders. While Hamm acknowledges that R_1 religion is more comprehensive than the behavior and thought of a religious leader, he concludes that none of these other elements of R_1 religion can be an autonomous source of religious moral inquiry. Theological doctrines, the most likely source, are not adequate, Hamm argues, because one cannot deduce ethical norms from theological premises (devoid of ethical terms) such as "God wills it."[9]

Hamm's argument against the autonomy of religious moral inquiry fails because he has a misconception about the ultimate justification of moral norms in most religious belief systems, particularly in R_1 religions. In these religious systems, the religious leader, such as Christ, Mohammed, or Moses, is thought to be an interpreter or prophet of morality received from a divine source. The religious leader expresses morality not simply derived from humanistic reasoning; for the religious believer, at least, it cannot be reduced to humanistic moral inquiry. And as pointed out above, the religious mode of consciousness is a plausible, legitimate form of human understanding and behavior. Hamm begs the question if he concludes without further convincing evidence (which he does not provide) that religious morality can be translated totally into humanistic morality. Hamm may be correct that some religions do not propose to have autonomous moral inquiry, but he does not prove that religions which claim otherwise are logically inconsistent in doing so.

The third objection to the validity of religious inquiry about morality is that it really can not/does not add anything to humanistic inquiry. If its prescriptive norms are identical/similar with those of humanistic moral inquiry, the religious language adds nothing to the content of humanistic morality. And if the two forms of moral inquiry contradict one another, there is good reason for holding the religious norms to be suspect because the function of humanistic moral inquiry is to lay down basic norms for human conduct that are the result of rational public consensus. A religious norm that prescribed racial discrimination would be an example of a norm that contradicts most consensual humanistic moralities and thus is held suspect. In the case of either the religious norm being identical to or contradicting humanistic morality, religious moral inquiry does not add any justifiable norms to those derived from humanistic moral inquiry. Secondly, if they contradict one another, the religious prescription ought not be followed, because humanistic inquiry is a good litmus test for religious inquiry.

There are two lines of standard response to this important concern. First, the religionist claims that even where the moral judgments are similar/identical, the motivational context is different and significantly so. The religionist's beliefs about morality are interrelated with his total belief system, and form an orientation toward life in general. It gives a reason, e.g., "imitate the religious leader," "because God wills it," "to gain eternal salvation," etc., that is not there in the humanistic motivation structure. As Toulmin has put it so aptly, "religion helps us put our hearts into it."[10]

The above point holds even if the moral judgments are similar/identical. But many religious ethicists go to great lengths to argue that religious demands on the moral life transcend humanistic moral demands. Religious morality can

246

require of a person greater individual commitment
and self-sacrifice, while the humanistic morality
typically does not do so — it permits the individual to more generally make decisions in view of
his personal interests. Religious morality does
add prescriptive content to humanistic moral inquiry. That does not necessarily mean that religious morality contradicts humanistic morality.
It merely means that it transcends those obligations that humanistic moral inquiry typically
prescribes for human conduct.

According to the view described above, religious moral inquiry and humanistic moral inquiry
are justifiable, distinct forms of inquiry about
moral knowledge. The starting points of their inquiries are different while the resulting norms can
be identical/similar and different (although not
necessarily contradictory).

The Desirability of Humanistic
Moral Inquiry in Public
School Curriculum

As indicated at the outset, the conclusion
that humanistic and religious morality are
logically autonomous forms of inquiry is not sufficient in itself to justify the desirability of
either/both of them in public school curriculum.
Argumentation is necessary to substantiate the desirability claim as well as to indicate some
general guidelines for any policy formulation. The
proposed thesis is that religious and humanistic
moral inquiry are conjunctively desirable in the
curriculum of public education. To substantiate
this position, we will proceed to examine the case
for each of them being desirably included (according to certain guidelines) in the public school
curriculum but only in conjunction with one another.

First let us examine some reasons why humanistic moral inquiry is desirable for public education in conjunction with religious moral inquiry.
Education, even in the most exact separation from

religion and religious education, is pervasively a value-laden, moral enterprise. Educating children to value certain subject matter, follow school/class regulations, make career choices, etc. are examples of influencing students in morally significant ways. Moral education, at least in the context of humanistic morality is desirable to make explicit what is already inherently implicit in education. Placing moral inquiry on the explicit level initiates the students into the forms of moral reasoning and values already operative in the curriculum and gives them some cognitive power to shape the ongoing direction of their education.

The second reason is that humanistic morality is at the basis of our Constitutional law and democratic ethos. And since one uncontested function of public education is to initiate the young into the forms of knowledge necessary for responsible citizenship, humanistic moral inquiry is necessary to achieve that societal mandate for education. Some curricular models accept the above rationale as the focal point for education in valuing. For example, the Salt Lake City School District has adopted the following ethical principles as knowledge objectives for their program in humanistic moral education.

1. Each individual has dignity and worth.
2. A free society requires respect for persons, property, and principles.
3. Each individual has a right to learn and the freedom to achieve.
4. Each individual, regardless of race, creed, color, sex, ethnic background, or economic status, has equal opportunity.
5. Each individual has the right to personal liberties.
6. Each individual is responsible for his/her own actions.
7. Each individual has a responsibility to the group as well as to the total society.
8. Democratic governments govern by majority vote.

248

9. Democratic societies are based on law.
10. Problems are solved through reason and orderly processes.
11. An individual should be tolerant of other religious beliefs and should have freedom to exercise his/her own.
12. Each individual has the right to work, to pursue an occupation, and to gain satisfaction from personal efforts.[11]

These moral principles, as well as other similar ones, are not just necessary for the citizenship functions in a democratic society. The entire fabric of our social life presupposes and is dependent upon principles of fairness, truth telling, promise keeping, etc., being observed by educated, autonomous individuals.

At the same time, the humanistic perspective on morality should not be the exclusive one taught in the schools. As we saw above, the religious perspective provides an added dimension to moral reasoning. If only the humanistic perspective were presented, it would create the impression that there is only one mode of moral inquiry (and it is sufficient). Instruction about religious morality is necessary to balance the perspective in the present religious pluralism of society. Our Constitution prohibits education from supporting any one religious denomination; but the Constitution does not countenance education undermining religion, either, as would be the case if only humanistic moral inquiry were taught in public education.

Robin Barrow points out another reason why the humanistic perspective should not be the exclusive one included in public education.[12] Religious inquiry (not just about religious morality) represents a paradigm of non-empirical consciousness and inquiry about the world. Without at least some systematic understanding of a non-empirical mode of inquiry, the student is denied an understanding of possible modes for interpreting human experience.

And as Hirst and others have persuasively argued, students ought to be initiated into the various forms of knowledge and modes of understanding that help them to become autonomous individuals who can use inquiry to ask their own questions about the good life and seek happiness.[13]

There are also some general guidelines that need to be specified as part of a policy proposal for the inclusion of humanistic moral inquiry in public education. For instance, the instruction cannot be done in a way that can be interpreted as indoctrination. Instruction in humanistic moral inquiry must be conducted in a manner which respects an open examination of reasons for accepting ethical principles, even where these ethical norms are a matter of general consensus. Moral indoctrination, the intent to have some believe certain moral principles as true without regard to reasons, does not respect the student as an autonomous individual.[14] Where there is no general consensus in society about a particular ethical norm or its application, both sides of the issue need to be presented in intellectual fairness and to avoid indoctrination.

As a second guideline, emphasis should be placed on skills in moral reasoning as well as instruction about a set of principles, such as those adopted by the Salt Lake City School District. Because one needs to continually apply ethical principles to different contexts, instruction in moral reasoning and argumentation must be included in any program of humanistic moral inquiry.

Thirdly, any program should respect the age of the students and to some extent, the sensibilities of the community. The latter part of the standard is not absolute, because the sensibilities/preferences of the local community on occasion cannot be tolerated by the larger community. Discussion about particularly sensitive moral issues, such as abortion, are not necessary to achieve the goals of good humanistic moral education. But this guideline leaves open the possibility that instruction in humanistic moral inquiry may necessitate on occasion variance with the opinions of some members of the local community.

So the humanistic perspective on morality is necessary to a good, general education, but that inclusion is dependent upon an inclusion with the religious perspective and in accord with the above guidelines for the manner of its inclusion.

The Desirability of Religious Moral Inquiry in Public School Curriculum

With respect to religious moral inquiry, an important guideline for its curriculum implementation must be defined at the outset. Because of our Constitutional separation between Church and State, instruction about religious moral inquiry cannot be similar, for example, to science instruction, where verifiable generalizations are taught as part of public knowledge. Instead, instruction concerning religious moral inquiry would be included in the study _about_ religion in society. The school/teacher would present the various religious moral positions with an attitude of neutrality and with the objective of furthering the student's understanding of religion. The educational objective would not be to have the student come to accept a particular religious position with respect to morality. The Supreme Court has clearly supported instruction about religion in public education with its landmark 1963 decision:

> "It is said, and I agree, that the attitude of government toward religion must be one of neutrality. But untutored devotion to the concept of neutrality can lead to invocation or approval of results which partake not simply of that noninterference and noninvolvement with the religious which the Constitution commands, but of a brooding and pervasive devotion to the secular and a passive, or even active, hostility to

251

> the religious .... Government must in-
> evitably take cognizance of the exis-
> tence of religion and, indeed, under
> certain circumstances the First Amend-
> ment may require that it do so. And it
> seems clear to me from the opinions in
> the present and past cases that the
> Court would recognize the propriety ...
> of the teaching about religion, as
> distinguished from the teaching of
> religion, in the public school."[15]

Inquiry about religious morality is only one aspect
of inquiry about religion. Since the instruction
is for the purpose of enhancing understanding, it
is neither necessary nor desirable for the school/
teacher to promote any of the pluralistic religious
moral positions as being true. It is sufficient
for inclusion in the curriculum that the religious
moral positions studied are representative of the
major religious traditions in American society.

Having presented the basic guideline, let us
examine the reasons supporting the policy recommendation for its inclusion in public education.
First, insofar as one of the major purposes of education is to provide a general understanding of
society, it is necessary to study the religious
dimension of life as it has been and is integral to
understanding the perspective of many people. And
this is true irrespective of whether one wants to
adopt the religious perspective for oneself or not.
The argument has been endorsed by the American
Association of School Adminstrators:

> "A curriculum which ignored reli-
> gion would itself have serious religious
> implications. It would seem to proclaim
> that religion has not been as real in
> men's lives as health or politics or
> economics. By omission it would appear
> to deny that religion has been and is
> important in man's history — a denial
> of the obvious. In day by day practice,
> the topic cannot be avoided. As an
> integral part of man's culture, it must
> be included."[16]

252

A second important reason for accepting instruction about religious morality in the curriculum is the expectation of general education to prepare the individual for making personal decisions about values, career directions, and other life choices. Having an understanding of the religious perspective and mode of understanding is an important ingredient for making informed choices about future life opportunities. It would be a grievous error for the religious perspective to be neglected in public school curriculum.

The reasons why religious moral inquiry should not be the exclusive moral perspective in the public school curriculum should be obvious from the above discussion. As was pointed out, public education presupposes certain moral principles for its maintenance and as integral to its missions. Since these moral principles ought not be expressed in religious language (for Constitutional reasons), humanistic moral inquiry is likewise necessary. So, while instruction about religious morality is desirable in the curriculum, it is <u>not</u> so to the exclusion of humanistic moral inquiry.

<u>Summary</u>

At the outset, it was contended that discussion about morality in the schools frequently subsumes morality into religion or reduces it to a humanistic form of inquiry. An alternative view was presented which holds that religious morality and humanistic morality are logically distinct, autonomous forms of inquiry that do not necessarily contradict one another concerning their prescriptive judgments about human conduct. They are conjunctively desirable and necessary for good public education, i.e., if the public school curriculum is good, it will contain instruction about morality from both the humanistic and religious perspectives. The instruction in both cases should avoid indoctrination and respect the Constitutional separation of Church and State.

253

The above position does not entail that
religious and humanistic morality be taught in the
same course or even during the same year. One
would expect, however, that the two forms of inquiry be presented in some complementary form.
Otherwise, it will be psychologically difficult for
the student to examine and integrate both forms
into his normative world-view.

Much contemporary discussion about moral education presupposes some false assumptions about
moral knowledge. By analyzing these presupposi-
tions and finding them wanting, we can construct
another basis for formulating rational policy
concerning moral and religious education. This
policy is consistent with Constitutional prescriptions, the purposes of general education, and the
nature of religious and humanistic inquiry.

NOTES

1. See, for example, Paul Kurtz, "What is Humanism?" in Paul Kurtz, ed. <u>Moral Problems in Contemporary Society</u>, Buffalo, N.Y.: Prometheus Books, 1973, pp. 1-14.

2. A. J. Ayer, <u>The Problem of Knowledge,</u> Baltimore, Md.: Penguine Books, 1956.

3. It has been particularly the works of Michael Polanyi, Thomas Kuhn, and Jurgen Habermas, that have underscored the weakness of the positivistic thesis with their demonstration of the personal, non-empirically explicit dimension in science. See Jurgen Habermas, <u>Theory and Practice</u>, Boston: Beacon Press, 1973; Michael Polanyi, <u>Personal Knowledge</u>, New York: Harper and Row, 1958; Thomas Kuhn, <u>The Structure of Scientific Revolutions</u>, Chicago: University of Chicago Press, 1962.

4. W. D. Ross, <u>The Rights and the Good</u>, Oxford: Clarendon Press, 1930.

5. Richard Purtill, <u>Thinking About Ethics</u>, Englewood Cliffs: N.J.: Prentice-Hall, Inc., 1976, p. 58.

6. Paul Hirst, <u>Knowledge and the Curriculum</u>, Boston: Routledge and Kegan Paul, 1974, p. 175.

7. Cornell Hamm, "Moral Education Without Religion," in D. B. Cochrane, C. M. Hamm, and A. C. Kazepides, eds. <u>The Domain of Moral Education</u>, New York: Paulist Press, 1979, p. 47.

8. Cornell Hamm, "Moral Education Without Religion," p. 39.

9. Cornell Hamm, "Moral Education Without Religion," p. 40.

10. Stephen Toulmin, <u>The Place of Reason in Ethics</u>, Cambridge: Cambridge University Press, 1961, p. 219.

11. Donald Thomas and Margaret Richards, "Ethics Education is Possible," <u>Phi Delta Kappan</u>, Vol. 60, No. 8 (April 1979), p. 579.

12. Robin Barrow, <u>Common Sense and the Curriculum</u>, Boston: George Allen and Unwin, 1976, p. 132

13. Paul Hirst, <u>Knowledge and the Curriculum</u>, pp. 30-53.

14. See I. A. Snook, <u>Indoctrination and Education</u>, Boston: Routledge and Kegan Paul, 1972.

15. Abington School District v. Schempp 374 U.S. 306 (1963).

16. American Association of School Administrators, Religion in the Public Schools, New York: Harper and Row, 1964, pp. 53-55.

Evolution vs. Creationism:
A Debate Between World Views

Ronald N. Giese

As children, many of us were exposed to the
fable of the blind men describing an elephant. The
person inspecting the knee declared, in effect,
that the elephant was a tree which swayed to and
fro. Meanwhile, the person examining the tail described the elephant as a rope and so on. A moral
of that fable was: Given a limited perspective,
people can draw conclusions which are valid for a
limited part of the world or issue. But, such conclusions can be, and most often are, woefully wrong
as a description of the whole.

Fables are useful tools with which to teach
important truths or concepts to children. Adults
can safely forget the fables, but not the truths
the fables taught. Otherwise, as adults they are
doomed to recreate the fable in another time and
place. The parent issue of our elephant, a "white
elephant" at that — something we sense to be too
valuable to throw out, but very bothersome to
keep — is the question that has perplexed humanity
from time immemorial, "whence the world and humanity?" The central issue of this article, a
first generation offspring of the parent question,
is still a white elephant of the same species.
Evolution is said to take eons of generations. Our
issue is, "which perspective(s) on origins shall we
teach our children?"

Time and reflection may provide resolution to
the parent question. This article will not. This
article will focus on the current perspectives
which must be considered to resolve the offspring
issue.

Science is well established as an area of
study by adults and as a subject in the curriculum
of public schools. Science as a subject gets its
credibility and content from the disciplines of
science — astronomy, chemistry, geology, physics,

257

etc. Religion is also a respected area of study by adults, though its place as a subject in our public schools is by no means established.

The debate over teaching of creationism in our public schools is not a war between science and religion as areas of study or between the two communities of scholars. The debate pits a small minority of scientists and fundamental religionists against the majority of the scientists and religionists. A popular expression says "you can't tell the players without a score-card." In this debate you cannot even tell teammates of the opposing sides by their uniforms — white lab coats and dark suits with turned collars. Teams must be identified by the goals (positions) they defend. Both goals, evolution and creationism, have defenders wearing each type of uniform and some wearing no specific uniform at all.

The major positions or goals being defended in this debate are:
(1) literal creationism - the Bible is the Word of God and is to be taken literally even as a science text.
(2) scientific creationism - the fossil record supports a creation model of "kinds" better than it supports a molecules to man evolution model. Scientific creationists accept microevolution as demonstrated fact (Thurman, 1978). Microevolution involves changes within the species. They reject an unwarranted inference macroevolution, i.e. the undemonstrated theory that species can, do and did evolve into other species. Thus, in creationist arguments against evolution, the word evolution should be understood to mean macroevolution. They seldom define the distinction they make which simply adds to the confusion.
(3) Theistic evolution - there is a divine plan behind evolution. The planner utilizes natural processes such as chance environmental changes, adaptations, and natural selection as mechanisms by which His designs are worked out.

(4) evolutionism - the driving force behind evolution is materialistic in nature and is explainable in terms of natural processes such as chance environmental changes, adaptations and natural selection. Evolutionists accept both the demonstrated process of microevolution and the theory of macroevolution so completely that they subsume both in the word evolution. Thus they often assume that the creationists' argument against evolution is directed toward evolution in any form, not just macroevolution.

The majority of the active opponents in the current debate hold either positions 1 and 2 or position 4. The opponents in this debate square off on the basic issue, "What is or is not science or a scientific theory." Let us then examine this issue as it applies to this debate.

Issue. What is science? Science is at once both a body of knowledge and a way of knowing. As a way of knowing, science, as all disciplines are, is based on assumptions. Among these assumptions are:

a. Every phenomenon results from a discoverable cause or set of causes.
b. All causes are materialistic in nature rather than supernatural.
c. The universe is not capricious, i.e. identical conditions operating on identical materials produce identical results.
d. The conclusions of science are tentative and are subject to change or discard as new discoveries are made.
e. The processes which we observe operating in the universe today always have and always will operate throughout the universe.
f. Science is objective, i.e. all conclusions, including one's own, are to be re-examined in the light of new evidence.
g. Given two or more possible explanations, the simplest, the most widely applicable, most probable, natural cause-effect explanations are accepted.

Creationists argue that evolution (macroevolution) violates assumptions c, d, and g and is, therefore, not within the scope of the body of scientific knowledge, nor is it consistent with science as a way of knowing. Evolutionists argue that creationism in any form fits neither aspect of science as it violates assumptions a, b, d, and e.

Creationists (Morris, 1974) argue that evolution violates assumption c as no one has been able to produce living organisms from chemicals in the laboratory much less in the uncontrolled conditions of non-laboratory environments. No one has, by selective breeding, produced new species (macroevolution), just varieties within species (microevolution). (A catch is that even if scientists could produce life or new species, this fact would in no way prove that this is what happened in nature.)

Creationists (Morris, 1974; Thurman, 1978) argue that evolution violates assumption d because there is no evidence or experiment that would prove evolution as invalid. Rather evolution is so flexible (nebulous) that contradicting evidence will never force a change of models, just a different application of the old model.

Assumption g is violated by evolution, claim the creationists (Moore and Slusher, 1974) because most "kinds" of organisms, creationists claim, appear in the fossil record as fully developed and at roughly the same geological point in time. The simplest explanation, say the creationists, is a creator and an act of creation.

Evolutionists argue that creationism violates the assumptions a and b because a creator is not discoverable, and more over, a creator (God) is by definition not a materialistic, but a supernatural cause.

Evolutionists (Cloud, 1977) also argue that assumption d is violated as there is no evidence that would disprove that a phenomenon is or is not the work of a God-Creator (Wallace, 1972).

Assumption e is violated by creationism in that the natural processes observed in the universe today do not include a supernatural creator and indeed such a creator's actions would be a discontinuity in the operation of natural cause and effect process (Moore, 1975).

Both sides claim that the other side is based on unfounded speculation and inference. The evolutionists point to the faith of the creationist in a divine creator (Moore, 1975). The creationists point to the belief of the evolutionists in the undemonstrated spontaneous generation of the first or firsts of living forms and to the evolving of new species (Thurman, 1974; Cloud, 1977). Both taunt with jeers like "anything impossible or not understood is explainable — given access to an all powerful creator — or given eons of geological time." Both sides claim that the other represents a religious point of view, e.g. Fundamentalist Christianity and scientific or secular humanism (American Humanist Association, 1977). They also hold that the driving force behind pressures to teach the opposing world view is religious zeal rather than academic interest. Both charge the other with attempted indoctrination and dogma.

Issue. Indoctrination and dogmatism. Most evolutionists and creationists agree that one cannot prove theories like evolution or creationism but rather competing theories are accepted or rejected by the weight of the evidence for them. They disagree on how well, if at all, the other's theory is supported by the fossil record and other lines of evidence. Thus, both charge the other side with indoctrination — teaching a partisan or sectarian point of view, and with dogmatism — unwarranted, arrogant positiveness in the statement of opinion as fact.

The debate over this issue is most fiercely fought over the textbooks used in schools (Nelkin, 1976). In practice, elementary and secondary school textbooks in all academic subjects, including science, are the total curriculum. They are studied and memorized verbatim (Smith, 1980). They are never analyzed by public school students to determine the author's point of view or biases. Texts are written to reflect the paradigms or models of the disciplines (views of the majority of scholars in that discipline). Kuhn (1970) argues that treating the paradigms as truth is normal and allows the disciplines to grow. Paradigms are only considered to be questionable when a revolution is occurring in a discipline. No such revolution is occurring or is seen as likely in biology as regards the paradigm of evolution. Thus evolution is treated as accepted fact rather than as a tentative explanation of "Whence humanity and other life forms?" Texts do not mention other paradigms, as the bulk of the community of scholars is satisfied. Kuhn's argument offers little comfort to dissident minorities.

The tendency of authors to reflect only the paradigm of the majority of scholars is exacerbated by the nature of texts. Textbooks, particularly public school texts, tend to distill facts, concepts and theory into bland statements that are best described as being monotone statements of "And that is how it is." One is hard pressed to find texts which describe any theories in such tentative language as "it's as if it were this way" or "this concept or relationship is derived from this data because ...." And, heaven forbid, that an author should point out things that cannot be explained by a theory or by a discipline. One often heard pragmatic reason for this is that, "Students at this age cannot handle ambiguity. They wonder why they have to learn this stuff anyhow, and they may well refuse to learn it if it isn't presented to them as fact."

Undergraduate college texts are only somewhat better but are more often enhanced by the assignment of journal articles which are more likely to reflect current investigations and the questions which remain unanswered. At the graduate level where these problems are posed, students are faced often for the first time with the tentativeness of knowledge and much of what they have been taught.

This scenario is all too reminiscent of Plato's notion as stated in The Republic of separate and unequal educations for unequals — philosopher-kings, guardians and artisans.

The creationists' attacks on texts often focus on one or both of the following arguments (Nelkin, 1976):
> (1) "Equal time or fairness" - if there is more than one point of view on issues, students should be taught about the various interpretations of the data even when a given interpretation represents the point of view of a minority of the scholars in an area.
> (2) Dogmatic statements must be eliminated or qualified to reflect the tentativeness of scientific knowledge. Further assumptions should be identified as assumptions or eliminated, but not stated as fact.

The "equal time" argument opens Pandora's box. Creationist literature indicates that there are two points of view on origins — creationism and evolution (Moore and Slusher, 1974; Morris, 1974). Not so. There are many points of view. Each of the world's religions represents at least one such viewpoint. Which ones should be included in texts? A thorough study of origins could be the focus of an entire course and science courses treat origins as only part of their content. How much time in an already crowded curricula should be devoted to this issue? Should equal time be extended only to the creationists but not to proponents of other perspectives? If others, which ones?

The decision to include controversial topics into the curriculum, even for objective study, is an anathema to public school people. There are two sides to every coin except in schools where only one sided coins are studied. A recent summary of three studies in each of three areas of the

curriculum, science, social studies and math, com-
missioned by the National Science Foundation found
that schools do not treat issues considered to be
at all controversial (Shaver, Davis, Helbrum, 1980).
Whatever else religions are they are controversial.

The National Association of Biology Teachers
through its executive director, William M. Moyer
(Moyer, 1980), feels that the opponents in the
creationism-evolution debate are so far apart that
discussion is impossible.

> It is impossible for a scientist and
> a creationist to carry on a meaning-
> ful dialogue because each begins from
> a different assumption ....

Moyer feels that exposing students to several world
views as science in science class is dangerous
(Moyer, 1980).

> ... keep theology out of the science
> curriculum. To do otherwise is to
> create dangerous confusion. If the
> world view of fundamentalist
> Christians is presented as science,
> why not that of the Hindus or the
> Buddhists?

Creationists argue that "scientific creationism" is science. It is they say more than
theology or simply the religious convictions of
fundamentalist Christians (i.e. the creationism of
Genesis). Further, they would argue that evolution
based on what they perceive as faith is unsupported
by experimentation. Evolutionist faith is part of
a religion creationists refer to as atheistic or
secular humanism.

In fact, it was this very point of view which
in 1969 brought the issue of creationism vs. evolution to national attention when equal time for
scientific creationism and evolution in science
textbooks was accepted by the California State
Board of Education (Nelkin, 1976; Thurman, 1978).
The board unanimously adopted a petition that
scientific creationism was supported by enough
scholarly research to be presented as a scientific

theory and that the current science instructional framework presented an unbalanced philosophical approach of atheistic humanism which is unconstitutional.

The accepted petition also required that dogmatic statements regarding origins be stated as conditional statements of speculation. This hit textbooks in their bindings.

By their very nature public school textbooks are surveys of one or more disciplines. They must overgeneralize, overstate, and oversimplify to cover whole areas of knowledge in a single book. Also to conserve space, they leave out qualifying phrases and words, the result being that hypotheses, tentative findings and inferences are stated as facts. For example, a statement that should read:
Based on knowledge of current habitats
of organisms with the same shell structure as the shells found in each rock
layer of this rock sequence scientists
infer that the environment of the area
switched from a freshwater brackish one
to a marine environment and back again
in a period of 4-7 million years. This
assumes an average deposition rate of ....
becomes
The fossil record shows a change from
a freshwater to marine environment and
back again in a period of 5 million
years.

When creationists are successful in forcing a change in the language used in texts to show the inferential nature of evolutionary statements, other topics of the texts which should also be inferential are not changed because there is no pressure to do so. There is economic pressure not to make such changes. The result is a distorted impression that the author-scientists are less convinced of evolution (which is stated to reflect the tentative nature of inference) than of other inferences or theories (stated as fact).

265

California represents a large segment of the textbook market. Publishers must listen and adapt if they want to sell their books there. The effect is not limited to California because publishers will sell the same modified text throughout the nation. Hence the concern at a national level.

Few antagonists can appreciate the refinements that their opponents force on them, at least while the contest rages. There are evolutionists who see that the reduction of dogmatic statements and the making of assumptions explicit are positive and desired if students are to get a true picture of science (Bonner, 1961; Southwick, 1970; Swan, 1970).

> Perhaps the greatest contribution creationists are currently making to science is their recognition of "creeping dogmatism" in the science of evolution. Through their efforts, it is likely that science textbooks in California will have to retreat from such dogmatic statements as "Life began in the primordial sea at least three billion years ago." An acceptable revision of this concept might be "Most scientists have interpreted from the fossil record that life began in the primordial sea at estimates exceeding three billion years ago." This is as it should be. Absolutes have no place in science. The scientist should carefully avoid dogmatic statements, couching all conclusions in relativistic terms. When the scientist fails to do this, other members of the scientific community must be ready to correct such errors. If evolutionists do not keep their own house in order, the creationists stand ready to attack their veracity. (Stansfield, 1977).

Issue. Legislation and the courts. Creationists tend to use the legislatures as their weapon
in the legal aspect of this debate. The evolutionists tend to counterattack through the courts.

State legislatures pass much legislation which
affects the schools and their curricula. They also
delegate authority for such regulations to State
Boards and departments of education and their textbook adoption committees. The most famous legislation regarding evolution and creationism in the
public schools was Tennessee's Butler Act which resulted in the Scopes trial in 1925. While most
concede that the Scopes trial was the turning point
in favor of the evolutionists in what is popularly
called the "monkey war," Scopes was fined, though
the fine was not collected on a technicality, and
the law remained in effect until it was repealed in
1967. Similar laws were passed in Mississippi and
Arkansas.

The moral reasoning or lack of it by the
politicians involved in the passage of the Butler
Act is revealing (de Camp, 1969). Representative
Butler's bill was passed by members of the House of
Representatives for political gain. They expected
the Senate to kill it. The Senate in turn passed
the bill for the same reason expecting the governor's veto. The governor signed the bill saying
nobody believes that this is going to be an active
statute. (The question is, Are religion-morality-
public school related laws being enacted today for
political gain with the knowledge that the courts
whose judges do not stand for re-election will de-
clare them unconstitutional? A charade at enormous
public emotional and monetary expense.)

The laws of Tennessee (repealed in 1967),
Arkansas and Mississippi all made it a crime to
teach evolution and/or required that a literal
Genesis account of creation be taught. They provided a legal basis for a religious dogma and for
censorship of an area of scholarship being presented in public schools. In 1968 the Arkansas law
was found to be unconstitutional as a violation of

267

the First and Fourteenth Amendments to the Constitution.

The First Amendment says in part that Congress shall make no law respecting the establishment of religion or prohibiting the free exercise thereof ....

The Fourteenth Amendment says no state shall make or enforce any law which shall abridge the privileges or immunities of citizens of the United States nor shall any state ... deny to any person within its jurisdiction the equal protection of the law.

In the test case of the Arkansas evolution law, Epperson v. Arkansas 393 U.S. 97 (1968) the U.S. Supreme Court found that "the law must be stricken because of its conflict with the Constitutional prohibition of state laws respecting an establishment of religion or prohibiting the free exercise thereof. The overriding fact is that Arkansas' law selects from the body of knowledge a particular segment which it prescribes for the sole reason that it is deemed to conflict with a particular religious doctrine; that is, with a particular interpretation of the Book of Genesis by a particular religious group."

In April 1973 the Tennessee General Assembly required biology textbooks to provide "an equal amount of emphasis on the origins and creations of man ... as recorded in ... the Genesis account in the Bible." The United States Court of Appeals for the Sixth Circuit ruled the law unconstitutional. This was because it was "a clearly defined preferential position for the Biblical version of creation as opposed to an account of the development of man based on scientific research and reasoning ... a preference by law is to seek to accomplish the establishment of religion which the First Amendment of the Constitution of the United States squarely forbids."

In 1977 the Marion Superior Court #5 citing

268

violation of the First and Fourteenth Amendments found the approval by the state's textbook adoption committee and subsequent use in public schools of the biology text Biology, A Search for Order in Complexity to be unconstitutional (Hendren v. Campbell). The book is written from a literal interpretation of Genesis creationism.

Currently other states are drafting legislation and Departments of Education are drafting positions speaking to the creationism vs. evolution debate. In 1980 a bill was introduced in the Florida legislature which requires that both scientific creationism and evolution and the evidence for and against each be taught. The bill's sponsors specifically wrote the bill to avoid the charges of establishment of religion (Biblical interpretation of Genesis) and against the establishment of "nontheistic or humanistic religion."

On the other hand the Iowa Department of Public Instruction drafted a position statement Creation, Evolution and Public Education. Iowa's position statement says, in effect, evolution belongs in the house of the scientific disciplines and science instruction whereas creationism belongs in the churches and other religious institutions and as such has no place in the science classroom.

Thus the debate goes back and forth among the courts, legislatures, Departments of Education, and state textbook adoption committees, never being resolved, but usually becoming more refined. Scientific creationists are now arguing for equal time between two "scientific theories" and against the presentation of evolution in dogmatic terms. Fundamentalist Christians support the scientific creationists' viewpoint not out of a concern for science per se but because they view evolution as an arch enemy. They see evolution as the scientific foundation and keystone which lend undue credibility to humanism, the relativity of cultural morals, values and notions of deity.

In every debate there are cheap shots or

statements made solely to score points rather than
to resolve the issue. Analytic philosophers refer
to cheap shots as fallacies of reasoning, _ad
hominem_, _ad populum_, slippery slop — _ad nauseam_.
But by whatever names these points are most often
made when the focus shifts from "What is valid?" to
"Who is right?" or "Who will prevail?" Some cheap
shots in this debate are

> -both sides of the California Textbook Contro-
> versy trying to tie the other to Russian com-
> munism in "creationism if unchecked will lead
> to an American equivalent of the Lysenko
> affair"; "communism developed from the theory
> of survival of the fittest."
> -the religionist who claims to know the "first
> cause of the evolutionist by name, God."
> -the evolutionist who claims God is unneces-
> sary and nonexistent because God is not
> demonstrable empirically.
> -both sides portraying former positions or
> states of knowledge as representatives of the
> other side.
> -both sides using the extremes of the other
> side as representing the whole of the other
> side.
> -both sides asking in mock bewilderment "which
> is the real theory of creationism or evolu-
> tion?", when both sides know that in the pur-
> suit of a theory or definition of a position
> variations of degree occur.
> -creationists pointing to gaps in the fossil
> record and saying these gaps disprove the
> very theory that identifies them and which
> often indicates where to look and what to
> look for to fill the gaps.
> -evolutionists glossing over gaps and uncer-
> tainties in their data.
> -creationists saying there are only two rea-
> sonable explanations to whence humans and
> evolutionists who say there is only one rea-
> sonable explanation.

Resolution "What shall we teach
our children about the question
whence 'humanity'?"

Education will not wait until the courts and
legislature have resolved the issue of whether or
not "scientific creationism" is or is not more
science than religion. Schools cannot stop
teaching evolution until there are no unfilled gaps
in the fossil record or until direct evidence of a
creator is found. Thus, one resolution to the
question is to ignore the debate and teach as we
have been — evolution in the schools and creationism in some religious institutions.

A better option, in the opinion of this author,
is a compromise to which none of the parties involved in the dispute except perhaps the courts
would likely support.

In the Abington School District v. Schempp
decision of 1963, the Supreme Court upheld the objective study of religion in public schools. Why
not an objective study of the sacred writings of
the world's religions on the topic of origins? To
ban such a study according to Phi Delta Kappa's
fastback 134 (Bergman, 1979), either by law or by
prevailing practice represents to many hostility to
religion which is unconstitutional. (It was just
this point which prompted the petition to include
creationism per se in California science textbooks
in 1969.) A milder conclusion to be drawn from the
omission of all references to religions on important issues of the curriculum are that religions,
or the questions they address, are unimportant,
outdated, or represent an invalid way of viewing
the world including its origins in the twentieth
century.

This option would allow students to explore
the relevance of religious world views, concerning
at least one topic relevant to them. It would
present to students some of humanity's best religious reasoning germane to the personal question of
developing youth, "Who am I?". Many creationists

271

would object, as they perceive their sacred writings "The Bible" to fall outside the scope of human reasoning. Some of their chief salespersons on this issue claim "there are only two options, evolution and creationism."

School persons in general would object to any issue being added to the curriculum let alone a controversial issue. School teachers, in particular science teachers, legitimately object that they have no training to add this dimension to their curricula.

A model for incorporating a study of religious world views concerning origins in public schools exists. The Australian Science Education Project in its unit on origins has students research various religions and analyze their positions regarding origins and the questions they seek to answer. The unit then describes the theory of evolution and the questions science is trying to answer throughout.

Summary

This debate between world views will continue ad infinitum — each side demanding that its view of the elephant in question is THE view or at the very least the most productive view. Whichever side represents a majority in a given "community" demands that its view be given equal time and presented fairly. Seldom, if ever, will voices be heard saying all world views answering important questions about origins should be presented as part of the human experience which should be passed on to students in our public schools.

REFERENCES

American Humanist Association Statement. Affirming evolution as a principle of science. The Humanist, 1977, 37.

Australian Science Education Project. Where humans came from. ASEP Toorak Victoria Australia, 3142, 1972.

Balanced treatment for scientific creationism and evaluation act. Senator Carlucci Proposed Senate Bill 70 Florida Legislature 1980.

Bergman, Jerry. Teaching about the creation/evolution controversy. Phi Delta Kappan Fastback 134, 1979. 25-30.

Bonner, John T. Perspectives. American Scientist, 1961, 49, 240.

Cloud, Preston. "Scientific creationism" - a new inquisition brewing? The Humanist, 1977, 37.

de Camp, L S. Prague. The end of the monkey war. Scientific American, 1969, 220, 15-21.

Hendren v. Campbell (Sup. Ct. #5 Marion County, Indiana). Printed in NABT - A compendium of information on the theory of evolution and the evolution-creationism controversy. 1977, 31-41.

Iowa Department of Public Instruction. Creation, evaluation and public education, mimeographed position paper. 1978.

Kuhn, Thomas S. The structure of scientific revolutions. 2nd ed., The University of Chicago Press, 1974.

Moore, John A. Perspectives. Biology and Medicine, 1975, 18.

Moore, John N. and Slusher, Harold. Biology: a search for order in complexity. Zondervan, 1974, preface.

Morris, Henry M. Scientific creationism. Creation-Life Publishers, 1974, 8-10.

Moyer, Wayne M. The problem won't go away. Bioscience, 1980, 30, 147.

Moyer, Wayne M. School is no place for theology. The American School Board Journal, 1980, 167, 32.

National Association of Biology Teachers. A compendium of information on the theory of evolution and the evolution-creationism controversy. 1977.

Nelkin, Dorothy. The science textbook controversies. *Scientific American*, 1976, 234, 33-39.

Shaver, James P.; Davis, O.L.; Helburn, Suzanne M. An interpretive report on the status of precollege social studies education based on three NSF-funded studies. *What are the needs in precollege science, mathematics, and social studies education? A view from the field*, NSF, SE 89-9, 1980, 3-18.

Smith, Herbert A. A report on the implications for the science community of three NSF-supported studies of the state of precollege science education. *What are the needs in precollege science, mathematics and social studies education? Views from the field*. NSF, SE 80-9, 55-78.

Southwick, J. Wanless. Letters to the editor. *Bioscience*, 1970, 20, 641.

Stansfield, William. *The science of evolution*. Macmillian, 1977, 11.

Swan, Emery F. Letters to the editor. *Bioscience*. 1970, 120, 640.

Thurman, L. Duane. *How to think about evolution and other Bible science controversies*. Intervarsity Press, 1978.

Wallace, Bruce. Science, biology and evolution. *BSCS Newsletter*, 49, 1972.

Public Schooling and Teaching
About Religion

William E. Collie

The very suggestion that public schools
legally can teach about religion comes as a surprise to many Americans. They most often are
victims of the commonly-held notion that "God has
been outlawed from the classroom" by some vaguely-
remembered Supreme Court action years ago. Therefore, any discussion of public education religion
studies must begin first with the legal issue before it can advance to other pertinent aspects.
Thus, while public education and religion have had
a long-established, though often volatile legal
relationship, we shall only examine that tie as it
pertains to the development of public education
religion studies.

A Source of Confusion

The major source of public confusion is a
still widely-held misunderstanding of the 1963
ruling of the United States Supreme Court in the
Abington School District v. Schempp and the related
Murray v. Curlett cases. This ruling declared
school-conducted opening exercises involving prayer
and Bible-reading unconstitutional. Because of the
basic similarity of the cases, the ruling for both
suits was given simultaneously, while one lengthy
dicta outlined the reasoning of the Court justices.
Simply put, the Court made a clear distinction between official public school conduct of activities
which could be interpreted as religious practice
such as prayers and Bible-reading exercises which
the Court judged unconstitutional and those instructional activities which could legitimately
take place which well might include study about
religion.

Justice Tom C. Clark's majority opinion in the
Schempp case strongly stated that education without
the study of religion was incomplete and that such

275

study was not prohibited by the First Amendment (freedom of religion) clause. In a concurring opinion, Justice Brennan further clarified the intent of the Court to support legitimate academic study:

> The holding of the Court today plainly does not foreclose teaching about the Holy Scriptures or about the differences between religious sects in classes in literature or history. Indeed, whether or not the Bible is involved, it would be impossible to teach meaningfully many subjects in the social sciences or the humanities without some mention of religion. To what extent, and at what points in the curriculum, religious materials should be cited are matters which the courts ought to entrust very largely to the experienced officials who superintend our Nation's public schools.[1]

That the Court actually had a responsibility to protect the right of the schools to teach about religion was suggested by this point in Justice Goldberg's concurring opinion:

> Neither government nor this Court can or should ignore the significance of the fact that a vast portion of our people believe in and worship God and that many of our legal, political and personal values derive historically from religious teachings. Government must inevitably take cognizance of the existence of religion, and, indeed, under circumstances the First Amendment may require that it do so. And it seems to me from opinions in the present and past cases that the Court would recognize the propriety of providing military chaplains and of teaching about religion, as distinguished from the teaching of religion, in the public schools.[2]

A Cause for Concern

Thus while the Supreme Court's ruling in the Schempp case gave a lengthy apologia for including teaching about religion as an integral part of the public school curriculum, instead the decision led to a widespread misperception that the schools no longer could give religion an empathetic, much less sympathetic, ear. That the potential of the Schempp ruling was overlooked in the public uproar over the practice issue should not be surprising. The ruling affected public school practices in thousands of communities large and small throughout the United States, practices which had been conducted largely without incident and mostly without question for generations. Prayer and/or Bible reading had become a stable component of school opening exercises as integral to the beginning of the school day as the Pledge of Allegiance to the flag. Thus reasoned, rational arguments for removal of religion from the position of practiced patriotism (God and country) to academic study provided small comfort to those who personally regarded the decision as a blow to the established school order they knew, had experienced, had accepted, and supported for future generations.

Certainly the passage of time since the 1963 decision has not lessened the conviction of many persons that the public good was not served when school-conducted prayer and Bible reading exercises were ruled unconstitutional. Lost in the emotion of perceived deprivation is the argument that for the good of all, the public schools must not serve as vehicles for the promotion of religious belief, even if those beliefs are held by a majority of the citizenry. For many persons in communities throughout the nation in which they perceive themselves to be in the religious majority, however, they remember the school-taught explanation that in a democracy the majority rules and therefore question why they cannot have prayer and Bible reading in their schools. They overlook the further explanation in democratic theory that the majority must protect the rights of the minority, even if that majority

277

is irreligious, areligious, or of a religious persuasion that finds such practices offensive.

For many persons the problem stems from their perception of how morality is conveyed. For them morality is "caught," not "taught." Rather than instruction being the primary teacher, they believe that the most potent force in the educational process is the modeling that takes place. Thus recurring practices like the Pledge of Allegiance, Bible reading, or repetition of a prayer are believed to have longterm impact as a centering force for the other activities that occur during the day. It is through those very activities the Court identified as religious practices that morality is believed to be conveyed and shaped, thus while academic study may be supportive of morality, it is at best only a secondary force and certainly an inadequate substitute. For many persons Bible reading and prayer are regarded as so central to the moral well-being of the nation that some "common denominator" form of both must be found which can be broadly acceptable to the believing community for the welfare of the nation. The attempt has led to several read-without-comment approaches to Bible reading programs in the schools reflecting an apparent failure to understand that such a literalistic approach to Bible reading violates the beliefs and practices of many Jewish and Christian faith communities, not to mention the sensibilities of those identifying themselves as irreligious or areligious. Court reviews at lower court levels, moreover, have consistently found such practices unconstitutional.

A Cause for Caution

To talk about the study of religion in public school raises concern with some members of the public because of their own religious background. For most people, knowledge about religion is largely experiential, not academic. It has come from our encounters with those overtly identified with religion in our own culture: the minister or priest,

278

the church school teacher, the television preacher. If our experiences have been positive and rewarding, then we generally approach the topic in like manner. If the experiences have been negative, we tend to resist having further contact. Further, religion studies often mistakenly are confused with religious studies of the church school type provided as religious education for induction into or the strengthening of a particular religious faith.

Within public schooling itself, acceptance for study about religion has come slowly for a number of very pragmatic reasons. First of all, because religion is an emotion-stirring area and its role in the classroom is not clearly understood, the potential for controversy involving teacher and administrator with the parents and general public is always a possibility. Further, because the academic study of religion has not been a part of most teachers' formal academic preparation, they often feel unsure and incompetent to deal with religion-related topics in the classroom. Additionally, because the religious dimension is a relatively new and still not widely accepted focus of study, few curriculum materials are available suitable for public school classroom use. Also, the existing curricular demands for classroom instructional time are already so great that the addition of new emphases is increasingly difficult to accomplish, however legitimate the concern. Finally, one must realistically recognize that there has been no great groundswell of public support calling for appropriate academic study about religion. Unless and until there is such strong public backing, public education religion studies' impact upon the elementary and secondary school curriculum will only gradually be felt.

A Case for Consideration

What has been the rationale for study about religion in public schools that meets acceptable standards? The test has clearly been one of academic appropriateness. If the public schools

are about the business of educating the young, when
they deal with religion, what is the educational,
the instructional intent? Broadly described, the
schools may study about the impact of religion (as
a phenomenon) or about religions (as belief systems) or about the much more open religious dimension of culture. Students may study the interactive
force of religion on all the other disciplines
studied in school — art, literature, history, the
social and the natural sciences. If the role of
education is to enable the person to understand the
complexities of the modern world, then every ex-
planatory system should be available for use, including religion studies.

From religion studies as an academic field
conducted in institutions of higher education, certain goals can be identified for public education
religion studies at the elementary and secondary
levels as well. Five general goals identified by
Piediscalzi and Collie as particularly appropriate
for American public schools include helping students develop a broad and discerning understanding
of:
> [1]the religious dimension of human exis-
> tence and the many and diverse ways in
> which it is embodied and expressed in
> historical groups and individual lives;
> [2]the way in which religions function in
> history and culture, with special em-
> phasis on how religions influence in-
> stitutions and in turn are influenced
> by them;
> [3]the meaning and significance of making
> a religious commitment and living by it;
> [4]the numerous and different ways in which
> religion may be studied; and
> [5]the difference between practicing and
> studying about religion.[3]

To exemplify how such study is taking place in
elementary and secondary schools, reference will be
made to units, courses, programs of study, or curriculum materials currently in use in the United
States in social studies.

The first goal for public education religion studies stresses understanding the religious dimension of human existence and the many and diverse ways in which it is embodied and expressed in historical groups and individual lives. On the primary level, the Learning About Religions/Social Studies Program (LARSS, Argus Communications) simply develops these concepts with young children in their first three levels which emphasize cross-cultural family studies, cross-cultural community studies, and ethnic studies in an urban setting.[4] Children begin the study of sacred space both for themselves and their family as well as for an Atoni family in Indonesian Timor as early as first grade. In the third level, they study the diversity of contemporary ethnic groups in San Francisco in Many Ways Around the Bay. Older students in American History or Problems of Democracy can see the religious dimension alive in Religious Issues in American Culture (Religious Issues Series, Addison-Wesley) in William Penn's letter defending diversity of belief among colonial settlers, while Thomas Barton's letter warns of problems which may result if like-minded followers are not kept "pure".[5] The entire series of Religion in Human Culture (Argus Communications) provides a compelling model for study, then proceeds to assist students in the study of five major religious traditions.[6]

The second goal's emphasis on the way in which religions function in history and culture is aptly shown by the materials previously referred to. In LARSS the community studies in level two focusing on the Mound Builders of Ocmulgee, Georgia and on Javanese life provide two studies that literally span thousands of years and are thousands of miles apart. The same identifiable forces are at work, though one culture is homogeneous while the other is quite diverse.[7] In the Religious Issues text on American Culture, the give-and-take influence of religion on institutions and vice versa is aptly traced in the study on "The Churches on the American Frontier" and provocatively raised in its unit "Religion: Personal and Social" with its revival sermon excerpts of Charles G. Finney and Billy Graham to the call for social change of the 1908 Social Creed of the Churches pressing for the abolition of child labor.[8] For middle grade students, the Allyn and Bacon series prepared by the Education Research Council has units entitled <u>Four World Views</u> and <u>Medieval Civilization</u> that traces the influence of religion on culture and history.[9]

The third goal emphasizing the meaning of making a religious commitment and living by it begins to receive simple this-is-what-believers-do treatment in the LARSS elementary materials. The impact of living by religious commitment in the face of adversity comes powerfully and disturbingly to life in the <u>Religious Issues</u> volume on American culture in the readings on "Blacks and the Churches" by Malcolm X and Martin Luther King and the constitutional conflict involved in the issue of Jehovah's Witnesses and saluting the Flag.[10] Most poignant of all, perhaps, are the butterfly pictures and narratives by the children of the Dachau concentration camp of World War II included in the filmstrip on "The Jewish Tradition" in the <u>Religion in Human Culture</u> series.[11]

The fourth goal to help students understand the numerous and different ways religion may be studied has been exemplified by the materials referred to previously. They demonstrate that religion can be studied as a part of history, anthropology or sociology and that such an examination of the religious dimension yields new insights into the culture that cannot otherwise be grasped.

The final goal to help students understand the difference between practicing and studying about religion is explicitly addressed in the initial training materials for the students in the <u>Religion in Human Culture</u> study of world religions. In the <u>Religious Issues</u> series, the distinction is shaped by the structure of the learning materials. For the elementary teachers of LARSS, the teachers' guide admirably sets the stage for introducing young children to this new and different approach to religion. Through experience the students involved in all of these programs will have a much broader understanding of the religious dimension of culture.

Will teaching about religion as advocated by the supporters of public education religion studies make our children more moral? Certainly no serious educator would make such a direct causative claim. To the extent, however, that such study encourages students to hesitate before making quick judgments about others' values, or to the extent that in the process of exploring how others have determined what was right for them to do, they begin to more closely examine their own actions, then perhaps moral growth can be claimed. At a minimum, if religion studies can assist students to better understand the cultural background, including religion, of the persons, subgroups, and societies they will come in contact with and to better equip them with questions and insights which will limit their tendency to prejudge and stereotype others, then its contribution to public schooling is justifiable.

A Continuing Challenge

At this juncture in our nation's development, it would appear useless to argue that we are so culturally unified that we can return to the past when Bible reading and prayer were a cultural overlay providing a patina of religious unity and common morality to the conduct of public schooling. Whatever service or disservice that exercise contributed to public schooling in the past, our energies now can better be applied to addressing those societal ills which call both our private and public morality into question. In order to deal with the increasingly complex and frustrating problems we face, we need to draw upon every available resource to better understand where we as a people of many cultures have been and where we as a multicultural society are heading. Study of the religious dimension of that journey should not be overlooked as we undertake our analysis. The message of our past is that we do not face the future in a cultural vacuum, and we need not do so if we only would draw upon the resources available to us.

The academic study of religion has contributed tools and insights which can enable us to read about religion in public schools in ways which are both educationally sound, and constitutionally appropriate. What is now needed is broad based community cooperation involving academicians, public school educators, religious leaders, and the general public to meet the challenge of changing the relationship between religion and the schools. This unified community backing should encourage the exploration of ways to appropriately teach our children about religion's influence on human existence and its powerful role in shaping our cultural heritage. At the same time, however, the community must defend the public school from attempts to use the schools for religious instruction presented in the guise of promotion of moral growth.

NOTES

1. Quotes from the dicta in Abington School District v. Schempp (1963) as reported in Peter Bracher et al., Public Education Religion Studies: Questions and Answers, PERSC Guidebook (Dayton, OH: Public Education Religion Studies Center, Wright State University, 1974), p. 1.

2. Ibid.

3. Nicholas Piediscalzi and William Collie (eds.), Teaching About Religion in Public Schools (Niles, Ill.: Argus Communications, 1977), pp. 15-16. For other statements of possible goals for public education religion studies see the PERSC Guidebook, op. cit., pp. 4-5 and Henry J. Hoeks, Studying the Sacred in the Schools: A Handbook for the Academic Study of Religions (Grand Rapids, Mich.: Calvin College for the Council on the Study of Religion in Michigan Schools, 1976).

4. Joan G. Dye, Teacher's Guide for Level 1: Learning About Religions: Social Studies (Niles, Ill.: Argus Communications, 1976), pp. 11-13.

5. Robert A. Spivey, Edwin S. Gausted, and Rodney F. Allen, Religious Issues in American Culture in the Issues in Religion series (Reading, Mass.: Addison-Wesley Publishing Company, 1972), pp. 11-18.

6. World Religions Curriculum Development Center, Religion in Human Culture (Niles, Ill.: Argus Communications, 1978).

7. Dye, op. cit.

8. Spivey, Gausted and Allen, op. cit., pp. 45-63; 84-101.

9. Four World Views and Medieval Civilization from The Human Adventure series prepared by the Education Research Council of America (Boston: Allyn and Bacon, Inc., 1975).

10. Spivey, Gausted and Allen, op. cit., pp. 74-81; 101-106.

11. World Religions Curriculum Development Center, op. cit. See the multimedia kit on The Jewish Tradition.

ABOUT THE EDITORS

THOMAS C. HUNT received the Ph.D. from the University of Wisconsin-Madison in 1971. Presently an Associate Professor of Educational Foundations at Virginia Tech, Dr. Hunt's major field is history of American education. His primary research interest is in religion, morality and education in its historical and current aspects.

MARILYN M. MAXSON received the Ph.D. from the University of Texas at Austin in 1977. She currently is an Assistant Professor of Curriculum and Instruction at Virginia Tech, where she teaches courses in Social Foundations of Education and Elementary Social Studies. Her major research interest is in the area of the inculcation of values in the schools.

ABOUT THE AUTHORS

JAMES C. CARPER is Assistant Professor of Foundations of Education and Coordinator of the Master of Arts in Teaching Program at Tulane University. He received the Ph.D. from Kansas State University. His interests in history of education and religion and schooling are reflected in articles and reviews which have been published in a number of scholarly journals. He is currently President of the Midwest History of Education Society.

WILLIAM E. COLLIE is Associate Professor of Education and Codirector of the Public Education Religion Studies Center at Wright State University in Dayton, Ohio. He is the co-editor with Nicholas Piediscalzi of the book, Teaching About Religion in Public Schools (Argus, 1977). He has frequently spoken and presented nationwide on the topic of his speciality, public education religion studies.

SAMUEL M. CRAVER holds the Ph.D. degree from the University of North Carolina. He has had teaching experience in the Charlotte-Mecklenburg schools and at the University of North Carolina, Auburn University, and Virginia Commonwealth University. He has been active in working for a rational approach to moral and ethics education in the public schools of Virginia.

JUNE EDWARDS, Ed.D., taught English and Social Studies for eight years in public schools in Illinois and Pennsylvania. She has taught at Alverno College, Louisiana State University, and Milwaukee Area Technical College. Currently she is a free-lance writer and part-time instructor in the College of Education, Marquette University. She is in the process of completing a book on censorship and the selection of literature in public high schools.

GARY D. FENSTERMACHER is Professor of Educational Foundations at Virginia Tech. His primary field is philosophy of education, and his research interest is in the study of teaching and teacher education.

SHIMON FROST, born in Warsaw, Poland, earned his Licence ès Lettres from the Sorbonne in Paris. He subsequently studied in the Graduate Department of the Teachers Institution of the Jewish Theological Seminary and received his Ed.D. from Teachers College, Columbia University. As of August, 1978, Dr. Frost has served as Acting Director and Director of the American Association for Jewish Education (AAJE), and prior to assuming this assignment he functioned as Director of AAJE's National Curriculum Research Institute.

RONALD N. GIESE is an Associate Professor of Education at the College of William and Mary. He has been a project staff member on two NSF funded science curriculum projects — Intermediate Science Curricula Science Study (ISCS) and Individualized Science Instruction System (ISIS). He has taught secondary science courses in both this country and in Ghana, West Africa. He is a theistic evolutionist.

JAMES F. HERNDON is Professor of Political Science at Virginia Tech. He holds the Ph.D. degree from the University of Michigan. His writings deal with church-state relations, interest groups and the legislative process, and mathematical models in political science.

SEYMOUR W. ITZKOFF is Professor of Education at Smith College. He received his doctorate from Columbia University. He has published extensively in philosophy, educational theory and music.

ROBISON B. JAMES (Ph.D., Duke University, 1965) is both Professor of Religion at the University of Richmond, where he has taught since 1962, and a member since 1976 of the Virginia General Assembly, where he serves on the House of Delegates Education Committee. Author of articles on theology and on public school ethics education, he is currently completing a book on the ethics of politics. He is co-founder of the three year old Virginia Association for Moral, Civic and Value Education.

WILLIAM F. LOSITO is Associate Professor of Education at the College of William and Mary. His specialized area of research interest is ethics and educational policy.

HARVEY G. NEUFELDT received the Ph.D. in History from Michigan State University in 1971. His research interests are in educational, religious, and intellectual history with special emphasis on education and the South, religion and schooling in nineteenth-century America, and higher education.

THOMAS F. SULLIVAN, a priest of the Archdiocese of Chicago, has been Assistant Professor of Religion and Religious Education at the Catholic University of America for the past five years. Before that he was Associate Superintendent of Schools in the Archdiocese of Chicago for nine years. He is the author of Focus on American Catechetics (N.C.E.A. Publications, 1972) and a Discussion Guide to Sharing the Light of Faith (U.S.C.C. Publications, 1979).